P9-DIB-792

Contents

ACKNOWLEDGMENTS

I would like to thank the people who have encouraged me in this endeavor, especially those who accompanied me on several new trips: my daughter Annie and her friends from the University of South Carolina, Dan Klingshirn and Tom Wissing; my sons Marshall, Ryan and Matthew and Ryan's wife Sarah; and my running colleagues, The Citadel Noon Runners. I am very appreciative of the support provided by a great local paddling club, the LowCountry Paddlers.

Ralph Earhart
January 2004

INTRODUCTION

After purchasing my kayak, I did not know where to paddle. I looked in kayak shops, bookstores, and libraries to find information about local kayaking and found very little information about landings and trip destinations. I bought a map and used it to expand my kayaking boundaries. The more I paddled, the more I realized that a trip guide for the recreational kayaker would be a useful resource.

The trips described in this guide are all within an hour of Charleston. The guide is for novices as well as more experienced kayakers.The trips begin at public boat landings in the ACE Basin south of Charleston and extend north of Charleston to the Santee River. Most of the trips take advantage of the river's current or tidal flow and do not require the kayaker to be in great physical condition. I have been to every landing in this guide and have taken each trip at least once. The time it takes to paddle a trip depends on a paddler's strength. I tried to paddle consistently on each trip, so you should be able to determine how long each trip will take after taking a few trips and comparing your time to mine.

Get your paddle out and get going!

ACE BASIN

The Ashepoo, Combahee, and Edisto (ACE) Basin represent one of the largest undeveloped estuaries on the east coast. The Nature Conservancy works with donors and local government to purchase land or have it donated. The South Carolina Department of Natural Resources (DNR) manages much of the land purchased or donated. An example of this practice occurred in 2002 when the Nature Conservancy and Beaufort County purchased Buzzard Island. Beaufort County retained 25% interest in the island and the Nature Conservancy transferred 75% to the DNR. This was the ninth island that was added in this manner. The island is over 140 acres and is open for public use. The ACE Basin has over 350,000 acres including pine and hardwood forests, brackish and salt-water marshes, and barrier islands and beaches. The basin provides a rich environment for fish, shellfish, and birds, including the bald eagle.

In the mid-1700s the tidal swamps along the rivers were cleared and used for growing rice. After the rice culture declined in the late 19th century, wealthy owners purchased many of the planta- tions for use as hunting retreats. The rice fields continue to be an important part of the landscape by providing a haven for waterfowl. Trips along these rivers reveal dikes and gates of the old rice fields. Some are in a dilapidated state while others are in a useable condition.

Combahee
Steel Bridge Landing
Cuckolds Creek Landing
Sugar Hill Landing
Fields Point Landing
Old Chehaw Landing

Ashepoo
Prices Bridge Landing
Chessie Creek Landing
HWY 303 Landing
Ashepoo Levee Landing
Brickyard Landing
Bennetts Point Landing

Edisto
West Bank Landing
Penney Creek Landing
Willtown Bluff Landing
Dahoo Landing
Toogoodoo Landing
Cherry Point Landing

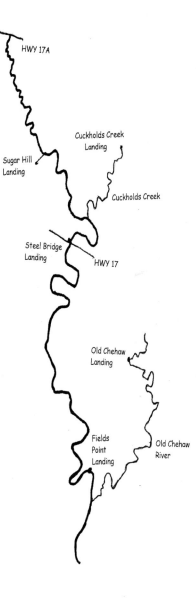

HWY 17A

Cuckholds Creek
Landing

Sugar Hill
Landing

Cuckholds Creek

Steel Bridge
Landing

HWY 17

Old Chehaw
Landing

Fields
Point
Landing

Old Chehaw
River

Combahee River

COMBAHEE RIVER

The Combahee River is the farthest river heading south from Charleston mentioned in this book. It is a fantastic river and any paddler who visits the ACE Basin should take at least one trip on it. On a mid-September trip on the river, I saw so many alligators I quit trying to be quiet and drift by them. I saw the largest alligator of all my kayaking adventures basking on a mud bank on the shore. Fish as big as my arm were jumping three feet out of the water.

Steel Bridge Landing

Directions: The landing is on HWY 17 on the right side heading south. Cross the Edisto River, then the Ashepoo River, and finally come to the Combahee River. The landing is immediately to the right after crossing the Combahee River Bridge. Start slowing down for the landing while on the bridge or you will zip by it. The landing is 46 miles from Charlestowne Landing and it takes about 1 hour to get there.

The bridge is on the county line, so police officers use it as a turn around spot. While putting my kayak in one day, two police cars came by. When I returned at the finish of my trip and was loading up, another came by. I felt safe at this landing, even though I was alone.

Tide: The high tide is about 3¼ hours behind Charleston Harbor and low tide is about 2½ hours behind.

The river is wide at the bridge and gets wider. On windy days a recreational kayaker should consider going upriver.

Trip 1: Paddle with the incoming tide up to Cuckolds Creek and then on to Cuckolds Creek Landing (9 miles and

Steel Bridge Landing

Trip 1: Paddle with the incoming tide up to Cuckolds Creek and then on to Cuckolds Creek Landing (9 miles and about 2¾ hours)

Trip 2: Paddle upriver with the tide to Sugar Hill Landing (11 miles and about 2½ hours) and come back with the tide.

3

about 2¾ hours). It takes about an hour to paddle to the Cuckolds Creek entrance and then another 1¾ hours to get to the landing. Plan for a 3 hour trip in order to stop and watch the alligators along the way. Time the arrival at Cuckholds Creek Landing before the tide changes there. Take a break at the landing and ride the outgoing tide back. This is an all day trip, but it is a lot of fun.

Trip 2: Paddle upriver with the tide to Sugar Hill Landing (11 miles and about 2½ hours) and come back with the tide. Time the trip to arrive at Sugar Hill Landing at high tide. The landing is not on the river. I had to ask a local boater on the river how to find it. After the Cuckolds Creek turnoff, there are three major left curves. There are houses on the right side of the river at the start of each turn. After the 3rd major left turn, there is a moderately long straight stretch. Get on the left side of the river. After passing a grassy island on the left, there is an "osprey nest on a stick" on the left. It is a nest on top of an old cypress tree that has lost its limbs. The landing is on the next creek to the left. If you miss this turnoff, you will pass a dilapidated old shed on the right side of the river. You can see this shed from the creek entrance. The landing is about a 10 minute paddle up the creek.

Safety Note:
Be very careful when driving away from this landing. It is difficult to see the traffic coming from the bridge when pulling onto the highway. If pulling a trailer, turn right and head away from Charleston until finding a safe place to pull off and turn around. I recommend driving to the Sugar Hill Landing turnoff and turning there. It has the visibility to make a left turn back onto the highway. (This is experience talking).

Cuckolds Creek Landing

Directions: Take HWY 17 south past the Edisto and Ashepoo Rivers and turn right onto HWY 119 towards White Hall. This turnoff is 3.8 miles from the intersection of HWY 303 with HWY 17. There is a brown sign on HWY 17 indicating Cuckolds Landing to the right. Go 4.4 miles down HWY 119 and it will intersect with HWY 66. Turn left on HWY 66 and immediately take the dirt road on the left. It goes past a church and onto the landing. The dirt road has a street sign naming it Cuckolds Lane. It is not well-marked and if you find yourself going over the bridge on HWY 66, you have passed it. You can see the landing from the bridge. Cuckolds Creek Landing is 47 miles and just slightly more than one hour from Charlestowne Landing.

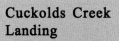

Cuckolds Creek Landing

Trip: Paddle down the creek to Steel Bridge Landing at HWY 17 (9 miles and about 2¾ hours).

The landing is clean and well-maintained. One of the locals told me he had been coming there for about four years and started cleaning up and hauling out trash every time he came. His personal clean-up campaign has encouraged others to maintain the landing.

Tide: The high tide is about 5 hours behind Charleston Harbor and low tide is about 4½ hours behind.

Trip: Paddle down the creek to Steel Bridge Landing at HWY 17 (9 miles and about 2¾ hours). The trip down the creek is spectacular. It is about a 1¾ hours paddle to the Combahee River. This is an easy ride if a pickup vehicle has been left at the Steel Bridge Landing. Plan the trip to arrive at the Steel Bridge Landing at its low tide—3 hours behind Charleston Harbor to avoid having to paddle against the incoming tide.

Sugar Hill Landing

Directions: Remain on HWY 17 for 1½ miles after the Steel Bridge Landing. There is a brown sign indicating the turn to Sugar Hill Landing to the right. This is HWY 33. The turnoff to Sugar Hill Landing Road (on a green street sign) is about 4 miles down the highway.

> **Sugar Hill Landing**
> **Trip:** Sugar Hill Landing to Steel Bridge Landing (11 miles and about 2½ hours).

Tide: The high tide is about 4 hours behind Charleston Harbor and low tide is about 3 hours behind.

Trip: Sugar Hill Landing to Steel Bridge Landing (11 miles and about 2½ hours). Leave a pickup vehicle at the Steel Bridge Landing and put in at Sugar Hill Landing. Plan to arrive at the Steel Bridge Landing at low tide to take advantage of the river current and the outgoing tide.

Fields Point Landing

Directions: Go down HWY 17 and cross the Edisto and Ashepoo Rivers. Continue down HWY 17 and turn left onto HWY 162, Wiggins Road. This turnoff is 3.9 miles past the HWY 303 turnoff. It is 44 miles from Charlestowne Landing. As you travel down HWY 162 you will pass the turnoff for Old Chehaw River Landing. The highway becomes a dirt road shortly before the white pillars at Wiggins. Here Fields Point Road veers off to the right. Follow Fields Point Road for 3.1 miles to the landing.

This landing has a one-lane ramp and plenty of parking. It is far from civilization. I left the landing on a Saturday in July and saw only four boats during a 4 hour trip. The river was very wide and the breeze made it comfortable on a day when the heat index in Charleston was over 100 degrees.

> **Fields Point Landing**
>
> **Trip:** Plan a trip for the morning—before the sea breezes start—planning for a tide change in the middle of the time allotted for the paddle.

Tide: Both high and low tide are about the same as Charleston Harbor.

Trip: Plan a trip for the morning–before the sea breezes start–by planning for a tide change in the middle of the time allotted for the paddle.

Old Chehaw Landing

Directions: Go down HWY 17 and cross the Edisto and Ashepoo Rivers. Continue down HWY 17 and turn left onto HWY 162, Wiggins Road. This turnoff is 3.9 miles past the HWY 303 turnoff. The landing is 6.8 miles down the road and it is well-marked. The landing is 48 miles from Charlestowne Landing. It has a little dock and a single ramp. The Old Chehaw River is narrow and has lots of curves. On a windy day, the many curves kept the waves from gaining much height.

Tide: The high tide is about 1¾ hours behind Charleston Harbor and the low tide is about 1½ hours behind.

Trip: Old Chehaw Landing to Wiggins and back (7 miles and about 2 hours each way). Plan for a tide change at Wiggins before paddling back.

Old Chehaw Landing

Trip: Old Chehaw Landing to Wiggins and back (7 miles and about 2 hours each way).

7

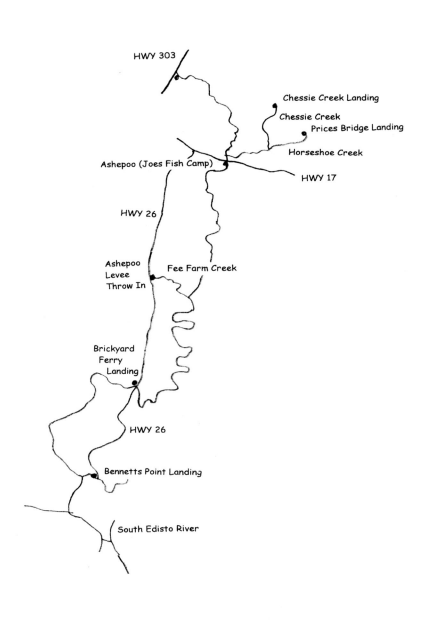

Ashepoo River

ASHEPOO RIVER

The Ashepoo River is my favorite river for paddling. There are several great trips on it. The boaters along the river are friendly. I have talked to folks on one trip, only to run into them on a later trip and we renew our conversations. The landings along the Ashepoo are the cleanest landings in the entire area. Boaters keep the landings clean and take pride in their cleanliness. The people using these landings have always been courteous and kind to me. One day as I was placing my kayak on top of my car, I told a boater who had just driven up to the landing that I needed another couple of minutes to secure the kayak before I moved the car. He said, "I've been fishing all day. I'm in no hurry. Take your time."

The Ashepoo is the shortest of the three rivers making up the ACE Basin. I enjoy the upper part of the river—above HWY 17—where both the creeks and the river itself are narrow. On the lower section of the river, a single road, HWY 26, goes by all the landings and therefore makes for efficient pickup points.

Prices Bridge Landing
Directions: Prices Bridge Landing is 40 miles from Charlestown Landing. Take HWY 17 south from Charleston to Jacksonboro. Veer right onto HWY 64 when leaving Jacksonboro. Go 6.8 miles along HWY 64 and immediately after the sign for Neyles, there is a brown sign indicating Prices Bridge Landing. Make a left turn onto State Route 199 (Maybank Lane). The landing is 3.2 miles down the road. The speed limit slows to 35 mph just before arriving at the landing.

Prices Bridge Landing deserves special note for its cleanliness. Local users of

Prices Bridge Landing

Trip 1: Prices Bridge Landing on Horseshoe Creek down to Ashepoo on HWY 17 (4 miles and about 1 hour each way).

Trip 2: Prices Bridge Landing on Horseshoe Creek, under the HWY 17 bridge, to a sandbar (6 miles and about $1\frac{3}{4}$ hours each way with the tide).

the landing have told me how hard they work to keep the landing clean of trash. One even told me he cuts the grass when the county gets behind on grass cutting!

Tide: The tides at Prices Bridge Landing are approximately 4½ hours behind Charleston Harbor. The tides at the HWY 17 bridge are about 4 hours behind Charleston Harbor.

Trip 1: Prices Bridge Landing on Horseshoe Creek down to Ashepoo on HWY 17 (4 miles and about 1 hour each way). Take this trip on the low portion of the tide to see the most wildlife. As the tide drains from the marsh, the alligators must leave the marsh in order to stay in water. If traveling with another car, leave the pickup vehicle in Ashepoo at Joe's Fish Camp. It is the boat landing immediately on the left after crossing the river. There is a $5 charge to park. Take an envelope, write your license number on it, enclose the money and put it into the box provided.

Trip 2: Prices Bridge Landing on Horseshoe Creek, under the HWY 17 bridge, to a sandbar (6 miles and about 1¾ hours each way with the tide). I did this trip early one late September morning and spotted three bald eagles! The sandbar is about ½ hour past Ashepoo. Plan to arrive there at low tide. Sometimes the sandbar is exposed (hooray!) and you can pull your boat up, have a picnic, and take a nice walk or swim along the sandbar. Other times the sandbar will be underwater. It depends on the river level and the phase of the moon. Plan to stop there, even if it is a few inches below the surface. In the summertime it is still a great place to get out and stretch your legs and cool off. Watch out for alligators! I got out one time to stretch when the water was about 18 inches deep. My daughter and I noticed something coming up the river. It turned out to be a good-sized alligator. She got back in her kayak. I just watched him swim past.

To find the sandbar: Continue down the river from the HWY 17 bridge and go under the railroad bridge. After passing houses on the right, there are well-maintained dikes and floodgates to the rice fields. Just after paddling by this area, there is a creek that enters from the right side of the river. At that point, the river will bend to the left. The sandbar is just around that left bend on the left side of the river. Locals come to this sandbar at low tide throughout the summer. It sometimes looks like "party central."

I paddled to the sandbar on an overcast and dreary Sunday in early September. As I was leaving the sandbar, I noted something big in the water headings towards it. It was a deer! The animal swam across the river, scampered across the sandbar, and swam to the near shore.

Planning Tip:
This is a great 6 hour trip from the time of departure to returning home. Plan on an hour to drive and unload, and another hour to load and return home. Easy paddling with the tide will take about 4 hours to go from Prices Bridge Landing to the sandbar and return. Of course turning at Joe's Fish Camp or planning for a vehicle pickup there can shorten the trip.

Chessie Creek Landing

Directions: Take HWY17 south from Charleston to Jacksonboro. Veer right onto HWY 64 when leaving Jacksonboro. Remain on HWY 64 past Neyles for another 1.6 miles. Get off HWY 64 by going straight as it bears to the right. Continue straight (not on HWY 64) for .2 mile. At the intersection, turn left onto HWY 458. A brown sign indicates this is the way to Bonnie Doone. It is HWY 458. Travel about 3.5 miles down this road and turn to the left at the sign for the Chessie Creek Public Boat Landing. Immediately after turning from HWY 458, turn right onto the dirt road. It leads to the landing.

Chessie Creek Landing

Trips 1 and 2: Take the same trips from this landing as from Prices Bridge Landing. The only difference is the starting point. The trip times and mileage are about the same.

Tide: The tides are approximately 4½ hours behind Charleston Harbor.

Use Chessie Creek Landing as an alternative starting point for the trips noted in the Prices Bridge Landing section of this guide. Chessie Creek intersects halfway between Prices Bridge Landing and Ashepoo. There are homes in the area of the landing. The locals are friendly and have offered to help me load my kayak when I was by myself. One summer morning I left this landing and after leaving the inhabited area I came upon an alligator that I followed down the creek for about 20 minutes.

Trips 1 and 2: Take the same trips from this landing as from Prices Bridge Landing. The only difference is the starting point. The trip times and mileage are about the same.

HWY 303 Throw-In

Directions: Take HWY 17 south. Remain on it past Jacksonboro. Do not veer onto HWY 64. Immediately after crossing the HWY 17 bridge over the Ashepoo, turn right onto Clover Hill Road. Continue for about 5 miles to HWY 303. Turn right onto HWY 303 (Green Pond Road). The bridge over the Ashepoo is in .2 mile. Pull off to the right and carry your boat to the river. There is a street immediately before the bridge, Water Court Street, that is the access for several homes along this part of the Ashepoo.

HWY 303 Throw-In

Trip 1: HWY 303 throw-in to HWY 17 (7 miles and about 2 hours with the tide) and then return with the tide.

Trip 2: HWY 17 (Joe's Fish Camp) to HWY 303 for a vehicle pickup (7 miles and about 2 hours with the tide).

This stretch of the Ashepoo is a "must see" destination. The river becomes extremely narrow near the bridge. It is difficult for one person to carry a boat down to the Ashepoo at this throw-in because the banks are steep and the shoreline is muddy, except at high tide. Do not let this inconvenience deter you from paddling the upper Ashepoo. The alternative to using this landing is launching at one of the other landings on the Ashepoo and paddling up to this location.

Tide: The tide is almost 5 hours behind Charleston Harbor.

Trip 1: HWY 303 throw-in to HWY 17 (7 miles and about 2 hours with the tide) and then return with the tide.

Trip 2: HWY 17 (Joe's Fish Camp) to HWY 303 for a vehicle pickup (7 miles and about 2 hours with the tide). The tide at the HWY 17 bridge is about 4 hours behind Charleston Harbor.

HWY 26 – Ashepoo Levee Throw In (Feefarm Creek)

Directions: Take HWY 17 south from Charleston and continue over the Edisto and Ashepoo River bridges. Turn left from HWY 17, 1.1 miles after crossing the Ashepoo River onto Bennetts Point Road (HWY 26). This turnoff is marked as the road to Bennetts Point. The throw-in is 8 miles down HWY 26 at a stream flowing under the road. There is plenty of room to pull off the road. Launch from the bank into the creek.

This is a relatively deep creek and schooners were able to go up it to the various plantations. The creek was named Feefarm Creek when a lawyer in earlier times was given a farm bordering the creek as a fee for services performed.

HWY 26– Ashepoo Levee Throw-In (Feefarm Creek)

Trip 1: Feefarm Creek to the Ashepoo River and return (2½ miles and about 1 hour each way).

Trip 2: Feefarm Creek to Brickyard Ferry Landing (15 miles and about 3½ hours).

Trip 3: Feefarm Creek to HWY 17 (18 miles and about 4 hours).

Tide: The tide is about 2½ hours behind Charleston Harbor.

Trip 1: Feefarm Creek to the Ashepoo River and return (2½ miles and about an hour each way).

Trip 2: Feefarm Creek to Brickyard Ferry Landing (15 miles and about 3½ hours). Drop a pickup vehicle at Brickyard Ferry Landing, paddle out Feefarm Creek to the Ashepoo, and then down to Brickyard Ferry.

Trip 3: Feefarm Creek to HWY 17 (18 miles and about 4 hours). Leave a pickup vehicle at Joe's Fish Camp and put in at the throw-in, paddling upriver to HWY 17.

Brickyard Ferry Landing (Bennetts Point Bridge)

Directions: Get to this landing by going 5 miles past the Ashepoo Levee Throw-In on Feefarm Creek. The landing is about 50 minutes from Charleston. It is marked with a brown sign on the right just before crossing the bridge. The landing is secluded. It is well-kept and I felt safe traveling alone. Visit Bear Island Wildlife Management Area from this landing. It is a 12,000 acre plot owned and operated by the South Carolina Department of Natural Resources. It provides quality habitat for wintering waterfowl.

Brickyard Ferry Landing

Trip 1: Brickyard Ferry Landing upriver with the tide.

Trip 2: Brickyard Ferry Landing to Bennetts Point Landing (9 miles and about 2 hours with the tide).

Tide: High and low tide are about 1½ hours behind Charleston Harbor.

Trip 1: Brickyard Ferry Landing upriver with the tide. I like this landing because I can go upriver if the tide is coming in, or downriver if it is going out. Either direction is good. Going upriver, the Bear Island Wildlife Management Area is on the right. There is no pickup point going upriver. Plan to go with the tide and turn around when the tide changes. This paddle can be made as long as you want, just plan the trip based on when the tide will change.

Trip 2: Brickyard Ferry Landing to Bennetts Point Landing (9 miles and about 2 hours with the tide). The Bear Island Wildlife Management Area is on the left. If a pickup vehicle has not been dropped at Bennetts Point, plan for the tide change at the time you reach Bennetts Point. There is a nice sandbar on the left about 2/3 of the way to Bennetts Point. It is above water for about an hour on each side of low tide. After passing a dock on the right side of the river, the river will make a turn to the left. The sandbar is just beyond the left turn. Stop and enjoy it.

In late January on a day with temperatures in the high 70s, I saw over a dozen large alligators basking in the sun on the tops of the mud banks within a few miles of the landing. I spotted one of the biggest alligators I have seen on my kayak trips in early December as he warmed himself in the grass alongside the river. I also followed an otter down the river for a distance on this same trip.

Bennetts Point Public Landing

Directions: Get to this landing by continuing over the bridge past Brickyard Ferry Landing for another 8 miles. Near the landing, the road makes a hard right turn. The boat landing is on the left by B&B Seafood. The trip to this landing is 48 miles from Charlestowne Landing with a travel time of about 1 hour and 10 minutes. If there are no parking spaces at the landing, park in the designated area just beyond B&B Seafood on the right side of the road.

Tide: Both high and low tide are about 1½ hours behind Charleston Harbor.

Trip 1: Bennetts Point Landing to Brickyard Landing (9 miles and about 2 hours). Bennetts Point Landing is on Mosquito Creek. Paddle on the incoming tide to Brickyard Ferry Landing. I left this landing one morning at 9:00, went with the tide up to Brickyard Ferry Landing, got out and had a picnic and enjoyed the view from the top of the bridge and returned by 1:30 in the afternoon. There is a large sandbar about 1/3 of the way up, on the right hand side. If you are there within about an hour of low tide, it should be above water. Get out and enjoy it.

Bennetts Point Landing

Trip 1: Bennetts Point Landing to Brickyard Landing (9 miles and about 2 hours).

Trip 2: Ride the tide downriver and take the cutoff to the right that goes to Rock Creek and St. Helena Sound (2 miles and about ½ hour with the tide) or go on past that turnoff and turn left for the cutoff on the intracoastal waterway to the Edisto River (3½ miles and about 45 minutes with the tide).

Trip 2: Ride the tide down river and take the cutoff to the right that goes to Rock Creek and St. Helena Sound (2 miles and about ½ hour with the tide). Or go on past that turnoff and turn left for the cutoff on the intracoastal waterway to the Edisto River (3½ miles and about 45 minutes with the tide). It was exciting to cross over from one river to the next. There is a sandy bank on the shores of the cut-through that makes for a nice pull-up area.

Author paddling past Bennetts Point. Spring 2003.

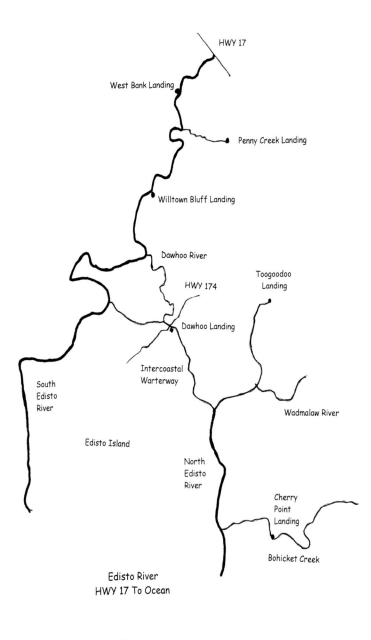

HWY 17

West Bank Landing

Penny Creek Landing

Willtown Bluff Landing

Dawhoo River

Toogoodoo
Landing

HWY 174

Dawhoo Landing

Intercoastal
Warterway

South
Edisto
River

Wadmalaw River

Edisto Island

North
Edisto
River

Cherry
Point
Landing

Bohicket Creek

Edisto River
HWY 17 To Ocean

Edisto River

EDISTO RIVER

The Edisto River is the longest free-flowing river in the state as well as the longest true blackwater river in North America. For the purpose of this guide, I divide the river into two sections–the ACE Basin section and the river section. The ACE Basin section begins at West Bank Landing, just south of HWY 17, and extends to the ocean at St. Helena Sound–close to Edisto Island State Park. The river portion extends from Colleton State Park down to West Bank Landing.

The trips in the ACE Basin are different from the river trips due to the tidal influence. When traveling alone on the river section, plan to paddle upriver and then turn and come back with the current. Of course, a pickup vehicle eliminates the need to paddle against the current. The sections of the river vary greatly. The North Edisto River is a separate river that is completely within Charleston County. Formed by the confluence of the Wadmalaw River, Toogoodoo Creek, and the Dawhoo River, it runs between Seabrook Island and Edisto Island. The North Edisto connects to the Edisto River by way of the intracoastal waterway.

EDISTO ACE BASIN TRIPS

West Bank Landing

Directions: West Bank Landing is downriver from the HWY 17 bridge. Go ½ mile past the bridge over the Edisto and turn left down HWY 30— Hope Plantation Road. There is a brown sign at the turnoff indicating Edisto River access. Follow along the road for 3.7 miles until it turns to a dirt road. The landing is immediately to the left.

West Bank Landing

Trip: West Bank Landing to Willtown Bluff (8 miles and about 2 hours with the tide).

Tide: High tide is about 4 hours behind Charleston Harbor and low tide is about 4¾ hours behind.

Trip: West Bank Landing to Willtown Bluff (8 miles and about 2 hours with the tide). There are two nice sandbars that appear as the tide goes out. One sandbar is on the left just past the Penny Creek entrance and another is on the left when making the final turn and before the Willtown Bluff Landing.

Penny Creek Landing

Directions: Take HWY 17 south from Charleston and turn left onto Parkers Ferry Rd (HWY 38). There used to be a brown sign noting Edisto River access to the left (Penny Creek and Willtown Bluff) and to the right (Martins Landing). The sign was down the year I wrote this book. The turnoff for Parkers Ferry Road is .3 mile from the green Parkers Ferry sign on HWY 17. Turn left from HWY 17, go 1 mile down Parkers Ferry Road where a brown sign indicates Penny Creek Landing to the right. Turn onto the street; it dead-ends at the landing.

Penny Creek Landing

Trip: Penny Creek Landing to Willtown Bluff (8 miles and about 2 hours with the tide).

This trip described below is one of my favorites within one hour of Charlestowne Landing. Do it, even if it means coming from Mount Pleasant. Penny Creek Landing is little more than a throw-in with ample parking. Be prepared to step in the mud to get to the creek when the tide is low. I enjoy this trip because there are many sandbars that provide for pull-offs to stretch and picnic. In particular, there is large sandbar just on the left side shortly after turning onto the Edisto from Penny Creek and another large one on the left side just before Willtown Bluff.

Tide: The high tide at the landing is 4 hours behind Charleston Harbor and low tide is about 3¾ hours behind. At the Edisto River junction, high tide is 3 hours behind and low tide is 3¾ hours behind.

Trip: Penny Creek Landing to Willtown Bluff (8 miles and about 2 hours with the tide). Penny Creek is narrow at the beginning and slowly opens up. The landscape changes from forest to marsh grass going downstream. It is about a one hour paddle from the landing to where the creek joins the river and it takes about another hour to get to Willtown Bluff Landing.

Tip: It is important to have confidence when turning onto a creek from a river. Pay careful attention to the terrain where Penny Creek enters the Edisto River. Remember certain trees and their position relative to the creek entrance just as you leave the creek to head down the river. Remember that some markers will be underwater at high tide.

Willtown Bluff Landing

Directions: Go south on HWY 17 and turn onto HWY 38, just like going to Penny Creek Landing. Go down HWY 38 for 5 miles and it will end. Turn right onto Willtown Road. This is a dirt road with a lot of loose sand. Along the road is a sign describing Willtown. Veer left at that sign to go to the landing. The trip is about 32 miles from Charlestowne Landing. Once in the water you can see why this is called a bluff. It is the highest land along the river.

Tide: The high tide is about 1½ hours behind Charleston Harbor and low tide is 2¼ hours behind.

Willtown Bluff Landing

Trip 1: Willtown Bluff to West Bank Landing (8 miles and about 2 hours).

Trip 2: Willtown Bluff to Penny Creek Landing on an incoming tide (8 miles and about 2 hours).

Trip 3: Willtown Bluff to Dawhoo Landing on a falling tide (10 miles and about 2½ hours).

Trip 1: Willtown Bluff to West Bank Landing (8 miles and about 2 hours). Leave a pickup vehicle at West Bank Landing or else plan to arrive there at high tide, take a break, and then return with the ebbing tide. You could continue to paddle about ½ hour past West Bank Landing to a little island that is just before a railroad bridge. There is a sandbar at the end of the island farthest from the bridge. It was about waist-deep at high tide the time I went. I recommend taking the additional time and paddling to the sandbar for a nice swim in the summer.

Trip 2: Willtown Bluff to Penny Creek Landing on an incoming tide (8 miles and about 2 hours). It is about 1¼ hours to the Penny Creek entrance and an additional hour from that entrance to Penny Creek Landing. Arrange for a pickup here or plan to arrive just before high tide, take a break, and return to Willtown Bluff with the falling tide.

Trip 3: Willtown Bluff to Dawhoo Landing on a falling tide (10 miles and about 2½ hours). Ride the falling tide down to the Dawhoo River and follow it to Dawhoo Landing. This is a good trip to take when low tide at Dawhoo Landing is in the afternoon since it gets paddlers off the wide Edisto River before the afternoon winds pick up.

Dawhoo Landing

Directions: Go south on HWY 17 and turn left onto HWY 17, the turnoff to Edisto Beach State Park. This turn is 6 miles after the only traffic light in Ravenel. When entering Adams Run, the speed limit drops to 35 mph. Pay attention. HWY 174 veers off to the right. It is marked, but pay attention or you will miss the turn and end up in Hollywood. Continue of HWY 174 and cross the bridge over the intracoastal waterway. The landing can be seen from the bridge and is accessed by turning right after coming off the bridge. It takes 35 minutes to get to the landing from Charlestowne Landing.

Dawhoo Landing

Trip 1: Dawhoo Landing on a rising tide to Willtown Bluff (10 miles and about 2½ hours).

Tide: The high tide is about 1 hour behind Charleston harbor and low tide is ¾ hour behind.

Trip 1: Dawhoo Landing on a rising tide to Willtown Bluff (10 miles and about 2½ hours). The turnoff to the Dawhoo River is within sight of the bridge. Turn right just before the intracoastal waterway marker number 132. Arrange for a pickup at Willtown Bluff Landing, or just plan to arrive there at high tide and return with the falling tide to Dawhoo Landing.

Toogoodoo Landing-North Edisto

Directions: Go south on HWY 17 and veer left on to HWY 162 heading toward Hollywood. Stay on this road. After passing the only traffic light in Hollywood, go 3.8 miles and there will be a brown sign indicating a left turn for Toogoodoo Creek access. Turn left and go straight down this road. The street sign says Storage Road. At the stop sign, cross the road, and continue to go straight. Across the road, the name changes to Parishville Road. It is 4.5 miles from the turnoff on HWY 162 to the landing.

Toogoodoo Landing

Trip: Toogoodoo Landing to Wadmalaw River (4 miles and about 1 hour).

Tide: The high tide is about 1 hour behind Charleston Harbor and low tide is ¾ hour behind.

Trip: Toogoodoo Landing to Wadmalaw River (4 miles and about 1 hour). I used this landing as a start and return location, planning my trip with the tide. Leave the landing by paddling to the right. Make a left turn to get on Toogoodoo Creek. A sandbar is on the left side of the river immediately after making the turn. This is a pleasant area to stop and take a swim.

Domestic animals as well as wildlife use the rivers. During an outing on the Toogoodoo Creek, I saw a large animal swimming from one shore to the other, but because of the distance, I could not determine the species. As I paddled closer, I determined it was a large dog. I watched him swim to the other bank and climb out through the plough mud, carefully avoiding an oyster bank.

Cherry Point Landing

Directions: Cherry Point Landing is at Rockville where Bohicket Creek joins the North Edisto River. Leave Charleston via the Wappoo Cut Bridge. Immediately after crossing the Wappoo Cut Bridge, turn right onto Maybank HWY (HWY 700). Cross over to Johns Island and continue all the way to Rockville. The speed limit drops to 35 mph just before Rockville. There is a brown sign just after the speed limit change that indicates Bohicket Creek Access. Turn left onto Cherry Point Road and go 1 mile. The landing is on the right. It is 24 miles from Charlestowne Landing.

> **Cherry Point Landing**
>
> **Trip:** Cherry Point Landing up Bohicket Creek and back.

Tide: The high tide is about ¼ hour behind Charleston Harbor and low tide is about the same as Charleston Harbor.

Trip: Cherry Point Landing up Bohicket Creek and back. The North Edisto River is to the right from the landing. Paddle to the left to go up Bohicket Creek. There is a shrimp boat facility on the left and the Bohicket Marina is on the right farther up. The Boy Scout camp is still farther up the creek. There is no good place for a pickup or to get out. Plan the trip according. If you plan to paddle for 4 hours, be in the water 2 hours before high tide and turn around after paddling 2 hours.

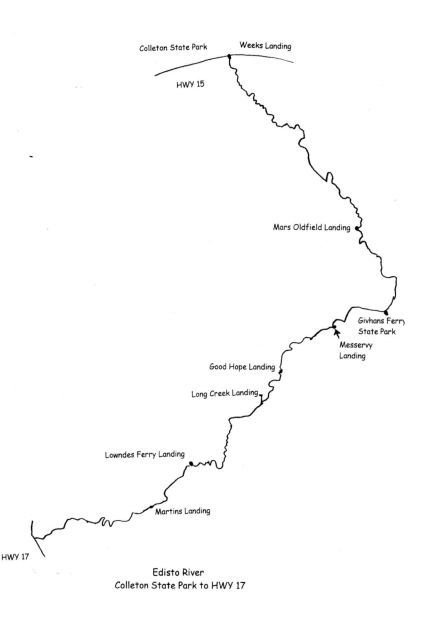

Colleton State Park   Weeks Landing

HWY 15

Mars Oldfield Landing

Givhans Ferry
State Park

Messervy
Landing

Good Hope Landing

Long Creek Landing

Lowndes Ferry Landing

Martins Landing

HWY 17

Edisto River
Colleton State Park to HWY 17

Edisto River

RIVER TOURS

I have done many trips by myself on the Edisto River. I make it a point to go against the current and then return. When paddling against the current, I go from side to side to slack areas of the river, I use eddies along the shoreline to help move along against the current, and I try to paddle at an angle to the current. Paddling alone against the current provides a good workout and ends with a relaxing ride back to the starting point. There is no need to plan around tides this far up the river. I recommend having a pickup vehicle for the easiest paddle. The trips on the Edisto River are easy to do with a pickup vehicle because many of the landings are on the same highway. This keeps backtracking to a minimum. Four of the landings can be associated with HWY 61 and any combination of these can be turned into trips that include a pickup vehicle. These are Weeks Landing (across from Colleton State Park), Mars Oldfield Landing, Givhans Ferry State Park Throw-In, and Messervy Landing. Three others can be associated with HWY 17A. These are Good Hope Landing, Long Creek Landing, and Sullivans Ferry Landing.

Weeks Landing (across from Colleton State Park)

Directions: Go out HWY 61, stay on it as HWY17A merges and leaves, and continue on HWY 61 through Givhans. Cross the bridge over the Edisto River and proceed to the blinking traffic light where HWY 61 intersects with HWY 15. Turn right onto HWY 15. Immediately after crossing the bridge over the Edisto, turn left to access the landing. There is no sign on HWY 15 indicating the landing turnoff. Weeks Landing is 1 hour from Charlestowne Landing. It is clean and has ample parking with a nice black-top surface.

Trip: Weeks Landing to Mars Oldfield Landing (11 miles and about 4½ hours) or to Givhans Ferry State Park (20 miles and about 6 hours). My daughter and I have done the trip all the way to

> **Weeks Landing**
>
> **Trip:** Weeks Landing to Mars Oldfield Landing (11 miles and about 4½ hours) or to Givhans Ferry State Park (20 miles and about 6 hours).

27

Givhans Ferry several times. We dropped the pickup vehicle at Givhans Ferry State Park, and then drove to Weeks Landing where we put in. The trip ends just before the HWY 61 bridge at Givhans Ferry. Givhans Ferry State Park does not open until 9 a.m. and now requires a $2 parking fee.

Mars Oldfield Landing

Directions: Go out HWY 61 and stay on it as you pass Givhans Ferry State Park. A brown Edisto River access sign is 6 miles past the HWY 61 bridge over the Edisto. Turn right at the sign. The landing is about a mile down the dirt road. The road ends at the landing.

At this point in the river the current is strong and little paddling is required. For the beginning paddler, the challenge is to keep the kayak in the middle of the river.

Trip: Mars Oldfield Landing to Messervy Landing (12 miles and about 4 hours). This is my favorite trip on this part of the Edisto. It can be shortened by taking out at Givhans Ferry State Park (9 miles and about 3 hours). I go past Givhans Ferry because it is difficult to carry the kayaks up the hill at the landing. The Messervy Landing is on the water and has a floating dock. Scenic wilderness flanks the river, and there are many places to pull off along the riverbank or onto sandbars when the water level is low.

Consider this a full day trip. The last time I went, I left Charlestowne Landing at 8:40 a.m. and returned at 3:30 p.m. The trip took 4 hours on the river, about a half hour of loading and unloading, and 2½ hours of travel time, including backtracking to the cars.

Mars Oldfield Landing

Trip: Mars Oldfield Landing to Messervy Landing (12 miles and about 4 hours). This is my favorite trip on this part of the Edisto. It can be shortened by taking out at Givhans Ferry State Park (9 miles and about 3 hours).

28

Messervy Landing

Directions: Go out HWY 61 and immediately after passing the road that goes right to Givhans Ferry State Park, turn left onto HWY 162, Old Beachhill Road. Go 1.8 miles and turn right at the street sign for Boat Landing Road. There is no brown sign indicating river access. The landing is about a mile down the road. It is 40 minutes from

Messervy Landing

Trips: Messervy Landing to Good Hope Landing (5 miles and about 1½ hours) or Long Creek Landing (8 miles and about 2¼ hours).

Charleston. The river floods a portion of this road when it is at flood stage (check the newspaper), and I would not go through the water in a car. The modern landing has two lanes and a floating dock. This landing is my auto drop-off point when I have two vehicles for a trip to the Mars Oldfield Landing to paddle down with the current. I have also used this as a turn-around point when I paddled solo up the river.

Trips: Messervy Landing to Good Hope Landing (5 miles and about 1½ hours) or Long Creek Landing (8 miles and about 2¼ hours). A great deal of vehicle backtracking, is required for this trip since the highway turnoff to both Good Hope and Long Creek landings are on HWY 17A and the Messervy turnoff is from HWY 61. Avoid some backtracking by taking the dirt road that parallels the river from Messervy Landing down to HWY 17A. The dirt road shortens the miles (but not the time) of backtracking.

Good Hope Landing

Directions: Go out HWY 61 from Charleston. When it joins HWY 17A, stay on HWY 17A and do not veer right on HWY 61 as you would if going to Givhans Ferry. Cross the Edisto, go .6 mile, and turn right onto HWY 91 (McDanieltown Road). Continue down this road for about 2.7 miles and pass

Good Hope Landing

Trip: Good Hope Landing to Sullivans Ferry Landing (5 miles and about 2 hours).

the turnoff to Long Creek Landing that is .4 mile down HWY 91. Good Hope Landing is marked with a brown access sign. Turn right from HWY 91 and continue down Good Hope Landing Road .4 mile to get to the landing. The landing is 40 minutes from Charleston.

Trip: Good Hope Landing to Sullivans Ferry Landing (5 miles and about 2 hours). Leave a pickup vehicle at Sullivans Ferry Landing which is downstream from the HWY 17A bridge over the Edisto. Put in at Good Hope Landing and ride with the current to Sullivans Ferry Landing.

I did this trip alone, leaving Sullivans Ferry Landing and paddling upstream to Good Hope Landing. It took me 2½ hours to paddle up and 1½ hours to paddle back. It was a great trip, but I was exhausted.

Long Creek Landing

Directions: Go out HWY 61 from Charleston. When it joins HWY 17A, stay on HWY 17A and do not veer right on HWY 61. Cross the Edisto, go .6 mile, and turn right onto HWY 91 (McDanieltown Road). Continue on down this road for about .4 mile. The turn to the right is well-marked with a brown sign noting Long Creek Landing. The landing is .6 mile down the dirt road. Long Creek Landing is 35 minutes from Charleston.

This landing is on a creek that flows into the Edisto. Paddle to the right when leaving the landing. I had to ask one of the locals for directions to the Edisto. There is a wide sandbank on the opposite side of the Edisto just as Long Creek junction.

Long Creek Landing

Trip 1: Long Creek Landing to Sullivans Ferry Landing (2 miles and about a ½ hour paddle).

Trip 2: Long Creek Landing to Messervy Landing and return (total trip 16 miles and about 4 hours).

Trip 3: Long Creek Landing to Martins Landing (9 miles and about 2½ hours).

Trip 1: Long Creek Landing to Sullivans Ferry Landing (2 miles and about a ½ hour paddle). Drop a vehicle off at Sullivans Ferry Landing on the way to Long Creek Landing and paddle with the current downstream.

Trip 2: Long Creek Landing to Messervy Landing and return (total trip 16 miles and about 4 hours). Paddle upstream about 8 miles to Messervy Landing, take a break, and paddle back. It takes about 2½ hours of good paddling to go up against the current and about 1¾ hours to come back with the current. Do not attempt this trip if the river is high because the current is too hard to paddle against. I tried it when the river was at 8.5 feet and it took 2 hours to paddle the 3 miles to Good Hope Landing. A local told me that the water level needed to be about 4 feet to have the current slow enough to take a trip of this length against the current.

Trip 3: Long Creek Landing to Martins Landing (9 miles and about 2½ hours). This is a great paddle going downstream. The logistics of this trip are complicated. Take HWY 17 south and go to Martins Landing. (Please see the directions to Martins Landing that follow). Leave a pickup vehicle at Martins Ferry. Continue down Parkers Ferry Road, remaining on it after it crosses County Line Road (HWY 317), where it changes to a dirt road and becomes HWY 137. Five miles after crossing County Line Road, HWY 137 intersects HWY 17A. Turn left on HWY 17A. Cross the bridge over the Edisto and follow the directions noted above to Long Creek Landing. Start at Sullivans Ferry Landing for a shorter trip, or Good Hope Landing for a longer trip.

Sullivans Ferry Landing

Directions: Go out HWY 61 from Charleston. When it joins HWY 17A, stay on HWY 17A and do not veer right on HWY 61. Cross the Edisto, go .6 mile, and turn left onto Camp Buddy Road. Follow this road for about a mile and it will intersect with Sullivans Ferry Road. Do not turn left onto Sullivans Ferry Road. (I did and ended up in someone's backyard. They were kind enough to give me the directions to the landing). At the intersection of Camp Buddy Road and Sullivans Ferry Road, continue straight on Camp Buddy Road. Go .3 mile, pass house number 1019 and then veer left before the next fence post. It appears to be someone's front yard. The little driveway leads to the landing.

As noted in my description of Good Hope and Long Creek Landings, this makes an excellent pickup point for trips down from those two landings. This landing is unique from many along the upper Edisto River because it is completely inhabited. In fact, when I went there the first time, I was afraid I was in someone's front yard and had to ask to make sure this was the public landing. Your vehicle should be safe here waiting for your return.

Sullivans Ferry Landing

This makes an excellent pickup point.

Lowndes Ferry Landing

Directions: Go out HWY 61 and get onto HWY 17 A. Go .6 mile after crossing the Edisto River and turn left onto Camp Buddy Road. These are the same directions as going to Sullivans Ferry Landing. However, at the intersection of Sullivans Ferry Road and Camp Buddy Road, turn right onto Sullivans Ferry Road. Note that some maps may indicate that Camp Buddy Road continues down to Lowndes Ferry. While I was at the intersection trying to decide what to do, a kind man stopped his truck and asked if he could help me. I told him where I was going and he told me that the Camp Buddy Road no longer goes to Lowndes Ferry despite what any map might say. He gave me the following directions and they worked well. Turn right onto Sullivans Ferry Road and go about 1 mile until passing horse pens on the left. Turn left on that road and go 3.8 miles to the landing. The Sand Hill Hunt Club is about 1 mile before the landing.

Trip: This landing is so far out of the way that I would not recommend using it unless planning to leave and return to the landing. The road to the landing is a bumpy dirt road and there is too much backtracking involved in trying to couple this with another landing. Martins Ferry Landing is only 4 miles downriver but it is difficult to coordinate dropping off a pickup vehicle. The trip upriver is against the current but it is worthwhile since it passes deeply wooded areas of the river. The time I went in early June, the water level was low and I was sometimes paddling through six inches of water. I left the landing and paddled 7 miles against the current up to the HWY 17A bridge and it took about 2½ hours. It took 1½ hours to return. I thought this was a desolate landing when I left in the morning. It was packed with young adults having a great time when I returned.

Lowndes Ferry Landing

Trip: This landing is so remote that I would not recommend using it unless planning to leave and return to the landing.

33

Martins Landing

Directions: Take HWY 17 south and turn right on Parkers Ferry Road (HWY 38). Penny Creek Landing is to the left from HWY 17. The turnoff for Parkers Ferry Road is .3 mile from the green Parkers Ferry sign on HWY 17. There used to be a brown sign indicating Edisto River access to the right and to the left. The sign was down on HWY 17 the year I wrote this book. Go 6 miles and turn left on a dirt road to get to the landing. This dirt road is about .3 mile long. The landing turnoff is not marked.

Martins Ferry Landing

Trip 1: Martins Ferry to West Bank Landing (11 miles and about 3 hours).

Trip 2: Martins Ferry to Lowndes Ferry and back (total trip 8 miles and about 2 hours).

The key is to go 6 miles and look for a dirt road going to the left. It is one of the roads that is not private and has a stop sign on it where it intersects with HWY 38. There may be a street sign indicating Martins Ferry Landing Road, but many times it is down too. If you miss the turnoff, you will cross a little bridge that is right after the turnoff. If you miss the little bridge, you will come to County Line Road, which is where the pavement ends and the dirt road begins. Turn around and go .9 mile back, cross the little bridge and look to the right.

Some of the guidebooks I have read indicate that this landing is affected by the tides. When I went, there was no tidal current impact. The current flowed swiftly downriver. Locals will agree that the river level goes up and down with the tides, but the river current offsets any incoming tidal current. The current "whips" by this landing but slows down a little further on as the river widens. Do not use this landing expecting an incoming tide to assist with the return trip.

Trip 1: Martins Ferry to West Bank Landing (11 miles and about 3 hours). Go downriver and arrange for a pickup at the West Bank Landing.

34

Trip 2: Martins Ferry to Lowndes Ferry and back (total trip 8 miles and about 2 hours). I have paddled upriver and the current was not bad, except where the river narrowed. It took me an hour to go the 4 miles to Lowndes Ferry Landing and about 45 minutes to return.

I did the trip to West Bank Landing one fine fall day with one of my friends. The water was like glass. Since the river is black, it reflected the sky and shoreline like a mirror. Unfortunately, I decided that we could paddle back up the river with the incoming tide. That is when I learned first hand that the water level may go up and down, but the current always flows out. It took us 3 hours to get to the West Bank Landing, but 6 hours to get back! While the scenery on the return trip was gorgeous, the trip was much too long. I took the trip one weekday when there were no boaters on the water. If I had seen any, I would have asked for a ride back. My paddling partner was tired and not very happy with the decisions I had made that day.

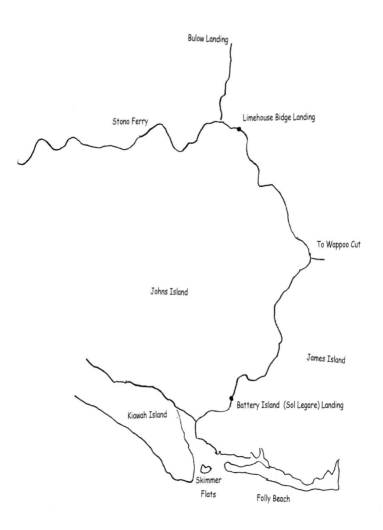

Bulow Landing

Stono Ferry

Limehouse Bidge Landing

To Wappoo Cut

Johns Island

James Island

Battery Island (Sol Legare) Landing

Kiawah Island

Skimmer
Flats

Folly Beach

Stono River

STONO RIVER

The Stono River runs between Folly Island and Kiawah Island, then between James Island and Johns Island, and continues inland to separate Johns Island from West Ashley and Hollywood. Because of its location surrounding Charleston, it has much history dealing with the Revolutionary War and the War Between the States.

Battery Island (Sol Legare Road) Landing

Directions: Go down Folly Road toward Folly Beach. Take either the James Island Connector (HWY 30) or the Wappoo Cut since the turnoff for the landing is almost at Folly Island. Turn right from HWY 171 (Folly Road) onto Sol Legare Road. The turnoff is not well-marked going out from Charleston. The turnoff is 2.4 miles from the stoplight by the James Island Presbyterian Church. The landing is at the end of the road. It is another well-done Charleston County Landing. The parking lot is paved, it has ample parking, and there are two lanes on the ramp.

Tide: The tides are about the same as Charleston Harbor.

Trip 1: Battery Island Landing to the Kiawah River (3 miles and about an hour each way). Leave the landing and paddle to the left toward the ocean. Turn right into the Kiawah River. Plan to do this trip toward the end of a falling tide and use the tide to carry you out and back on the Stono. Use the slack water time to be on the Kiawah River.

Trip 2: Battery Island Landing to Folly Island sandbars (5 miles and about 1½ hours). Go toward the ocean and bear left to the sandbars off Folly Island. Skimmer Flats, a major nesting area for pelicans and other shore birds, is between Kiawah Island and Folly

Battery Island Landing

Trip 1: Battery Island Landing to the Kiawah River (3 miles and about an hour each way).

Trip 2: Battery Island Landing to Folly Island sandbars (5 miles and about 1½ hours).

37

Island. The sandbars back here have a lot of nice sand for swimming and picnicking at low tide. Across the Stono River is a beach on Kiawah Island. Plan this trip to avoid the windiest parts of the day or do it on a day when a high pressure area has settled in. The river is very wide and a building wind can create good-sized waves for the recreational kayaker. I took this trip on a day when a high pressure area had settled over Charleston just a few days before. The water was like glass and it was a great trip.

Special note:
Paddling down the river towards the ocean, the water becomes very broad. Afternoon winds will create waves. If planning to be out in the area between Kiawah Island and Folly Island, be prepared for chop once the afternoon begins, or else plan to return up the river before noon.

Limehouse Bridge Landing

Directions: Take HWY 17 south from Charleston. Turn left from HWY 17 toward Kiawah Island on SC 20. A brown sign on HWY 17 indicates the Limehouse Bridge turnoff. The landing has ample parking, floating docks, and a 3-lane ramp. It is 8 miles from Charlestowne Landing.

Tide: The high tide is about 1¾ hours behind Charleston Harbor and low tide is about 1½ hours behind.

Trip 1: Limehouse Bridge to Riverland Terrace (9 miles and about 2 hours) or Wappoo Cut (10 miles and about 2¼ hours). I do not like being in this section if it is windy or if I will be there in midday when winds tend to pick up. It is interesting to look at Charleston and Johns Island in this area. There are beautiful homes along the river. Plan the trip to arrive at either of these landings at low tide in Charleston. Please read the section of this book about Wappoo Cut to learn about Elliotts Cut. Boat traffic can create problems getting through that narrow section.

Trip 2: Limehouse Bridge up Rantowles Creek to Bulow Landing (5 miles and about 1¼ hours with the rising tide). Paddle underneath the bridge. There is a large sandbar on the right side of the river just past the bridge (less than 1 mile from the landing) at low tide. It is a good place to stop and relax. Boaters flock to this sandbar on summer weekends. Rantowles Creek is slightly past the sandbar, on the right side of the river. There is a fine beach on the left side immediately after entering the creek. Continue up Rantowles Creek under the HWY 17 bridges. After passing under the bridge, the water opens up. The left side of this bay is a huge mud flat. Keep to the right to stay in the channel. Crab pot bouys indicate deep water. The creek leaves this

---

Limehouse Bridge Landing

Trip 1: Limehouse Bridge to Riverland Terrace (9 miles and about 2 hours) or Wappoo Cut (10 miles and about 2¼ hours).

Trip 2: Limehouse Bridge, up Rantowles Creek to Bulow Landing (5 miles and about 1¼ hours with the rising tide).

Trip 3: Limehouse Bridge to Stono Ferry Golf Course (7 miles and about 2 hours).

bay and goes under power lines before getting to Bulow Landing. Do this trip on a rising tide.

Trip 3: Limehouse Bridge to Stono Ferry Golf Course (7 miles and about 2 hours). I have ridden the tides down there and back several times. Fish and dolphin are active in the shallower areas of this section. I was surprised to see dolphins this far inland.

Bulow Landing

Bulow Landing is on Rantowles Creek, which empties into the Stono River just upriver from the Limehouse Bridge. This is a nice creek to go down with the outgoing tide. The tide runs very quickly through here and with a falling tide, you can get to the Stono River in about ¾ hour.

Directions: Take HWY 17 South from Charleston. Remain on HWY 17 and pass the turnoff to Johns Island and the Limehouse Bridge. Cross the Rantowles Creek Bridge on HWY 17 and look for the brown sign indicating the Bulow Landing turnoff. This is Davison Road. It is .3 mile after the bridge. Turn right onto Davison Road and go 1.8 miles. A dirt road goes off to the right. This is Bulow Landing Road. There is no sign for the landing. If you pass this dirt road, the very next road is County Line Road. Turn right on it and head back to Bulow Landing Road. The landing is .6 mile down this dirt road. At the time I wrote this guide, there had been heavy equipment traffic on this sandy road. The road is very soft and treacherous if there has been a lot of rain. Drive slowly and carefully down it.

Tide: The tide is approximately 2 hours behind Charleston Harbor.

Trip: Bulow Landing to Limehouse Bridge (5 miles and about 1¼ hours with the tide). Take the falling tide and plan to stop on the beach on the intracoastal waterway. Turn left toward Limehouse Bridge and the sandbar is on the left side of the river. Since this is such a short trip when running with the tide, I like to return to Bulow

Bulow Landing

Trip: Bulow Landing to Limehouse Bridge (5 miles and about 1¼ hours with the tide).

40

Landing. The area north of HWY 17 is very wide and much of it is a mud flat at low tide. It is not important to know where the channel is when leaving Bulow Landing at high tide, but it is important to know where the channel is when paddling through at low tide. When returning, the channel runs along the far right side of the mud flat. Just after going under the HWY 17 bridge, take every right turn and bear right whenever there is an option in order to remain in the channel. Power lines across the creek indicate where the creek narrows and heads directly to the landing.

Earhart at Folly Island sandbars. Summer 2002.

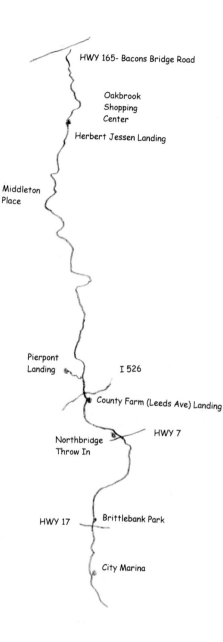

HWY 165- Bacons Bridge Road

Oakbrook
Shopping
Center

Herbert Jessen Landing

Middleton
Place

Pierpont
Landing

I 526

County Farm (Leeds Ave) Landing

Northbridge
Throw In

HWY 7

HWY 17

Brittlebank Park

City Marina

Ashley River

ASHLEY RIVER

The Ashley River passes Old Fort Dorchester and famous plantations such as Drayton Hall and Middleton Place. I enjoy the Ashley River because it is close, not too busy, and has easy access along its shores. There is no need to adjust the times of low and high tide from the times listed in the newspaper until upriver from the County Farm (Leeds Avenue) Landing. The City Marina and Brittlebank Park throw-in are on the Ashley River. I discuss them in the chapter titled *Immediately Within the Charleston Area*.

Northbridge Throw-In

Directions: This throw-in is on the West Ashley side of the HWY 7 bridge that crosses from North Charleston to West Ashley. The area was not designed for parking and boat launching, but many people use it to get to the river. There are large ruts in the dirt roads that lead to the water. I recommend pulling off on the north side of the bridge, parking on the grassy shoulder, and carrying the kayak down to the water. The shore is sandy and gently sloping. This is a terrific place to go for those who live close by and can only spend a short time on the river.

Tides: The tide is about ½ hour behind the harbor tide.

Trip 1: Northbridge to County Farm Landing (3 miles and about 1 hour). If the tide is coming in, go upriver past the County Farm Landing.

Trip 2: Northbridge to Charleston (6 miles and about 2 hours). If the tide is going out, head down toward the city. Time the trip to turn around when the tide changes.

Trip 3: Northbridge to Charlestowne Landing (4 miles and about 1¼ hours

Northbridge Throw-In

Trip 1: Northbridge to County Farm Landing (3 miles and about 1 hour).

Trip 2: Northbridge to Charleston (6 miles and about 2 hours).

Trip 3: Northbridge to Charlestowne Landing (4 miles and about 1¼ hours each way).

each way). Paddle down the Ashley River and go up the creek to Charlestowne Landing. Charlestowne Landing can be seen from the Ashley River. The creek to the landing is on the right-hand side after paddling past Dolphin Cove Marina. Plan the trip to be there about low tide and paddle up towards Charlestowne Landing on slack water. Return to Northbridge with the incoming tide. There is no place to pull over at Charlestowne Landing; however, there are a few spots just past it.

County Farm (Leeds Avenue) Landing

Directions: From Charlestowne Landing, get on I-526 and head toward North Charleston. The boat landing can been seen when crossing the bridge over the Ashley River. Get off I-526 at the Leeds Avenue exit. When getting off, turn right. There is a brown sign indicating County Farm Boat Landing immediately after going around a bend in the road. Turn right a the stop light. If you miss the stop light turn, you will pass the county jail to the right. After turning right at the light, follow that road around for about a ½ mile to the landing. This is a major landing and is extremely busy on weekends. Courtesy is critically important.

Tide: The tide is about ¾ hour behind Charleston Harbor.

Trip 1: Leeds Avenue Landing, up the river to Drayton Hall (3½ miles and about 1¼ hours), or Middleton Place (8 miles and about 2½ hours). Use the tide to go up and back. For the trip to Middleton Place, which is a long trip, plan to take an incoming tide to get there. Return with the falling tide. It is too far to paddle to Middleton Place without tidal help.

Trip 2: Leeds Avenue Landing to Northbridge and back (3 miles and about 1 hour each way). This is a good short trip. Plan to be at Northbridge at the time of low tide—about ½ hour after Charleston Harbor low tide.

County Farm Landing

Trip 1: Leeds Avenue Landing, up the river to Drayton Hall (3½ miles and about 1¼ hours), or Middleton Place (8 miles and about 2½ hours).

Trip 2: Leeds Avenue Landing to Northbridge and back (3 miles and about 1 hour each way).

44

Pierpont Landing

Directions: Go out HWY 61 toward Summerville. After crossing HWY 7 and driving 2.7 miles on HWY 61 there will be a traffic light on Parsonage Road. A brown sign indicates Ashley River Access. Sometimes tree branches block the sign. Follow Parsonage Road toward the river and then bear left at the end. The parking lot is adequate and there is a one-lane ramp.

Pierpont Landing

Trip: Pierpont to Northbridge (7 miles and about 1½ hours).

The landing is a neighborhood landing, right next to a set of apartments. It is on a creek that winds around for about a mile before entering the Ashley River. The creek has several blind turns. Be careful and listen for boats. Keep close to shore when hearing a boat coming.

Tide: This landing is far enough away from downtown to require a calculation for when the tides change. It is about 1 hour behind published Charleston tides.

Trip: Pierpont to Northbridge (7 miles and about 1½ hours). Take an outgoing tide and ride down the Ashley River past the County Farm Landing to the Northbridge with the tidal current. Stop on the riverbank by the Northbridge, take a break, and then return up the Ashley with the tide.

Herbert Jessen Landing (Near Oakbrook Shopping Center in Summerville)

Herbert Jessen Landing

Directions: This landing is at the end of a road intersecting Dorchester Road by the Oakbrook Shopping Center in Summerville. From Charlestowne Landing take I-26 and go west. Take the very next exit onto Dorchester Road and go left. Go 14 miles down Dorchester Road, driving past Ashley Phosphate Road. After the final entrance to King's Grant subdivision is a major intersection with a traffic light.

Trip 1: Jessen Landing to Middleton Place (3½ miles and about 1½ hours with the tide).

Trip 2: Jessen Landing to Bacons Bridge Road (2 miles and about 1 hour).

There is a sign that says Ashley River Access. The landing is ½ mile down the road. This landing is paved, clean, and neat.

Tides: The high tide at this landing is about 2½ hours behind Charleston Harbor and the low tide is almost 3½ hours behind.

Trip 1: Jessen Landing to Middleton Place (3½ miles and about 1½ hours with the tide). Head to the left and paddle down the river. King's Grant is on the left. This is a much easier paddle to Middleton Place than coming upriver from Leeds Avenue. There is no place to pull over at Middleton Place. Pull over after passing Middleton Place, take a break, and then return.

Trip 2: Jessen Landing to Bacons Bridge Road (2 miles and about an hour). Paddle to the right (upriver) from this landing toward the headwaters of the Ashley River. Old Fort Dorchester State Park is on the right shortly after beginning the trip. Depending on the amount of recent rainfall and the depth of the tide at the time of a trip, a paddler may have to negotiate fallen trees. The river becomes very shallow and there are a lot of fallen trees after Bacons Bridge Road. This is an excellent two hour trip in any kind of weather because it is shady in the summer and well-protected from winds in the winter.

Paddling from the Ashley River toward Charlestowne Landing. Fall 2002.

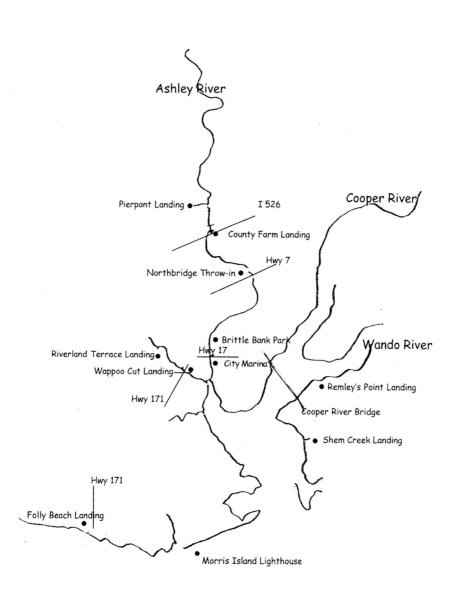

Ashley River

Cooper River

Pierpont Landing ●   I 526

● County Farm Landing

Hwy 7

Northbridge Throw-in ●

● Brittle Bank Park

Riverland Terrace Landing ●   Hwy 17

Wappoo Cut Landing ●   ● City Marina

Wando River

● Remley's Point Landing

Hwy 171

Cooper River Bridge

● Shem Creek Landing

Hwy 171

Folly Beach Landing ●

● Morris Island Lighthouse

Immediately Around Charleston

IMMEDIATELY AROUND CHARLESTON

There are many enjoyable trips within the immediate Charleston area. The landings are within short distances and are easily accessed.

Charleston Harbor

Harbor trips are noted for their beauty. I enjoy the harbor at sunset and sunrise. As with many open areas of water, it is generally calmer closer to sunrise and sunset than during the afternoons. Breezes (and this means waves) develop as the day heats up. One of the local sailing schools does not start class until 11 a.m. in order to be on the water during the best sea breeze time. Unless a high-pressure area has settled over Charleston, avoid being on the harbor when it is choppy. Plan the final leg of a trip to begin about 11 a.m.

There is a lot of merchant ship and motorboat traffic on the harbor. Too many paddlers have stories about encounters with merchant ships. *Paddler Magazine* listed Charleston Harbor as a "Southeast Sea Kayak Hotspot." *(Paddler Magazine,* July/ August 2002, page 76.) The article alerted experienced kayakers to be careful of the busy working harbor. Pay careful attention to the ship traffic, and stay out of their way. Merchant ships have minimal maneuverability in the confines of the harbor, but they do tend to have predictable courses. Paddlers say, "When a merchantman blows his horn at you, he is likely telling you to get ready to be squashed." Motorboats come from all directions. A collision situation exists when the bearing of an approaching boat does not change and the distance gets closer. Don't assume that motorboaters are paying attention to what is in front of them. Raise your paddle and wave if

Immediately Around Charleston

Mount Pleasant Area
Remleys Point Landing
Shem Creek Landing

West Ashley/James Island Area
Wappoo Cut Landing
Riverland Terrace Landing

City of Charleston
City Marina
Brittlebank Park Landing
Seven Bridge Challenge

49

the boat is closing in and its bearing does not change. A considerate boater will immediately turn as soon as he sees you.

Trips in the harbor can be easy paddles if planned carefully around the tide changes. For the easiest trips, plan to paddle with the tide, timing the trip to return after the tide changes. The tides for this area can be assumed to be the tides published for the Charleston area in the newspapers, radio, and TV. There are slight variations, but not enough to require a calculation.

Mount Pleasant Area

Remleys Point Landing
Directions: After crossing the Cooper River Bridge turn left at the second stoplight. There is a brown sign indicating Remleys Point Landing to the left. Turn left onto Mathis Ferry Road. After .4 mile, another brown sign indicates Remleys Point Landing to the left. Turn left and go 1.5 miles. There is a blue sign indicating a left turn to go to Remleys Point Landing. Turn left onto 2nd Street. Stay on this street, which ends in the landing's parking lot.

This landing is directly on the harbor and near the Cooper River Bridges. The landing is large and serves many people who live east of the Cooper. The landing's parking lot is large with three wide lanes on the boat ramp. Barriers have been built around the landing so that the ramp area is not subject to waves from the river. It is busy on summer weekends.

Tide: Use the Charleston Harbor tide tables.

Remleys Point Landing

Trip 1: Remleys Point on a rising tide up the Cooper River or the Wando River.

Trip 2: Remleys Point to Shem Creek (4 miles and about 1½ hours on an outgoing tide).

Trip 1: Remleys Point on a rising tide up the Cooper River or the Wando River. If the tide is coming in, go up the Cooper River past the old Navy Base and toward North Charleston. Or go up the Wando River past the port and explore the various creeks that branch off the Wando. Be careful paddling by the container port on the Wando. Ships leave at all times.

Trip 2: Remleys Point to Shem Creek (4 miles and about 1½ hours on an outgoing tide). Go under the Cooper River bridges. Arrange for a pickup at the Shem Creek landing. It takes about 1 hour to paddle with the tide to Crab Bank, a sandy island where Shem Creek enters the harbor. Get out here, stretch, picnic and enjoy the scenery. Then paddle up Shem Creek to the landing. This last leg will take 20-30 minutes, depending on how hard the tide may be coming out.

One gorgeous day in September, I paddled around Crab Bank and came upon approximately 200 pelicans sitting on the bank. It was a spectacular sight. I paddled in close and then coasted along the bank with the tide. The pelicans just stood and watched me.

Shem Creek
Directions: After crossing the Cooper River Bridge, get on Coleman Boulevard (HWY 703) at the bottom of the bridge. This used to be the only route to Sullivans Island and Isle of Palms before the Isle of Palms Connector opened. After crossing the Shem Creek bridge, the highway makes a big turn to the left. There is a traffic light at the end of the turn and a brown sign indicating the Shem Creek access to the left. Turn left onto Simmons Avenue. The street ends in three blocks at the landing.

There is no parking immediately at the boat landing. Go ahead and take your boat off and set it in the grass at the head of the ramps. The parking lot cannot be seen from the landing. It is around a turn to the left. It is lined for vehicles with trailers. If it is a weekend

Shem Creek Landing

Trip 1: Shem Creek on a falling tide into the harbor toward Sullivans Island.

Trip 2: Shem Creek to Remleys Point. See Trip 2 in the Remleys Point section.

or a summer day, park on the street just outside the parking lot.

Tide: Use the Charleston Harbor tide tables.

Trip 1: Shem Creek on a falling tide into the harbor toward Sullivans Island. Take the outgoing tide and go past all the restaurants and fishing boats into the harbor. There is a nice sandbar (Crab Bank) protecting the entrance to Shem Creek from the harbor. The trip along Shem Creek should be peaceful, but watch out for boats, especially the fishing boats. Keep out of their way. This is a narrow, shallow channel and large fishing boats have little maneuvering room. It takes about ½ hour to paddle with the tide out to Crab Bank. This bird sanctuary is closed from April 1–October 15 in order to protect the nesting areas. When the sanctuary is not closed, this small sandy island is a great place to picnic while viewing the harbor.

Trip 2: Shem Creek to Remleys Point. See Trip 2 in the Remleys Point section. If the tide is coming in and you only have a short amount of time to paddle, arrange for a pickup at Remleys Point Landing. It will take about 1½ hours to get from the Shem Creek Landing to the Remleys Point Landing.

Many people leave Shem Creek and paddle to Fort Sumter. This trip requires paddling across the shipping lanes and unless the trip is done early in the day, it is subject to afternoon winds that produce waves on the return. The best trip to Fort Sumter is from the Wappoo Cut Landing.

WEST ASHLEY/JAMES ISLAND AREA

Wappoo Cut Landing

Directions: Get to this landing by heading out from Charleston toward Folly Beach on HWY 171. Do not take the James Island Connector. Turn right from 171 just before crossing the drawbridge over the Wappoo Cut to get to the landing.

The Wappoo Cut Landing is to the City, James Island, and West Ashley areas what Remleys Point is to the East Cooper area. It has a large paved parking area, floating docks, and four ramps that can be used simultaneously. I like this landing because it is convenient to me, well-lit, and provides excellent access to the views on Charleston's west side.

Tide: Use the Charleston Harbor tide tables. Plan around the tides when planning a trip from Wappoo Cut. The tides run fast through here at peak times. A novice should not try to paddle against the tide during the peak two hour period. It will not be dangerous; it just will not be fun.

Trip 1: Wappoo Cut to Charlestowne Landing (4 miles and about 1½ hours). Leave Wappoo Cut on the first two hours or last two hours of an incoming tide. Turn left and paddle with the tide up the Ashley River. The marina area, the City's Brittlebank Park, and The Citadel are all on the right. Continue past The Citadel. Go to the other side of the river and proceed up Old Towne Creek to paddle past Charlestowne Landing. Charlestowne Landing can be seen from the Ashley River, especially if the Landing's sailing ship is tied up in the creek.

Wappoo Cut Landing

Trip 1: Wappoo Cut to Charlestowne Landing (4 miles and about 1½ hours).

Trip 2: Wappoo Cut to the Battery (3 miles and about 1 hour on an outgoing tide).

Trip 3: Wappoo Cut to Limehouse Bridge (10 miles and about 2¼ hours).

Trip 4: Wappoo Cut to Fort Sumter (7 miles and about 1½ hours).

Trip 2: Wappoo Cut to the Battery (3 miles and about 1 hour on an outgoing tide). Plan to be on the Cooper River side of the Battery at dead low tide. Ride the outgoing tide and have a magnificent trip along the west side of Charleston, going past the Coast Guard Station and traveling along the Battery. Be careful traveling along the Battery. The wakes from passing boats hit the seawall and reflect back with almost the same force. There is nothing to be concerned about; just realize that any wave that passes under will come back from the other direction with about the same force. There is a little beach where the seawall ends. Take a break and wait for the incoming tide to start running. Ride it past the Battery and into the Wappoo Cut.

Trip 3: Wappoo Cut to Limehouse Bridge (10 miles and about 2¼ hours). Go with an incoming tide through Elliotts Cut and continue up the Stono River with the tide. Elliotts Cut is very narrow and has seawalls. Waves bounce off the seawall on one side, go to the other side, and bounce back. At times of heavy boat traffic there are large "confused" waves in this area. Avoid Elliotts Cut during the times of heavy boat traffic to avoid this rough situation. I came through Elliotts Cut one Sunday at noontime. I managed to paddle up very close to the stern of a sailboat motoring up the waterway. I maintained that position going through the Cut. The sailboat acted as an "icebreaker" to cut through the waves for me.

At one time during the Civil War, the Confederates captured a Union vessel in the Stono River and brought it through this area to Charleston. The Union vessel drew only eight feet, but the cut was so shallow that it took them three days to pull it through. Shortly after that adventure, the southern engineers made a concerted effort to deepen Elliotts Cut.

Trip 4: Wappoo Cut to Fort Sumter (7 miles and about 1½ hours). Do this trip when low tide in the harbor is noon or earlier. Leave on the outgoing tide and ride it along James Island to the sandbars by Fort Sumter. Plan to leave Fort Sumter in time to get into the Ashley River before the afternoon winds pick up.

Riverland Terrace (Fire House) Landing

Directions: Go out HWY 171 toward Folly Beach—do not take the James Island Connector. Immediately after crossing the Wappoo Cut Bridge, turn right onto Maybank Road. Go down Maybank Highway .8 miles where the highway bears left at a stoplight. Veer right. After 1 block a brown sign indicates Elliotts Cut access. Turn right and go to the end of the road.

Riverland Terrace Landing

Trips: Do the same trips from here as from Wappoo Cut Landing.

The Fire House Landing is in the Wappoo Cut and provides access to the Wappoo Cut from the James Island side. This is a good departure site for trips on the Stono. It is small and peaceful, especially when compared to the activity that takes place at the Wappoo Cut Landing.

Tide: Use the Charleston Harbor tide tables. The tides run fast through here at their peak times.

Trips: Do the same trips from here as from Wappoo Cut Landing.

I enjoy using Fire House Landing to get out on the Stono River. Just a word of caution, Elliotts Cut—the final section before the Stono River—can be tricky and dangerous when there is lots of boat traffic. Read the Wappoo Cut section for more description.

City of Charleston

City Marina
Directions: The City Marina is on the west side of the city off Lockwood Boulevard. It is south of the HWY 17 bridges. There is a parking fee and the water is inaccessible for several hours around low tide. The City Marina is in a great location and worth the cost of parking, but the lack of access to the water for hours at a time makes this, unhappily, a poor landing.

Brittlebank Park
Directions: Brittlebank Park is on Lockwood Boulevard across from the Charleston Police Department. There is plenty of free parking. The river is inaccessible for several hours around low tide unless leaving from the floating dock. It is a lengthy trek out to the end of the dock. Plan to have help in carrying your boat. I do not recommend using this landing because of the length of time that the water is inaccessible from the shoreline.

Seven Bridge Challenge
No description of Charleston Harbor trips can be complete without describing the Seven Bridge Challenge. The Seven Bridge Challenge tests kayaking ability and knowledge of tides. There are seven bridges crossing the Charleston Harbor area: Wappoo Cut Bridge, James Island Connector from West Ashley to James Island, James Island Connector from the City to West Ashley, the two HWY 17 Ashley River Bridges, and the two Cooper River Bridges. The Seven Bridge Challenge is to pass under all seven on the same trip. The personal challenge is to see how quickly you can paddle under all seven. The challenge requires paddling in both directions on the Cooper and the Ashley Rivers. Careful tidal planning is required.

> **Seven Bridge Challenge**
>
> The Seven Bridge Challenge is to pass under all seven on the same trip.

View of Shem Creek as author paddles inland. Summer 2002.

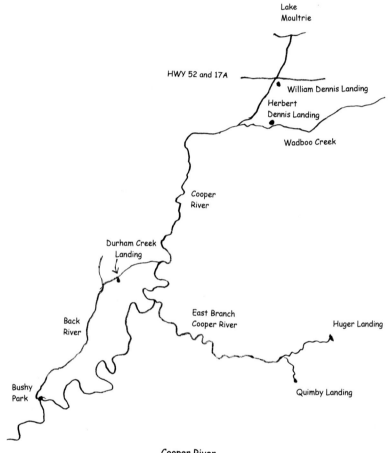

Cooper River
Bushy Park To Lake Moultrie

Cooper River

COOPER RIVER

The upper Cooper River area is great for paddling. The river becomes narrow upriver from Charleston. The scenery is magnificent where the west branch and east branch join. The lower part of the Cooper River below Bushy Park is wide. Wide rivers are rough in windy conditions. At the time I wrote this guide, kayaks were not permitted downriver from Bushy Park due to naval security issues.

Bushy Park Landing

Directions: Follow signs to the Naval Weapons Station. I recommend going on I-26 to I-526. Get off at the North Rhett exit and turn left at the bottom on the ramp. This is North Rhett and it changes to Henry Brown Boulevard, a 55 mph expressway to the Weapons Station. At the traffic light at the end of the expressway, turn right onto Red Bank Road, and proceed through the Weapons Station area. As the road ends, turn left toward Bushy Park. The landing is about ½ mile down the road.

This is a major landing. There are multiple ramps leading to both freshwater and saltwater. The freshwater landing (on the left) is on the Back River. This river connects upstream through Durham Creek to the Cooper River. The saltwater side (on the right) goes directly to the Cooper River. Getting to this landing has been complicated since September 11, 2001, because of the drive through the Weapons Station area. During an alert status, the road may be closed. When Red Bank Road is closed, get to Bushy Park by going down Cypress Gardens Road, and then past Durham Creek Landing. See the section on Durham Creek Landing.

Bushy Park Landing

Trip 1: Back River to Durham Creek Landing (8 miles and about 2 hours with the tide).

Trip 2: Cooper River to Durham Creek Landing (21 miles and about 6 hours with the tide).

Trip 3: Ride with the tide and turn back at the tide change.

Tide: High tide on the Cooper River side is about 1 hour behind Charleston Harbor and low tide is about ¾ hour behind. The Back River side is approximately 6 hours behind Charleston Harbor.

Trip 1: Back River to Durham Creek Landing (8 miles and about 2 hours with the tide). A paddler needs to know when to veer right to get on Durham Creek. It is a logical turn, but I always worry about finding the correct turn when on a new trip. I recommend doing the trip from Durham Creek Landing to Bushy Park before doing this one in order to be able to recognize the turnoff to Durham Creek.

Trip 2: Cooper River to Durham Creek Landing (21 miles and about 6 hours with the tide). Put in on the saltwater side and go upriver to the Durham Creek entrance, then to the Durham Creek Landing. The turnoff to Durham Creek is by green marker #9.

Trip 3: Ride with the tide and turn back at the tide change.

Durham Creek Landing

Directions: Follow the signs to Cypress Gardens. Get on HWY 52 and proceed through Goose Creek. Shortly after passing through Goose Creek is a brown sign for Cypress Gardens. The road is not well-marked, but it is old HWY 52. There is another turnoff from HWY 52 in a few more miles. Turn right at another brown sign for Cypress Gardens. This is Cypress Gardens Road and will lead straight to the landing. If making the first turn (noted above), go 2.1 miles, and then turn right onto Cypress Gardens Road. Go 4 more miles and the landing is on the left just after crossing the bridge. It is a large, busy landing. It is 25 minutes from Charlestowne Landing.

Durham Creek connects Back River to the Cooper River. It runs fast midway through the tide. The landing is extremely busy on summer weekends and

Durham Creek Landing

Trip 1: Durham Creek, up the Cooper River with the tide.

Trip 2: Durham Creek to Back River and return (total trip 16 miles and about 4 hours).

the boaters are very anxious to get out of Durham Creek and onto the Cooper River. Keep very close to the right side of the creek.

Tide: The tide is about 4 hours behind Charleston Harbor.

Trip 1: Durham Creek, up the Cooper River with the tide. Go to the right toward the Cooper River and then north (left) on the Cooper toward Pimlico. It took me about a half hour to get to the Cooper River. The Cooper River becomes very wide at this point with old rice fields. A kayak should be able to cross the rice fields without too much problem. I recommend staying in the river channel just to avoid getting stuck in the weeds. Water does not move quickly through the rice field area and one time when paddling over them, I found myself in an area thick with insects. The insects were not a problem when I got back in the channel.

It is challenge for kayakers new to this section of the river to figure out the path of the river channel. Motorboats stay in the channel and they can be followed. Pay attention to the river markers to stay in the channel and remember the slogan: red to the right when returning from sea. Keep the red markers to the right and green markers to the left when heading upriver. Find the tide change time at Pimlico and plan to turn around when it changes. High tide at Pimlico is about 3¼ hours behind Charleston Harbor and low tide is about 4 hours behind.

Trip 2: Durham Creek to Back River and return (total trip 16 miles and about 4 hours). Paddle with the tide to Bushy Park; take a good break, and then return. Leaving a pickup vehicle at Bushy Park makes this a pleasant one-way trip. The landing at Durham Creek is about 7 miles from Bushy Park along Bushy Park Road. It is easy to leave Charleston, go through the Weapons Station area, drop off a vehicle at Bushy Park, and head on to the Durham Creek Landing.

Wadboo Creek

Directions: Wadboo Creek is in the Moncks Corner area. Take I-26 and veer off at the Goose Creek HWY 52 exit. Follow HWY 52 through Moncks Corner. Right after crossing over the Tail Race Canal, turn right onto HWY 402. The landing is 2.2 miles away and is on the left side before crossing the bridge. This landing is 50 minutes and 34.2 miles from Charlestowne Landing.

Wadboo Creek Landing

Trip 1: Wadboo Creek into the swamp.

Trip 2: Wadboo Creek to William Dennis Landing, by HWY 52 bridge (3 miles and about 1 hour).

Take this creek back into Wadboo Swamp or paddle to the Cooper River by going under the bridge.

Tide: Low tide is about 5 hours behind Charleston Harbor and high tide is about 4 hours behind. The current is affected by water releases from the Pinopolis Dam on Lake Moultrie. It is possible for the tide to be coming in when the dam releases water, and the current turns around. One time I headed upstream against the tide. The current picked up rapidly and the water had a lot of eddies throughout. Then shortly later the hard current stopped. I experienced a release of water. I was able to paddle against it, but it was difficult.

Trip 1: Wadboo Creek into the swamp. There are three different ways to leave the landing. Go into the swamp by heading straight out. Going to the left takes you nowhere; going to the right takes you toward the Cooper River. The tidal range is about 3-4 feet here. It can be affected by water release from the dam on the Cooper River. I paddled about 30 minutes into the swamp before the creek became narrow and the fallen trees kept me from going any farther. Pay attention to the tides to avoid being caught upstream and having to ford over downed trees.

Trip 2: Wadboo Creek to William Dennis Landing, by HWY 52 bridge (3 miles and about an hour). Go under the bridge. It takes about 20 minutes to get to the Cooper River. Turn right onto the Cooper and paddle past Santee Canal State Park on the left. The William Dennis Landing is upriver, on the right, just before the HWY 52 bridge. A good trip is to paddle into the swamp, then turn around and go into the Cooper River and up to the William Dennis Landing.

William Dennis Landing

Directions: This landing is just outside Moncks Corner and can be seen when going over the bridge across the Tail Race Canal. Take the first right after the HWY 52 bridge, go .3 mile, and turn right onto Carswell Drive. The landing is .8 mile down this road.

Tide: Low tide is about 5 hours behind Charleston Harbor and high tide is about 4 hours behind. The current is affected by water releases from the Pinopolis Dam on Lake Moutrie.

Trip: Use William Dennis Landing as a take-off point to go up the Tail Race Canal to go to the locks for Lake Moultrie (3 miles and about 1 hour). A sign at the locks says that boats without power are not permitted to use the locks, though many tell me that kayaks are allowed through. It is about a one hour paddle to the locks. I do not recommend swimming in the Tail Race Canal. The current can be very powerful with lots of eddies when water is released from the dam.

William Dennis Landing

Trip: Use William Dennis Landing as a take-off point to go up the Tail Race Canal to go to the locks for Lake Moultrie. (3 miles and about 1 hour).

Witherbee District- Creeks Flowing into the Cooper River

Two public boat landings in the National Forest flow into the East Branch of the Cooper River. These creeks are more open than the ones flowing into the Santee River from the Wambaw District of the national forest.

Huger Area Landing

Directions: Take I-26 toward Columbia and turn off onto I-526 heading towards Mount Pleasant. After crossing the Cooper River, exit to Clements Ferry Road (North). Clements Ferry Road changes to a two-lane highway. Go 3.9 miles past the traffic light with a convenience store on the left to a road that veers to the left. The sign indicates to take it to go to HWY 41. It is HWY 100 (Reflectance Road). If you miss it, you'll still end up on HWY 41. Turn left onto HWY 41. In about 11 miles, veer left onto HWY 402. Two miles along 402 is the Huger National Forest area. There is no sign indicating river access. Turn into this area and bear left. Follow the dirt road until it ends at the boat landing. The Huger Area Landing is 45 minutes from Charlestowne Landing.

I have always felt very safe at national forest landings. This landing is in the forest, but the only people I have run into here have been boaters.

Tide: The high tide is about 4¾ hours behind Charleston Harbor and the low tide is 4¼ hours behind.

Trip: Huger Landing, downstream with the tide. Paddle to the right, under the railroad bridge. Huger Creek and Quimby Creek join up shortly downstream and form the East Branch of the Cooper River. Plan this trip around a tide change in the East Branch.

Huger Area Landing

Trip: Huger Landing, downstream with the tide.

64

Quimby Bridge Landing

Directions: The directions are the same as for the Huger Area Landing, except that it is slightly closer (32 miles from Charlestowne Landing). After traveling 11 miles on HWY 41, turn left onto Cainhoy Road. This turnoff is just before HWY 402 veers off. Do not go on HWY 402. The landing is ¼ mile down Cainhoy Road on the right, just before a bridge that crosses the creek. Quimby Creek Landing is paved and has ample parking.

Tide: High tide is about 4½ hours behind Charleston Harbor, and low tide is behind about 4¼ hours behind.

I left this landing one morning at 10 a.m. when low tide was predicted for 2½ hours later. I returned to the creek two hours after the predicted low tide (4½ hours later) and expected to have the tide sweep me up the creek. I was surprised to find that I had to paddle against the current. At the landing, I asked a local fisherman why the tide was not running as I expected. He told me that with all the recent rain—we just had a tropical storm go through the area two days before—the swamps were full and the incoming tide could not offset the water draining from the swamps. He pointed out that the water was rising because of the incoming tide, but the drainage from the swamps had created a top current that went the other way.

Trip 1: Quimby Creek, downstream with the tide and back. It takes about 20 minutes to intersect with the Cooper River East Branch. Continue downstream until the tide changes. The trip to the Cooper River is a magnificent 12 miles paddle (one way). On a warm day in December, I managed to see two alligators on this trip!

Trip 2: Quimby Creek to Huger Landing and back (8 miles and about 3 hours). This requires paddling against the tide, but is not too strenuous if done around the time of high or low tide at the landings.

Quimby Creek Landing

Trip 1: Quimby Creek, downstream with the tide and back.

Trip 2: Quimby Creek to Huger Landing and back (8 miles and about 3 hours).

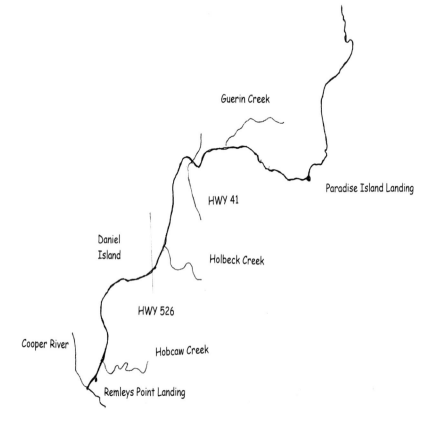

Guerin Creek

Paradise Island Landing

HWY 41

Daniel
Island

Holbeck Creek

HWY 526

Cooper River

Hobcaw Creek

Remleys Point Landing

Wando River

WANDO RIVER

The Wando River is relatively short, having its headwaters in the Francis Marion Forest close to HWY 17 near McClellanville. Aside from Remleys Point Landing, which is really in Charleston Harbor, the only other public boat landing on the river is the Paradise Island Boat Landing. The shores of the Wando have become increasingly developed during the last several years. The upper part of the river is beautiful. On an October trip I saw a bald eagle. Shrimp "boiled the water" as I paddled through the shallows and one shrimp even jumped into my boat.

Paradise Island Landing

Directions: Cross the Cooper River Bridge and continue on HWY 17 for 11 miles. Turn left at the brown sign indicating Wando River access onto HWY 1453 (Chandler Road). The landing is 1.2 miles down the road. This landing is 21 miles 30 minutes from Charlestowne Landing.

Tide: High tide is about 1½ hours behind Charleston Harbor and low tide is about 1 hour behind.

Trip 1: Paradise Island Landing upriver to the Francis Marion Forest (5 miles and about 1½ hours) and back.
Paddle to the right after leaving the landing and you will go under the Paradise Island Bridge in about 1 hour. Continue on until the river becomes too narrow to proceed because of fallen trees. This situation may happen about 1½ hours after leaving the landing.

Trip 2: Paradise Island Landing down to HWY 41 bridge (7 miles and about 1½ hours) and back. Paddle downriver with the tide, planning to return when the tide changes. There is a convenience store with a landing on the water. It is a good place to pull over

Paradise Island Landing

Trip 1: Paradise Island Landing upriver to the Francis Marion Forest (5 miles and about 1½ hours) and back.

Trip 2: Paradise Island Landing down to HWY 41 bridge (7 miles and about 1½ hours).

67

and buy a snack. The landing requires a fee, so plan for that if leaving a pickup vehicle there.

The only other public landing on the Wando River is Remleys Point– immediately before the Wando merges with the Cooper River. Remleys Point is included in the *Immediatley Within the Charleston Area* of this guide. This is a 20 mile trip. Leave a pickup vehicle at Remleys Point if you decide to paddle it.

FRANCIS MARION NATIONAL FOREST

The Francis Marion National Forest is named for the Revolutionary War hero, Francis Marion, the Swamp Fox. He and his men roamed this area and continually harassed the more powerful British troops stationed in Charleston. General Marion's men would attack the British and then disappear into the swamp. They cut the British supply lines between North Carolina and Charleston. His harassment kept British troops in the South so they could not join up with British forces in Virginia.

After the Revolution, the land was used for more than 150 years for plantations that produced indigo, rice, and cotton. In 1936, President Roosevelt directed the Forest Service to purchase the land from private owners to form this forest. Much of the land was depleted after decades of poor agricultural practices, logging without reforestation, wildfire, and lack of wildlife management.

In September 1989, Hurricane Hugo came ashore with 135 mph winds that destroyed most of the older trees in the forest. Hugo's destruction blocked over 500 miles of roads and wiped out recreation areas and trails. Before Hugo, the Francis Marion Forest was one of the leading national forests in the East for quality of timber production.

Rivers and creeks through the national forest provide a unique view into Lowcountry history. Kayak trips in the forest are different from other areas because the creeks flow through wonderfully wooded areas. The water in the creeks is brown, unlike the blackwater of the ACE Basin creeks.

A detailed map of the forest area is available for purchase at the ranger's district headquarters and at the Seewee Visitors Center on HWY 17 between Awendaw and McClellanville. There is much private land within the national forest. Paddlers should comply with state law and owners' rules when on private land. Red paint and signs mark the boundaries between the national forest land and private property. Stay on the national forest land unless having specific permission from the landowner.

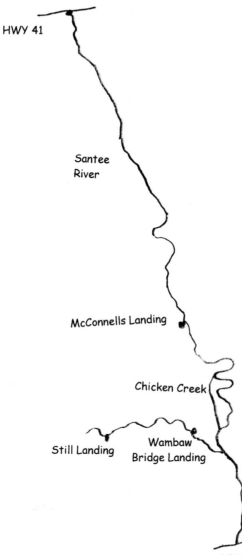

HWY 41

Santee
River

McConnells Landing

Chicken Creek

Still Landing

Wambaw
Bridge Landing

HWY 17

Santee River

SANTEE RIVER

Still Landing on Wambaw Creek

Directions: Take HWY 17 north towards McClellanville. Just before McClellanville, turn left at the blinking traffic light onto HWY 45 (French Santee Road). There is a gas station/convenience store on the left just before the turn. Drive 4 miles down HWY 45 and turn right onto Mill Branch Road (Forest Service 211) and drive 3 miles. At that point there is a small forest service sign indicating Still Boat Landing to the left. Go ½ mile down this dirt road to the landing on Wambaw Creek. The landing is 1 hour from Charlestowne Landing. It is secluded and clean and has ample parking.

Tide: The tide is about 5½ hours behind Charleston Harbor.

Trip: Still Landing to Wambaw Bridge Landing (4 miles and about 1¼ hours). Go right from the landing toward the Santee River to the Wambaw Bridge Landing. There is a tree crossing the creek about 1/3 of the way down. It must be forded at low tide. The trip to the bridge and back is a great trip for a solo kayaker. Leave a pickup vehicle at the bridge and go one way. It takes me about ½ hour longer to do this trip against the tide.

Still Landing on Wambaw Creek

Trip: Still Boat Landing to Wambaw Bridge Landing (4 miles and about 1¼ hours).

71

Wambaw Bridge Landing

Directions: Use the directions to Still Boat Landing but do not take the turnoff to Still Landing. Continue on Mill Branch Road for another 2.3 miles towards Elmwood Campground. At the campground, turn right onto FS 216 and go .4 mile to another turnoff. Turn left and go .2 mile to the bridge. Altogether, this trip is about six miles on dirt roads. The boat landing is across the bridge and on the right. Wambaw Bridge Landing is slightly over an hour from Charlestowne Landing. This landing can also be reached directly from HWY 17. See the directions for McConnells Landing.

A one-lane ramp goes down by the bridge to the creek. There is ample parking along the roadside, but please make sure to leave room for others to access the ramp with boat trailers.

Tide: The tide is about 5 hours behind Charleston Harbor.

Trip 1: Ride with the tide up the creek toward Still Boat Landing (4 miles and about 1¼ hours). Leave a pickup vehicle at Still Landing for a one-way trip. The creek gets narrower upstream. I have come upon deer as I paddled this creek. On seeing me, they crashed through the forest as they tried to get away.

Trip 2: Wambaw Bridge to the Santee River, up Chicken Creek to the Santee River, and back (10 miles and about 1¾ hour each way). Go out to the river, turn right, and paddle through Chicken Creek to where it intersects the Santee River again. Chicken Creek is a small creek through the woods that cuts out the curves on the Santee River. In planning this trip, plan to reach the

Wambaw Bridge Landing

Trip 1: Ride with the tide up the creek towards Still Boat Landing (4 miles and about 1¼ hours).

Trip 2: Wambaw Bridge to the Santee River, up Chicken Creek to the Santee River, and back (10 miles and about 1¾ hours each way).

Trip 3: Wambaw Bridge to the Santee River, up Chicken Creek, and then to McConnells Landing (11 miles and about 2¾ hours).

further junction of Chicken Creek and the Santee River at the time of high tide–about 2½ hours behind Charleston Harbor (the same as McConnells Landing). It takes about an hour to reach the Santee River from the landing.

Directions for Chicken Creek: Turn left from Wambaw Creek and paddle about ½ mile to the entrance of Chicken Creek. It is the first creek on the left side of the river. There is a small island in the Santee River just across from the entrance. It takes about ¾ hour to ride with the tide through Chicken Creek.

Trip 3: Wambaw Bridge to the Santee River, up Chicken Creek, and then to McConnells Landing (11 miles and about 2¾ hours). Instead of turning around where Chicken Creek intersects the second time with the Santee River, go on up the Santee River, through a major curve and then to McConnells Landing. It takes about an hour to get from Chicken Creek to the landing.

Note:
If there has been a lot of rain, the Santee River may be flowing out, even though the tide is coming in. Do not plan this trip without verifying that the tide offsets the river current.

McConnells Landing (Pleasant Hill Landing)

Directions: Leave Mount Pleasant heading towards Georgetown. Turn left from HWY 17 at the Hampton Plantation sign. This is 6.6 miles after the blinking traffic light at McClellanville. The road will change to a dirt road and become FS 204. The Wambaw Creek bridge is 4.4 miles down this road. Continue past the bridge for another 3.6 miles and turn right onto FS 204F. This is a well-marked turnoff. It is 59.4 miles from Charlestowne Landing to McConnells Landing. The landing is almost 1½ hours from Charlestowne Landing, but I've included it for those who live east of the Cooper, and I highly encourage those living west of Mount Pleasant to take a trip from this landing. The landing was renovated in 2002 and is an excellent landing—especially for being so far "off the beaten path."

Tide: The high tide here is about 2½ hours behind Charleston Harbor and low tide is almost 4 hours behind.

Trip 1: McConnells Landing to Wambaw Creek Bridge, via Chicken Creek (11 miles and about 3 hours). Leave a pickup vehicle at Wambaw Bridge while driving to McConnells Landing. Paddle down the Santee River through Chicken Creek and then up Wambaw Creek to the bridge. Chicken Creek is about an hour's paddle from the landing and is just after the large first S curve. Plan on 2 hours to paddle from the landing through Chicken Creek, to the entrance of Wambaw Creek. Paddle up Wambaw Creek to finish the trip. The total trip length depends on how fast the tide is running. Since the main trip is on a falling tide, the trip up Wambaw Creek will probably be against the falling tide. To find Wambaw Creek from the Santee River, turn right after leaving Chicken Creek and take the next big creek on the right. There is a

McConnells Landing (Pleasant Hill Landing)

Trip 1: McConnells Landing to Wambaw Creek Bridge, via Chicken Creek (11 miles and about 3 hours).

Trip 2: McConnells Landing to Wambaw Creek Bridge, remaining on Santee River—not going through Chicken Creek (13 miles and about 3½ hours).

74

boat shelter on the left side of the Santee just after the entrance to Wambaw Creek. Wood duck house #30, on the right side of the Santee, is another sign of the creek entrance. There is a turnoff to the left about 5-10 minutes after entering the creek at wood duck house #29. Do not take that turn, continue straight. The bridge is located about ½ hour farther up the creek.

Trip 2: McConnells Landing to Wambaw Creek Bridge, remaining on Santee River—not going through Chicken Creek (13 miles and about 3½ hours). Leave a pickup vehicle at Wambaw Bridge, and drive on to McConnells Landing. Paddle downriver, remaining on the Santee River, rather than going down Chicken Creek. After passing Chicken Creek, remain on the right side of the river. Take a hard right turn onto the next "creek." Wood duck house #41 marks this right turn. This narrow creek is really the Santee River. The Santee River is very wide before the turn. Just before this turn, there is a branch that heads off to the left and the main body of water appears to go straight. Going straight will put you on the North Santee River. Do not do that!

I made a full day trip of taking the falling tide from McConnells Landing, through Chicken Creek, to Wambaw Creek and then paddling back up the Santee River, not taking Chicken Creek. The Santee River paralleling Chicken Creek is narrow and has lots of curves. I was concerned that I might be in the wrong body of water because the rest of the Santee River is wide and this section is narrow.

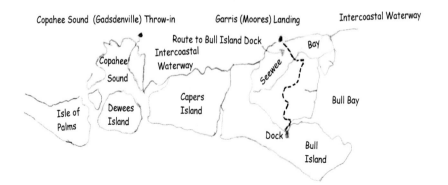

Copahee Sound (Gadsdenville) Throw-in   Garris (Moores) Landing   Intercoastal Waterway

Route to Bull Island Dock

Intercoastal Waterway

Copahee Sound

Isle of Palms

Dewees Island

Capers Island

Seewee Bay

Bull Bay

Dock

Bull Island

Gadsdenville Landing and Garris (Moores) Landing

Bull Bay

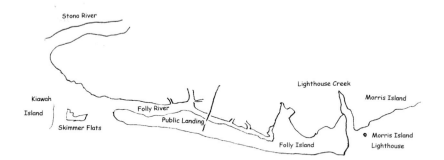

Stono River

Kiawah Island

Skimmer Flats

Folly River

Public Landing

Lighthouse Creek

Morris Island

Folly Island

Morris Island Lighthouse

Folly Beach

Folly Beach

CLOSE TO THE OCEAN TRIPS

Many kayakers want to get out on real saltwater. I hesitate to go down the rivers all the way to the ocean because the mouths of the rivers are wide and the water can become very choppy in the afternoons. I recommend three areas that are close to the ocean but are protected from freshening winds.

Garris Landing (Moores Landing for Bull Bay)

Directions: Take HWY17 north through Mt. Pleasant. After passing a brown sign indicating Wando River Access (for Paradise Island) on the left, go 2.5 miles farther on HWY 17. The turnoff to Garris (Moores) Landing is to the right on to HWY 584. There is a green sign for Cape Romain National Wildlife Area and a sign for the Bull Island ferry. Go 3.5 miles down HWY 584 and turn right at another Cape Romain and Bull Island ferry sign onto HWY 1170. Garris Landing is 1.5 miles down that road. This landing is 50 minutes from Charlestowne Landing.

The U.S. Fish and Wildlife Service maintains this landing. It has a gate and operating hours. Currently the hours are 6 a.m. to 9 p.m. The landing is inaccessible outside of these hours. The landing has plenty of parking and even restrooms! A 1,000-feet-long pier is beside the boat ramp. Since this landing is close to Bull Bay, it is one of the main landings that recreational shrimpers use and is extremely busy during recreational shrimp baiting season, the first week in September to mid-November.

Tide: The tide is about the same as Charleston Harbor.

Trip: Garris Landing to Bull Island dock (6 miles and about 1½ hours). Leave the landing about 2 hours before low

---

Garris Landing (Moores Landing for Bull Bay)

Trip: Garris Landing to Bull Island dock (6 miles and about 1½ hours). Leave the landing about 2 hours before low tide and ride the falling tide out to Bull Island.

tide and ride the falling tide out to Bull Island. Wait for the tide to turn and paddle back with it. Paddling through the various channels cutting through the mud flats at low tide is like paddling in a maze. The mud flats disappear at high tide and the scenery is completely different. The ferry leaves the landing twice a day, generally at 9:30 and 12:30. Watch it for guidance to get through the maze.

Several sections of the paddle have direct water access to Bull Bay. If wind conditions are above 15 knots, the water may be choppy in these sections. Take the wind condition into account when planning this trip.

Directions through the maze: Leave the landing and paddle left up the intracoastal waterway for a short distance. Just before green channel marker #73, turn right into a creek entrance that has markers on each side. Follow that creek out, paying close attention to the markers. The key to staying in the channel is to watch for markers ahead. The first creek ends at an intersection with a larger creek. The choice is to go right or left. There are no markers to the right, so turn left. This creek ends at another intersection and another right or left choice is required. There are markers each way. The last time I paddled this trip, there was a white triangular marker at this turn. Turn right. From this point on, make turning decisions based on being able to see a marker ahead. Remember that the ferry goes through here, so the channel is deep enough for it. If the water gets shallow, retrace your trip until you see where you made the wrong turn. It's an adventure, but once at the dock, you will know how to do it the next time with fewer wrong turns! Besides, part of the fun of being in a kayak is getting in very shallow water.

After resting and stretching at the boat dock, there are three choices for the return trip. The first choice is to go back the way you came. Another way to return is paddling back the way you came but trying to take short cuts to get to the intracoastal waterway. This is likely to end up on a variety of mud flats. A completely different choice is to go into Bull Bay, experience a little ocean activity, and return through the bay. If it is windy or rough, make a decision based on the skill and confidence of the least experienced paddler. It is fun for the recreational kayaker to be out on the bay if it is not choppy. Go straight out from the landing towards the ocean, turn left into the bay and proceed along the shore. Do not take the first major creek to the left. The second major creek to the left is the "cut through" to get off the bay. Take it and paddle toward the mainland. Almost any wide creek ends at the intracoastal waterway. Watch for the pilings of the Garris Landing pier. After reaching the intracoastal waterway, turn left. This sounds very confusing, and it is. Be willing to explore.

I have ended up on the mud flats several times paddling back. I lost sight of the markers and ended up turning toward the intracoastal waterway too soon. It was no problem; I just did not end up on the waterway where I expected. One Sunday I got myself in just inches of water on an incoming tide on large mud flats. The worse that could happen would be waiting a few minutes for the water to rise. I saw a spectacular massing of dolphins jumping and splashing in just inches of water. Apparently they had found a school of fish and were herding them and feasting.

Copahee Sound Throw-In (Gadsdenville Landing)

Directions: Take HWY 17 north through Mount Pleasant. Continue on HWY 17 past the turnoff for the Isle of Palms Connector and go 6.6 miles to a brown sign indicating Copahee Sound Access to the right. Turn right onto Gadsdenville Road and go .7 miles to the end of the road. The landing is at the end of the road sticking out into the marsh. It has a primitive ramp.

Copahee Sound Throw-In

Trip 1: Copahee Sound Throw-In to Capers Island (4 miles and about an hour).

Trip 2: Copahee Sound Throw-in to Dewees Island (5 miles and about 1½ hours).

I was at the landing about 1½ hours before low tide. There was not enough water in the creek to paddle out. Since the creek bed is mostly sandy, I was able to pull my boat along. Plan to leave or arrive at this landing more than two hours later than low tide.

On a trip in July, I paddled by some men with a seine. They told me that there were big shrimp that came out of the creek at low tide and that they had once caught over 100 pounds of shrimp with the seine in 20 minutes. There are a lot of shrimp in this area and it is fun to see the water "boil with shrimp" when paddling through.

Tide: The tide is about 15 minutes ahead of Charleston Harbor.

Trip 1: Copahee Sound Throw-In to Capers Island (4 miles and about an hour). It takes about ½ hour to paddle to the intracoastal waterway. Pay attention to landmarks at each turn. I use a stand of trees as the mark for the final turnoff into the landing. After leaving the landing, proceed down the narrow creek for about ¼ mile where it intersects a bigger creek. The stand of trees is on the left. You will miss the landing on the return trip if you miss this stand of trees. Turn right and stay in the creek to the intracoastal waterway.

The creek intersects the intracoastal waterway at green marker #99. This is the marker that boaters from Charleston use to make the turn to

Capers Island. Go straight across the waterway to Capers Inlet. Paddle all the way to the front of the island. This is a fantastic place to explore and swim.

Trip 2: Copahee Sound Throw-In to Dewees Island (5 miles and about 1½ hours). When reaching the waterway, turn right and paddle the waterway to the inlet between Dewees and Isle of Palms. Turn left. Dewees is developed, but the beaches are public. Paddle out towards the ocean, past a few sets of docks to get to the best beach area.

Folly Beach Landing

Directions: Take HWY 171 to Folly Beach. It is 13 miles from Charlestowne Landing. The boat landing is immediately to the right after crossing the bridge to Folly Beach. It is a large, well-maintained, completely paved parking lot and landing. The landing overflows with vehicles on weekends. Do not park in spaces marked for trailers. Park on the street or along the wall at the back of the lot.

Tide: High tide is about ½ hour behind Charleston harbor and low tide is about 10 minutes ahead of Charleston.

Trip 1: Folly Beach Landing to Morris Island Lighthouse (6 miles and about 2 hours). This trip passes through an area with a lot of Civil War history. Late in 1863 there were more than 17,000 union troops on this area of Folly Island and Morris Island. The soldier population grew to over 22,000 troops later in the war. This is the launching point for the Battle of Secessionville made famous in the movie *Glory*.

There is no direct route behind Folly Beach to the Morris Island Lighthouse. The Folly River does not parallel the beach. Paddle under the bridge. After passing the second major opening to the

Folly Beach Landing

Trip 1: Folly Beach Landing to Morris Island Lighthouse (6 miles and about 2 hours).

Trip 2: Folly Beach Landing to sandbars behind Charleston County Park (3 miles and about 1 hour).

81

left, there is a little island on the left side of the channel. Immediately after that island, the river bends to the left. Take that left bend. Though it looks like the channel goes straight ahead, it only leads to a huge oyster flat. After making the left, look for a clump of trees way back and to the right. The clump of trees is on the main channel that goes to Lighthouse Creek. Do not turn right until clearly seeing the base of the trees. Motorboats use this channel at low tide. If you find yourself in shallow water, you have made a wrong turn. There is a sandbar about 2/3 of the way to Lighthouse Creek. It is after a major bend to the left and is above water for about 1¼ hours on each side of low tide. Even if it is not above water, it is a good place to get out and stretch. After leaving the sandbar, paddle on to Lighthouse Creek and turn right. Paddle down the creek to the sandbar that the lighthouse sits on.

I have come upon several pods of dolphins in the Folly River. They played with each other and appeared to enjoy having me around. I have seen them jump clear out of the water. I have seen more pelicans on the Folly River trip than on any of my other trips.

Trip 2: Folly Beach Landing to sandbars behind Charleston County Park (3 miles and about 1 hour). Paddle with the outgoing tide to the sandbars behind Charleston County Park. Plan to arrive near low tide so the return trip is on the rising tide. The sandbars are a terrific place to enjoy a nice picnic and swim.

Note: Plan to arrive at the lighthouse sandbar at low tide. This requires paddling against the outgoing tide on the first 1/3 of the trip. The trip goes with the tide after turning right at the clump of trees. When returning, the trip goes against the tide after turning left at the clump of trees. The final 1/3 of the trip back to the bridge, against the tide, may feel like it is taking a long time, especially after swimming and a full day in the sun.

82

APPENDIX

ROAD SIGNS

It is essential to know how to read road signs to find the landings. Did you ever notice the little black and white signs that appear on the top of some stop signs? Those are the signs indicating secondary roads. The first set of numbers signifies the county or local area and the second set is the road number. These road numbers coincide with the road numbers listed on maps. Many times these secondary roads have a street sign along with the highway number. For example, the secondary road sign (on top of the stop sign) for Prices Bridge Landing is HWY 199. A street sign, Maybank Lane, is right next to the stop sign. You can look for street sign names, but it is easier to look for the secondary road number. Maps generally list the secondary road numbers. Roads without a road number are not state roads. For example, the road to Lowndes Ferry Landing on the Edisto is not state maintained, and the roads in the Francis Marion Forest do not have state numbers on them since the United States Forest Service maintains them—they have forest service numbers instead.

WIND

Almost any time is a good time for kayaking. If it is windy, paddle inland on the rivers. If it is hot, paddle out towards the ocean and get the breezes from the open areas of water.

Charleston winds generally pick up in the afternoon. I prefer kayaking on large bodies like the harbor in the early morning or early evening to avoid the afternoon sea breeze. I do not enjoy being on open bodies of water (such as wide sections of a river close to the ocean or in Bull Bay) when the wind is predicted to be above 15 knots. If a high barometric pressure system settles over the area, the water tends to lie down all day. Take advantage of high-pressure days to be out on large bodies of water in the afternoon. The wind is no problem inland. In the heat of summer, there is very little wind inland and that is the time to move out toward the ocean.

Wind creates waves on all bodies of water and even on the more narrow rivers and creeks. When the wind and the tide come from the same direction, the water tends to be much smoother than when they run in opposite directions. When winds and tides run against each other, the waves tend to be steeper and break. On a windy day, you can verify this phenomenon by paddling on a curvy river. When the stretch of river has the wind and tide running together, the water will be relatively smooth. Take a turn around a bend and when the wind and tide go in opposite directions, the water is choppy. Be aware of this when paddling on a windy day.

RAINY WEATHER

Some years will be wetter than others. In 2003, the Edisto River remained flooded through July. When there is a lot of rain, the rivers will be flooded and difficult to paddle against. Do not expect the tide to offset the draining of the forest and swamps. Check the newspaper for the river flood status when planning to paddle upstream on a river.

TIDES

Tides impact all of the trips in this guide except for the upper Edisto River trips. The US Government publishes tide tables and lists the time and height difference at various stations with respect to a reference station. For example, there may be eight or nine reference points in the

Ashley River. The Cosgrove Bridge is one. The time difference between the Cosgrove Bridge and the Customs House Wharf is 25 minutes later for high tide and 18 minutes later for low tide. These tables are available on the internet. To make matters easier, several internet sites actually provide the time of high and low tide at these stations and no calculation is required.

As of the writing of this guide, there are several internet sites to choose from. To obtain a listing of stations and their time and height difference from reference points, go to: www.co-ops.nos.noaa.gov/tides03/tpred2.html#sc. My favorite site that provides the actual times of the tides at the stations is www.harbortides.com; however, it was not active at the time this guide went to press. If those sites are not available, try one operated by the University of South Carolina Biology Department: tbone.biol.sc.edu/tide (no www with this one) or www.tidesonline.com (pick Charleston or Savannah). Since internet sites do go up and down, do a search for "tides" every now and then an explore what the internet has to provide.

Use the tide change times or differentials when planning trips. For example, Penny Creek Landing on the Edisto River is four hours behind Charleston Harbor. If Charleston Harbor has a low tide at 9:00 a.m., then Penny Creek will be low at 1:00 p.m. (four hours later). I know I can ride with the tide down Penny Creek almost anytime until noon.

TIDAL FACTS

Generally there are two high tides and two low tides each day. The tide changes approximately every six hours. The tide changes later the farther one is from the ocean, and planning is required in order to take best advantage of the tide changes. Willtown Bluff is three hours behind and Penny Creek landing, further away from the ocean, is four hours behind.

Tides are influenced by prevailing winds and other weather activities. You cannot set your watch by the tide changes, but you can get close. I have supplied the approximate differences between the Charleston Harbor tide and the boat landings in this guide. Use this differential for planning purposes. There are web pages that provide the exact times of high and low tides for many of the most used landings. Weather conditions, especially wind, can effect the high and low tide, as well as the height of the tide.

I divide the tidal flow into thirds. The first two hours and last two hours of the six hour tidal period are when the current runs the slowest. Most people have little problem paddling against the tide during these two periods. The farther away from the middle third of the six-hour tide, the easier the paddling becomes. The middle third of the tidal period (hours three and four) are the most difficult to paddle against. Avoid paddling against the tide during these two hours unless you are ready for a strenuous workout.

I use this concept when doing a short trip from the Wappoo Cut to a small beach on the east side of the Battery. I paddle out of the Wappoo Cut with an outgoing tide and then wait for the tide to change and ride the incoming tide back. To provide more flexibility for taking this trip, I have found that I can leave Wappoo Cut at the beginning of the incoming tide and do the same trip. At this point it is not difficult to paddle against the incoming tide since it is in the first third of its cycle. When I turn around at the Battery, I can ride back on the middle third of the tide and shoot across the Ashley River and into the Wappoo Cut quickly and with little effort. Knowing I can paddle out on the first two hours for the incoming tide gives me a larger window of opportunity to take this trip.

The time of the tide change moves about an hour each day. If it is low tide in Charleston Harbor today at 3:00 p.m., it will be low tomorrow at about 4:00 p.m.

The tide is "opposite" every seven days. If it is low tide in Charleston Harbor at 4:00 p.m. this Saturday, it is going to be high tide at about 4:00 p.m. next Saturday. For planning purposes, expect a low tide in two weeks about 4:00 p.m. This is not precise, but it helps in planning. A tidal trip taken one weekend cannot be done the next weekend. It can be done at about the same time in two weekends.

Tide tables predict the tide and current based on the moon. There are many other factors to consider. If there has been a lot of rain, the rivers will be full of the rainwater run off and, even though the water level goes up and down with the tide, the current may continue to flow out, even on an incoming tide. This is an important consideration when planning to use an incoming tide to help return up river. If the swamps are full, if drainage ditches beside the roads are filled with water, and most certainly, if the rivers are rising because of a period of rain, expect the current to continue out—sometimes even hard—during an incoming tide. Winds from the east and south push the tide up the rivers, causing high tide to come sooner and last longer. The spring and fall equinoxes will cause the tide to rise a lot higher than normal, creating more of a current as it goes in and out.

Planning around the tides can be challenging, but it is important to learn how the tidal currents work. Paddlers "zip along" when going with the tide. It feels like paddling through syrup when going against it. If the tidal current is too strong, take a break! It will always change and slow down or go the way a little later.

PADDLING CLUB

Many kayakers would rather paddle with a club and enjoy the benefits of the club's experience and camaraderie. I highly recommend contacting the LowCountry Paddlers.

Their web sit is: www.lowcountrypaddlers.net. The following is from their web page: *We are a socially and economically diverse organization with one common link…a love of paddling. Whether kayak or canoe expert or beginner we all enjoy the camaraderie and the beauty of South Carolina's waterways. We have monthly meetings on the third Monday of each month followed by a club paddle the following Saturday. You are more than welcome to both.*

DISCLAIMER

Every effort has been made to make this guide as accurate as possible. Many things can change after a guide is published. The author accepts no responsibility for any injury or inconvenience sustained by any person using this book. It is strongly suggested that recreational kayakers wear PFDs at all times while out on the water.

Burn Care

Steven E. Wolf, MD
David N. Herndon, MD
Shriners Burns Hospital
Blocker Burn Unit
University of Texas Medical Branch

LANDES
BIOSCIENCE
AUSTIN, TEXAS
U.S.A.

VADEMECUM
Burn Care
LANDES BIOSCIENCE
Austin

Copyright © 1999 Landes Bioscience
All rights reserved.
Printed in the U.S.A.

Please address all inquiries to the Publisher:
Landes Bioscience, 810 S. Church Street, Georgetown, Texas, U.S.A. 78626
Phone: 512/ 863 7762; FAX: 512/ 863 0081

ISBN: 1-57059-526-7

Library of Congress Cataloging-in-Publication Data

Burn Care / [edited by] Steven E. Wolf, David N. Herndon.
     p. cm.
  "Vademecum."
  Includes index.
  ISBN 1-57059-526-7
1. Burns and scalds--Patients--Care Handbooks, manuals, etc. 2. Burns and scalds--Treatment Handbooks, manuals, etc. I. Wolf, Steven E. II. Herndon, David N.
[DNLM: 1. Burns--therapy. WO 704 B9603 1999]
RD96.4.B8625 1999
617.1'1--dc21
DNLM/DLC   99-24714
for Library of Congress   CIP

Dedication

We wish to recognize all those who went before us to pave the path of burn care at UTMB and the Shriners Burns Hospital in Galveston. The development and growth of these units was begun primarily through the efforts and support of Truman G. Blocker, Sally Abston, and James C. Thompson. We dedicate this work to them.

Contents

Editors

Steven E. Wolf, MD
Assistant Professor
Department of Surgery
Clinical Fellow (1996-1997)
Shriners Burns Hospital and Blocker Burn Unit
University of Texas Medical Branch
Galveston, Texas, USA
Chapters 1, 8, 10, 12

David N. Herndon, MD
Jesse Jones Professor of Surgery
Chief of Staff,
Shriners Burns Hospital and Blocker Burn Unit
University of Texas Medical Branch
Galveston, Texas, USA

Contributors

Juan P. Barret, MD
Clinical Fellow (1997-1999)
Shriners Burns Hospital
   and Blocker Burn Unit
University of Texas Medical Branch
Galveston, Texas, USA
Chapters 4,11

Peter Dziewulski, MD, FRCS (Plast)
Consultant Plastic and Reconstructive
   Surgeon
St. Andrews Centre for Plastic Surgery
   and Burns
Essex, United Kingdom
Clinical Fellow (1997-1998)
Shriners Burns Hospital
   and Blocker Burn Unit
University of Texas Medical Branch
Galveston, Texas, USA
Chapter 4

Doraid Jarrar
Research Fellow
Department of Surgery
Brown University
Providence, Rhode Island
Fellow (1996-1998)
Shriners Burns Hospital
   and Blocker Burn Unit
University of Texas Medical Branch
Galveston, Texas, USA
Chapter 8

Marc G. Jeschke, MD
Fellow (1996-1999)
Shriners Burns Hospital
   and Blocker Burn Unit
University of Texas Medical Branch
Galveston, Texas, USA
Chapter 9

Ron Mlcak, RT
Director of Respiratory Therapy
   and Inter-Hospital Transportation
Shriners Burns Hospital
Galveston, Texas, USA
Chapter 2

Victor M. Perez, MD
Clinical Fellow (1998-1999)
Shriners Burns Hospital
   and Blocker Burn Unit
University of Texas Medical Branch
Galveston, Texas, USA
Chapter 6

Edgar J. Pierre, MD
Resident in Anesthesia
University of Miami
Miami, Florida, USA
Fellow (1994-1997)
Shriners Burns Hospital
   and Blocker Burn Unit
University of Texas Medical Branch
Galveston, Texas, USA
Chapter 10

Peter I. Ramzy
Fellow (1997-1999)
Shriners Burns Hospital
  and Blocker Burn Unit
University of Texas Medical Branch
Galveston, Texas, USA (1997-1999)
Chapter 7

Art Sanford, MD
Clinical Fellow (1998-1999)
Shriners Burns Hospital
  and Blocker Burn Unit
University of Texas Medical Branch
Galveston, Texas, USA
Chapters 3,12

Arjav J. Shah, MD
Resident in Anesthesia (1995-1999)
University of Texas Medical Branch
Galveston, Texas, USA
Chapter 5

Preface

The purpose of this handbook is to define treatment techniques developed at one facility consisting of two burn units that treat children and adults respectively. The protocols are the same for both age groups unless specified. This is the compilation of work done by the residents, fellows, and faculty of the University of Texas Medical Branch Blocker Burn Unit and the Shriners Hospital for Children—Galveston Burns Hospital. Each chapter will touch on the pathophysiology of the process in question. However, the bulk of the information will be in regards to specific protocols followed in these two burn units. Chapters will be on subjects ranging from initial resuscitative care to reconstruction and rehabilitation. Chapters on specific injuries from electricity and chemicals will also be included. For a complete discussion on issues related to burn care, the reader is referred to the textbook, *Total Burn Care.*[1]

REFERENCE
1.   Herndon DN. Total Burn Care. (1996) WB Saunders, London UK.

Acknowledgments

We wish to acknowledge the efforts of several, without which the following handbook could not have been developed. The burn fellows and residents shouldered most of this work. The efforts of all the nurses and therapists should also be recognized. Lastly, the tireless work of our partner, Dr. Manu Desai cannot go unmentioned. His innumerable contributions to burn care are described in these pages.

General Considerations

Steven E. Wolf

Burn injury represents a significant problem worldwide. As a reference, over 1.2 million people are burned in the United States every year, most of which are minor and treated in the outpatient setting. However, approximately 60,000 burns in the USA are moderate to severe and require hospitalization for appropriate treatment. Of these, it is estimated that 5,000 die each year from complications related to the burn. The significance of burn injury to society is supported by the finding that only motor vehicle collisions cause more trauma-related deaths. These deaths occur in a bimodal distribution either immediately after injury or weeks later due to multiple organ failure, a distribution that is similar to the pattern of all trauma-related deaths. Two-thirds of all burns occur at home and commonly involve young adult males and children. Young adults are burned frequently with flammable liquids, while toddlers are most often scalded by hot liquids while in the kitchen. A significant percentage of burns in children are, unfortunately, due to child abuse. These generalizations bring to mind that most of these injuries are preventable, and therefore amenable to prevention strategies.

Burns in survivors are complicated by significant morbidity. The ravages of scarring are evident in terms of both function and cosmesis. Even after successful treatment, many patients develop significant scar contractures requiring intense rehabilitative efforts that often culminate in operations for scar release to return function. Other complications such as amputation of limbs and direct thermal injury to vital organs such as the brain and eyes further cause disabilities. Burns in cosmetically important areas including the face and hands leave these patients with devastating marks of the injury that lead to difficult social challenges.

The results of burn have been recognized by the medical community, and significant amounts of resources and research have been directed towards improving these dismal statistics. These efforts have resulted in dramatic improvements. Between 1971 and 1991, deaths attributed to burns decreased by 40% with a concomitant 12% decrease in deaths associated with inhalation injury.[1] Much of this improvement was likely related to effective prevention strategies that decreased the number and severity of burns. Approaches such as legislation mandating nonflammable children's sleepwear,[2] changes in the National Electrical Code to decrease oral commissure burns,[3] elevating hot water heaters from the ground and increased smoke alarm use to decrease injuries in structural fires[4] have been shown to decrease the incidence and severity of injuries in the target populations. Other areas for prevention efforts through further legislation and education of at-risk populations are also actively being pursued through the work of the American Burn Association and other organizations.

Burn Care, edited by Steven E. Wolf and David N. Herndon. © 1999 Landes Bioscience

Improved patient care in those that sustained severe burns has also improved survival. In 1949, Bull and Fisher reported a 50% mortality rate for a burn of 49% TBSA in children aged 0-14, 46% TBSA for patients aged 15-44, 27% TBSA for those of age 45 and 64, and 10% TBSA for those 65 and older.[5] These dismal results have improved markedly. The latest reports indicate a 50% mortality rate for 98% TBSA burns in children 14 and under and 75% TBSA burns in other young age groups[6,7] (Fig. 1.1). These improvements are further illustrated by the following. Investigators have shown that the significant risk factors for mortality after burns using modern treatment techniques are age > 60 years, burn size greater than 40% of the total body surface area (TBSA), and inhalation injury. Using a logistic regression analysis in their patient population, only someone with all three risk factors would have a predicted mortality greater than 33%.[8] Therefore, a young patient with almost any size burn using modern treatment techniques should be expected to live.

Advances in treatment techniques are based on improved understanding of resuscitation, enhanced wound coverage, better support of the hypermetabolic response to injury, more appropriate infection control, and improved treatment of inhalation injuries. Further improvements can be made in these areas, and investigators are active in all these fields to discover means to further improve survival.

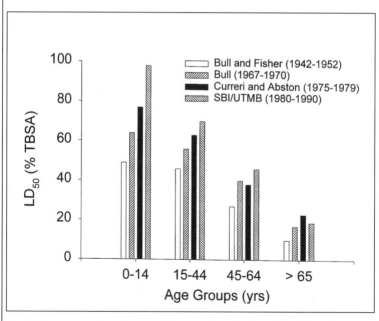

Fig. 1.1. Improvements in burn mortality over time. An increasing LD_{50} indicates improved survival. The most dramatic improvements have been in children.

With improvements in mortality, survivors of these devastating injuries will have special needs. Many of the problems are related to the ravages of scarring and the psychosocial aspects of reintegration into society. Improvements have been made in these fields such that a survivor of a massive burn with disfiguring scars can lead a relatively normal life.[9] New advances in skin replacement and scar management are likely to decrease the effects of scarring. New modalities of psychosocial care and treatment may improve the well being of these patients.

Many of the improvements in burn care originated in specialized units dedicated to the care of burned patients. These units consist of experienced surgeons, physicians, nurses, therapists, dietitians, pharmacists, social workers, psychologists, and prosthetists with the dedicated resources to maximize outcome from these often devastating injuries (Table 1.1). Because of the dedicated resources, burned patients are best treated in such places. The American Burn Association has established guidelines to determine which patients should be transferred to specialized burn units. Patients meeting the following criteria should be treated at a designated burn center:[10]

1. Second and third degree burns of greater than 10% TBSA.
2. Full-thickness burns over 5% TBSA.
3. Any burn involving the face, hands, feet, eyes, ears, or perineum that may result in cosmetic or functional disability.
4. High-voltage electrical injury including lightning injury.
5. Inhalation injury or associated trauma.
6. Chemical burns
7. Burns in patients with significant co-morbid conditions (e.g., diabetes mellitus, COPD, cardiac disease).

Patients meeting the following criteria could be treated in a general hospital setting:

1. Second and third degree burns of less than 10% TBSA
2. No burns to areas or special function or risk, and no significant associated or premorbid conditions.

Table 1.1. Personnel required for a specialized burn unit

Specialized Burn Units
Burn Surgeons
Dedicated Anesthesiologists
Psychiatrists/Psychologists
Physiatrists
Nurses
Occupational Therapists
Physical Therapists
Dietitians
Pharmacists
Social Workers
Prosthetists

REFERENCES

1. Brigham PA, McLoughlin E. Burn incidence and medical care in the United States: Estimates, trends, and data sources. J Burn Care Rehabil 1996; 17:95-107.

2. Cusick JM, Grant EJ, Kucan JO. Children's sleepwear: Relaxation of the Consumer Product Safety Commission's flammability standards. J Burn Care Rehabil 1997, 18:469-476.

3. Rabban JT, Blar JA, Rosen CL, Adler JN, Sheridan RL. Mechanisms of pediatric electrical injury. New implications for product safety and injury prevention. Arch Pediatr Adloesc Med 1997, 151:696-700.

4. Mallonee S, Istre GR, Rosenberg M, Reddish-Douglas M, Jordan F, Siverstein P, Tunell W. Surveillance and prevention of residential-fire injuries. N Engl J Med 1996, 335:27-31.

5. Bull JP, Fisher AJ. A study in mortality in a burn unit: Standards for the evaluation for alternative methods of treatment. Ann Surg 1949; 130:160-173.

6. Herndon DN, Gore DC, Cole M, Desai MH, Linares H, Abston S, Rutan TC, VanOsten T, Barrow RE. Determinants of mortality in pediatric patients with greater than 70% full thickness total body surface area treated by early excision and grafting. J Trauma 1987; 27:208-212.

7. McDonald WS, Sharp CW, Deitch EA. Immediate enteral feeding is safe and effective. Ann Surg 1991; 213:177-183.

8. Ryan CM, Schoenfeld DA, Thorpe WP, Sheridan RL, Cassem EH, Tompkins RG. Objective estimates of the probability of death from burn injuries. N Engl J Med 1998, 338:362-366.

9. Blakeney P, Meyer W, Robert R, Desai M, Wolf SE, Herndon DN. Long-term psychosocial adaptation of children who survive burns involving 80% or greater total body surface area. J Trauma 1998, 44:625-632.

10. Committee on Trauma, American College of Surgeons. Resources for optimal care of the injured patient. 1999.

Pre-Hospital Care and Emergency Management of Burn Victims

Ron Mlcak

Advances in trauma and burn management over the past three decades have resulted in improved survival and reduced morbidity from major burns. Because the care of the burn patient is quite expensive and labor-intensive, regional burn centers have evolved. This regionalization has created an effective and coordinated pre-hospital management, transportation and emergency care system which has resulted in a marked improvement in the clinical course and survival for the thermal injured patient.

For burn patients, there are usually two phases of transport. The first is the entry of the burn patient into the emergency medical system with treatment at the scene and transport to the initial care facility. In the second phase, the patient is assessed and stabilized at the initial care facility and then transported to a burn intensive care unit.[1] With this perspective in mind, this chapter reviews current principles of optimal pre-hospital care and emergency management of the thermal injured patient.

PRE-HOSPITAL CARE

Prior to any specific treatment, the patient must be removed from the source of injury and the burning process stopped. Always suspect an inhalation injury and administer 100% oxygen by face mask. As the patient is removed from the source of injury, care must be taken that the rescuer does not become another victim.[2] All care givers should be aware of the possibility that they may be injured by contact with the patient or the patient's clothing. Universal precautions, including wearing gloves, gowns, mask and protective eye wear should be used whenever there is likely contact with blood or body fluids. Burning clothing should be removed as soon as possible to prevent further injury to the patient.[3] Remove all rings, watches, jewelry and belts as they retain heat and can produce a tourniquet-like effect causing vascular ischemia.[4] If water is readily available, pour it directly on the burned area. Early cooling can reduce the depth of the burn and reduce pain, but cooling measures must be used with caution to avoid hypothermia with its clinical sequela. Ice or ice packs should never be used since they may cause further injury to the skin and produce hypothermia.

Initial management of chemical burns consist of removing the saturated clothing, brushing the skin if the agent is a powder and irrigation with copious amounts of water. Irrigation with water should continue from the scene of the accident through the emergency evaluation in the hospital. Efforts to neutralize the chemicals are contraindicated due to the additional generation of heat, which would further contribute to tissue damage. The rescuer must be careful not to come into contact with the chemical.

Removal of a victim from contact with an electrical current is best accomplished by turning off the current and by using a nonconducting device to separate the victim from the source.[5]

ASSESSMENT OF THE BURN PATIENT

Assessment of the burn patient is divided into a primary and secondary survey. In the primary survey, immediate life-threatening conditions are quickly identified and treated. In the secondary survey a more thorough head-to-toe evaluation of the patient is undertaken.

Initial management of the burn patient should be the same as for any other trauma patient, with special attention directed at the airway, breathing, circulation and cervical spine immobilization.

AIRWAY

Exposure to heated gases and smoke resulting from the combustion of a variety of materials results in damage to the respiratory tract. Direct heat to the upper airways results in edema formation which may obstruct the airway. One must suspect airway injury in those patients who have facial burns, singed nasal vibrissae, carbonaceous sputum and tachypnea.[5] One hundred percent humidified oxygen by face mask should be given initially to all patients, even when no obvious signs of respiratory distress are present. Upper airway obstruction may develop rapidly following injury, and the respiratory status must be continually monitored to assess the need for airway control and ventilatory support. Progressive hoarseness is a sign of impending airway obstruction, and endotracheal intubation should be done early before edema obliterates the anatomy of the area.[3]

BREATHING/VENTILATION

The patient's chest should be exposed to adequately assess breathing, and whether there is a circumferential burn that might restrict ventilation. Airway patency alone does not assure adequate ventilation. After the airway is established, breathing must be assessed to insure adequate chest expansion. Impaired ventilation and poor oxygenation may be due to smoke inhalation or carbon monoxide intoxication.

Endotracheal intubation is necessary for unconscious patients or those in acute respiratory distress, or in patients with burns of the face or neck which may result in edema causing obstruction of the airway.[3] Establishment of a secure airway is of utmost priority for patients in respiratory distress secondary to thermal injury. If endotracheal intubation is indicated it should be performed early and by the most experienced clinician.

CIRCULATION

Blood pressure obtained by a cuff is not the most accurate method of monitoring a patient with a large burn in the initial phase because of the pathophysiologic changes that accompany such an injury. Accurate blood pressure measurements may be difficult to obtain because of edema of the extremities; the pulse rate may be somewhat more helpful in monitoring the appropriateness of fluid resuscitation, however it may be elevated in the early postburn period.[6] To assess for adequate perfusion use skin color and capillary refill in nonburned sites.

CERVICAL SPINE IMMOBILIZATION

In those patients who have been in an explosion or deceleration accident, there is the possibility of a spinal cord injury. Appropriate cervical spine stabilization must be accomplished by whatever means necessary including cervical collars to keep the head immobilized until the condition can be evaluated.

SECONDARY ASSESSMENT

After completing the primary assessment a through head-to-toe evaluation of the patient is imperative,[7] and a careful determination of trauma other than burn wounds should be made. As long as no immediate life-threatening injury or hazard is present, the secondary examination can be performed before moving the patient and precautions such as cervical collars, backboards and splints should be used.[8] Secondary assessment should include the patients past medical history, medications, allergies and the mechanism of injury.

IV ACCESS

Never delay transporting burn victims to an emergency facility due to the inability of establishing IV access. If the local/regional EMS protocol prescribes an IV line be started, that protocol should be followed. The Pre-Hospital Burn Life Support course recommends that if a patient is less than 60 minutes from a hospital, an IV is not essential and can be deferred to the admitting hospital. If an IV line is established, Ringers lactate solution should be infused at 500 ml/h in an adult and 250 ml/h in a child 5 years of age or older. In children less than years of age, no IV lines are recommended if the receiving hospital is close by.[4]

2

WOUND CARE

Pre-hospital care of the burn wound is basic and simple because it requires only protection from the environment with application of a clean dressing or sheet to cover the involved part.[4] The patient should be wrapped in a blanket to minimize heat loss and for temperature control during transport.

PAIN CONTROL

The first step in diminishing pain is to cover the wounds to prevent contact by exposed nerve endings. If it is approved for use in the local/regional EMS system, narcotics may be given for pain, but only intravenously in small doses and only enough to control the pain. The intramuscular or subcutaneous route should never be used,[4] as drug absorption is decreased due to peripheral vasoconstriction. This might become a problem later on when the patient vasodilates and gets an increase in absorption from the area and possible toxicity.

TRANSPORT TO A HOSPITAL EMERGENCY DEPARTMENT

Rapid, uncontrolled transport of the burn victim is not a priority, except in cases where other life-threatening conditions coexist. In the majority of accidents involving major burns, ground transportation of victims to the hospital is available and appropriate. Helicopter transport is of greatest use when the distance between the accident and the hospital is 30-150 miles or the patient's condition warrants.[9] Whatever the mode of transport selected, it should have appropriate size and emergency equipment available, as well as trained personnel such as a nurse, physician, paramedics or respiratory therapist who are familiar with trauma patients.

ASSESSMENT AND EMERGENCY TREATMENT AT INITIAL CARE FACILITY

PRIMARY SURVEY

The assessment of the patient with burn injuries in the hospital emergency department is essentially the same as we have outlined for the pre-hospital phase of care. The only real difference is the availability of more resources for diagnosis and treatment in the emergency department. As with other forms of trauma, the primary survey begins with the ABCs and the establishment of an adequate airway. Endotracheal intubation should be accomplished early if impending respiratory failure or ventilatory obstruction is anticipated because it may be impossible with the onset of edema following the initiation of fluid therapy. Not usually thought of and of equal importance is how to secure an endotracheal tube, particularly since traditional methods often do not adhere to burned skin. One method of choice includes securing the endotracheal tube with tape under the ears as well as over the ears.[10] While doing assessments and making interventions for life-threatening problems in the primary survey, precautions should be taken to maintain cervical spine immobilization until injury to the spine can be ruled out.

2

SECONDARY SURVEY

Following the primary survey, a thorough head-to-toe evaluation of the patient should be done. This includes obtaining a history as thorough as circumstances permit, including an AMPLE history: allergies, medications, preexisting diseases, last meal and events of the injury. The history should include the mechanism and time of the injury and description of the surrounding environment, such as injuries incurred in an enclosed space, the presence of noxious chemicals, the possibility of smoke inhalation and any related trauma. A complete physical exam with a careful neurological exam should be done. Those patients with facial burns should have their corneas examined with fluorescent staining. Routine admission labs should include a CBC, serum electrolytes, glucose, BUN and creatine. Pulmonary assessment should include arterial blood gases, chest X-rays and carboxyhemoglobin.[11]

All extremities should be examined for pulses, especially with circumferential burns. Pulses can be assessed by Doppler ultrasound flow meter. If pulses are absent the involved limb may need urgent escharotomy. If there is associated respiratory compromise due to a circumferential burn then escharotomies should be done to relieve chest wall constriction and improve ventilation. Escharotomies may be performed at bedside under intravenous sedation. Mid-axial incisions are made through the eschar but not into subcutaneous tissue of the eschar to assure adequate release. Pulses should be monitored for 48 h.[11]

EVALUATION OF WOUNDS

After the primary and secondary surveys are completed and resuscitation is underway, a more careful evaluation of the burn wound is performed. The wounds are gently cleaned and loose skin and blisters debrided since blister fluid contains high levels of inflammatory mediators which increase burn wound ischemia. The blister fluid is also a rich media for subsequent bacterial growth. Deep blisters of the palms and soles may be aspirated instead of debrided to improve patient comfort. After burn wound assessment is complete, the wounds are covered with a topical antimicrobial agent or a biological dressing and an absorbent burn dressing is applied.

An estimate of burn size and depth assist in determination of severity, prognosis and disposition of the patient. An accurate assessment is important since burn size affects fluid resuscitation, nutritional support and surgical interventions. The size of the burn wound is most frequently estimated by using the "Rule of Nines" method. A more accurate assessment can be made of the burn injury, especially in children, by using the Lund and Browder chart (Fig. 2.1), which takes into account changes brought about by growth.[4]

Fig. 2.1. Burn diagrams.

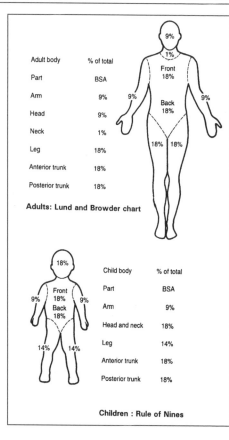

Adult body — % of total

Part	BSA
Arm	9%
Head	9%
Neck	1%
Leg	18%
Anterior trunk	18%
Posterior trunk	18%

Adults: Lund and Browder chart

Child body — % of total

Part	BSA
Arm	9%
Head and neck	18%
Leg	14%
Anterior trunk	18%
Posterior trunk	18%

Children : Rule of Nines

FLUID RESUSCITATION

Establishment of intravenous lines for fluid resuscitation is necessary for all patients with major burns including those with inhalation injury or other associated injuries. These lines are best started in the upper extremity peripherally, and a minimum of two large caliber IV catheters should be established through nonburned tissue if possible, or through burns if no non burned areas are available. The most critical aspect of the early care of the burn patient is to restore and maintain adequate tissue perfusion and vital organ function. Fluid needs are based on the extent of the burn and should be infused initially as Ringers lactate solution at 2-4 ml/kg%BSA. The two most common formulas for estimating fluid needs are the Parkland formula which is 4 ml/kg/%BSA burned, and the modified Brooke formula, which is 2 ml/kg/%BSA burned.[4,12,13] These have been combined and presented as the consensus formula of 2-4 ml/kg/%BSA burned.[4] All the formulas call for one-half of the total amount to be given over the first 8 h from the time of injury and the second half to be given over the following 16 h (Table 2.1).

Table 2.1. Fluid calculations

Consensus Formula
   2-4 ml/kg/%BSA burned
   Give 1/2 of the total amount over the first 8 h from the time of the injury and the 2nd
   half to be given over the following 16 h.
Example: 80 kg man with a 40% TBSB:
   4 ml x 80 kg x 40% TBSB =12800 ml
   Total fluids first 24 h = 12800 ml
   Total fluids first 8 h: 12800/2 =6400 ml = 800 ml/h
   Total fluids next 16 h: 6400/16 =400 ml/h

Table 2.2. Galveston formula

Resuscitation Formula
   1. Fluid administration-Ringers lactate
   First 24 h:
      a. 5000 ml/M2 burn + 2000 ml/TBSA m^2
      b. administer $^1/_2$ in first 8 h postinjury and the 2nd half in the next 16 h.
Example: 15 kg child with an 87% TBSB, height 96 cm.
            Body Surface (m^2) =.60
            Total Burn (m^2)=.52
            2000 ml x .6 TBSAm^2 = 1200 ml
            5000 ml x .52 TBSABm^2 =2600 ml
            Total fluids first 24 h = 3800 ml
            Total fluids first 8 h = 1900 ml = 237 ml/h
            Total fluids next 16 h = 1900 ml = 118 ml/h

Pediatric burned patients should be resuscitated using formulas based on body surface area, which can be calculated from height and weight using standard nomograms. The Shriners Hospital for Children Burns Institute formula recommends initial resuscitation with 5000 ml/m^2/BSA burned/day plus 2000 ml/m^2/BSA total/day Ringers lactate.[14] This formula also calls for one-half of the total amount to be given over the first 8 h and the second half to be given over the following 16 h (Table 2.2).

All resuscitation formulas are designed to serve as a guide only. The response to fluid administration and physiologic tolerance of the patient is most important. Additional fluids are commonly needed with inhalation injury, electrical burns, associated trauma and delayed resuscitation of patients. The appropriate resuscitation regimen administers the minimal amount of fluid necessary for maintenance of vital organ perfusion, and the subsequent response of the patient over time will dictate if more or less fluids are needed. Inadequate resuscitation can cause diminished perfusion of renal and mesenteric vascular beds. Fluid overload can produce undesired pulmonary or cerebral edema.

Urine Output Requirements

The single best monitor of fluid replacement is urine output. Acceptable hydration is indicated by a urine output of more than 30 ml/h in an adult (5 ml/kg/h) and 1 ml/kg/h in a child. Diuretics are generally not indicated during the acute resuscitation period. Patients with high voltage electrical burns and crash injuries with myoglobin and/or hemoglobin in the urine have an increased risk of renal tubular obstruction. Therefore in these patients sodium bicarbonate should be added to the IV fluids to alkalinize the urine, and urine output should be maintained at 1-2 ml/kg/h as long as these pigments are in the urine.[4] The addition of an osmotic diuretic such as mannitol may be needed to assist in clearing the urine of these pigments.

Decompression of Stomach

To prevent any regurgitation with an intestinal ileus, a nasogastric tube should be inserted in all patients with major burns to decompress the stomach. This is especially important for all patients being transported in aircraft at high altitudes. Additionally, all, patients should be restricted from taking anything by mouth until the transfer has been completed. Decompression of the stomach is usually necessary because the anxious, apprehensive patient will swallow considerable amounts of air and distend the stomach.

Temperature Control

The patient must be kept warm and dry since hypothermia is detrimental to the trauma patient and can be avoided or at least minimized by the use of blankets or warm solutions. The patient must be kept warm and wet dressings changed if possible prior to transfer.

Pain Control

The degree of pain experienced initially by the burn victim is inversely proportional to the severity of the injury.[8] No medications for pain relief should be given intramuscularly or subcutaneously, since fluid shifts are from the vascular spaces to the interstitial (third) space, rendering such dosing ineffective and allowing for uncontrolled and unpredictable uptake when fluid resuscitation occurs.[3]

Tetanus Immunization

Recommendations for tetanus prophylaxis are based on the condition of the wound and the patient's immunization history. All patients with burns of greater than 10% BSA should receive 0.5 ml tetanus toxoid. If prior immunization is absent or unclear, or the last booster dose was more than ten years ago, 250 units of tetanus immunoglobulin is also given.[4]

SUMMARY

Burn injuries present a major challenge to the health care team, but an orderly, systematic approach can simplify the initial pre-hospital care and emergency management. A clear understanding of the pathology of burn injuries is essential in providing quality burn care. Successful management of burn victims requires careful attention to treatment priorities, protocols and meticulous attention to details.

REFERENCES

1. Boswick, JA ed. The Art and Science of Burn Care. Rockville: Aspen Publishers, 1987.
2. Dimick AR, Triage of burn patients. In: Wachtel TL, Kahn V, Franks HA eds. Current Topics in Burn Care. Rockville: Aspen System 1883; 8-15.
3. Wachtel TL. Initial care of major burns, Postgraduate Medicine. 1989; (85)1:178-196.
4. Nebraska Burn Institute, Advanced burn life support providers manual. Lincoln, 1987.
5. Radiation Injury: Nebraska Burn Institute: Advanced Burn Life Support Manual. Lincoln: Appendix I, 1987.
6. Bartholomew CW, Jacoby WD. Cutaneous manifestations of lighting injury. Arch Dermatol 1975; 1466-1468.
7. Committee on Trauma, American College of Surgeons. Burns, In: Advanced trauma life support course book. Chicago: Am. College of Surgeons 1984; 155-163.
8. Rauscher LA, Ochs GM. Prehospital Care of the Seriously Burned Patient. In: Wachtel et al, eds. 1-9.
9. Trunkey DD. Transporting the Critically Burned Patient. In: Wachtel et al ed. 9:11-14.
10. Mlcak RP, Helvick B. Protocol for securing endotracheal tubes in a pediatric burn unit. J Burn Care 1987; 8:233-237.
11. Herndon D et al. Shriners Burns Institute and the University of Texas Medical Branch at Galveston. Resident's Manual, 1992; l-17.
12. Archauer B ed. Management of the Burned Patient. Norwalk: Appleton and Lange, 1987.
13. Baker S et al. The injury fact book. Lexington: Lexington Books, 1984.
14. Herndon D et al. The management of burned children. J Burn Care and Rehabil 1993; 14:3-8.

Resuscitation

Art Sanford

3

Along with early excision and grafting, one of the central tenets of current burn care is fluid resuscitation of the burn victim. Many different methods have been proposed, all valid, but with no universal acceptance for one formula. They vary in their use of crystalloid and colloid components and are in continuing evolution as we understand the pathophysiology of the burn wound better. The most important principle in burn resuscitation is that any of these formulas are only guidelines and individual fluid requirements are to be judged by clinical and hemodynamic parameters as endpoints. Without adequate resuscitation, tissue perfusion suffers and the burn shock cascade is perpetuated. Delay to adequate resuscitation is one of the factors identified with increased mortality.

One of the many functions of the skin is to maintain fluid and electrolyte hemostasis. After burn injury, the integrity of skin is lost and leakage of plasma occurs. This is complicated by edema secondary to loss of endothelial integrity and further sequestration of fluid in tissues not directly affected by the burn itself. Thermal injuries of greater than 30% have been demonstrated to initiate a cascade of inflammatory mediators leading to capillary leak that leads to the anasarca in unburned areas and pulmonary edema. These mediators include histamine, bradykinin, and serotonin but the exact mechanism to initiate the cascade has not been elucidated. Attempts at modulation of the cascade are reported, but have not been successfully applied in a clinical setting. Adequate resuscitation aims to counter these effects and reduce this process of postburn shock.

Intravenous access should be established early in the initial evaluation of the burn patient after the airway has been secured according to standard trauma protocols. Peripheral, large bore IVs provide excellent access and can actually administer greater volumes of fluid due to diminished resistance of the catheter secondary to a shorter length. Central venous access may be difficult to establish with the crowding of people around the torso of a newly arrived trauma victim, and also carry risks of pneumothorax or inability to control bleeding from inappropriate placement. In children it can be particularly difficult to establish intravenous access, and the intra-osseous route can be used emergently for fluids and medicines.

Calculations of fluid requirements are based on the amount of body surface involved in second or third degree burns (not first-degree burns). The "Rule of Nines" has been used to estimate the body surface area burned (Fig. 3.1), but this does have limitations in the pediatric population where the head is proportionally larger than the body when compared to the adult. Modifications of this burn diagram are available (Fig 3.2) or nomograms are available as well (Fig 3.3) to calculate body surface area and percent burn. On a more practical note, knowing that

Burn Care, edited by Steven E. Wolf and David N. Herndon. © 1999 Landes Bioscience

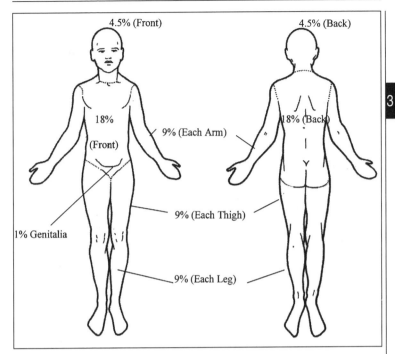

4.5% (Front)   4.5% (Back)

18% (Front)   18% (Back)

9% (Each Arm)

1% Genitalia

9% (Each Thigh)

9% (Each Leg)

Fig. 3.1. "Rule of Nines"

Area	Birth-1yr.	1-4yr.	5-9yr.	10-14yr.	15yr.	Adult
Head	19	17	13	11	9	7
Neck	2	2	2	2	2	2
Ant. Trunk	13	13	13	13	13	13
Post. Trunk	13	13	13	13	13	13
R. Buttock	2.5	2.5	2.5	2.5	2.5	2.5
L. Buttock	2.5	2.5	2.5	2.5	2.5	2.5
Genitalia	1	1	1	1	1	1
R. U. Arm	4	4	4	4	4	4
L. U. Arm	4	4	4	4	4	4
R. L. Arm	3	3	3	3	3	3
L. L. Arm	3	3	3	3	3	3
R. Hand	2.5	2.5	2.5	2.5	2.5	2.5
L. Hand	2.5	2.5	2.5	2.5	2.5	2.5
R. Thigh	5.5	6.5	8	8.5	9	9.5
L. Thigh	5.5	6.5	8	8.5	9	9.5
R. Leg	5	5	5.5	6	6.5	7
L. Leg	5	5	5.5	6	6.5	7
R. Foot	3.5	3.5	3.5	3.5	3.5	3.5
L. Foot	3.5	3.5	3.5	3.5	3.5	3.5

Fig. 3.2. Relative % TBSA with age

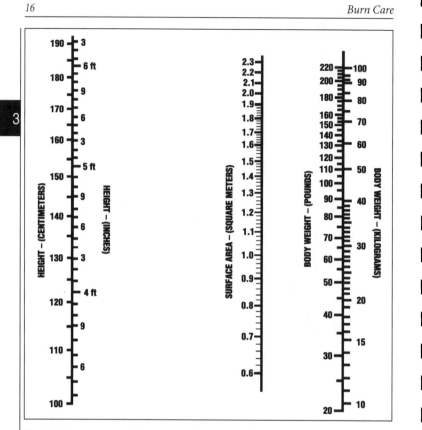

Fig. 3.3. Nomogram to calculate body surface area and percent burn

the patient's palm (not the examiner's) is equal to 1% of total body surface, body surface area (BSA) burned can be estimated by "patting out" the burned areas when a quick evaluation is needed.

The modified Brooke and Parkland (Baxter) formulas are the most commonly used early resuscitation formulas at this time. They use 2-4 cc/kg/%BSA burn of Lactated Ringers solution respectively. The calculated needs are for the total fluids to be given over 24 h. Because of the previously mentioned fluid shifts in the immediate postburn period, one half of these calculated needs are given in the first 8 h postinjury, and the remaining one half are administered in the next 16 h. It is important to remember that if resuscitation is delayed for a period that "burn time" begins from the injury, not initiation of treatment, so it may be necessary to administer even larger volumes to catch up with needs. Again, these are only estimates of needs and fluid administration must be adjusted to maintain urine output at 1/2-1 cc/kg/h.

For example, a 70 kg person with a 50% TBSA burn resuscitated immediately would require between 7 and 14 liters of resuscitation fluid, at a rate of 437 cc/h-875 cc/h for the first 8 h depending whether 2 or 4 cc/kg/%TBSA is chosen, respectively. The subsequent 16 h would need between 219 cc/h and 437 cc/h, again based on this same range. A more complex calculation, for a 60 kg person with a 75% TBSA burn presenting 4 h postinjury resuscitated at 2 cc/kg/%TBSA would require 1.125 liters/h for the first 4 h of resuscitation (the first 4.5 liters need to be given over 8 h but because of the delay in instituting treatment, all of this volume must be given in the remaining 4 h of the initial segment of "burn time"). Regardless, clinical condition and urine output must be the final determinants. Use of albumin in early resuscitation is currently not advocated with the understanding that increased capillary leak would allow the administered protein to pass to the injured tissues and actually increase osmotic pressure of the tissues and hence edema. Once endothelial integrity has been restored at 6-8 h postinjury, albumin administration may proceed to attempt to maintain plasma oncotic pressure. In general, minor burns (less than 15% BSA burn) do not require intravenous supplementation and can be managed with close attention to oral intake.

Continuing fluid replacement must also take into account ongoing losses until the burn wounds and donor sites have healed as demonstrated by complete reepithelization. After the initial 24 h, approximate ongoing losses are 1 cc/kg/%BSA burn to be replaced in addition to standard maintenance fluids, again adjusted based on urine output and clinical evaluation. Electrolytes and protein will also be lost until the wound is closed and need appropriate replacement. Another important consideration is the large volume of "insensible losses" burn patients suffer secondary to ventilators and the air-fluidized sand beds of up to one liter per day.

Children pose a special challenge to resuscitation efforts. Body composition of a child consists of relatively more free water compared to an adult and there is also a relatively larger surface area per kilogram in a child, hence resuscitation formulas for adults usually underestimate the needs of a child. Infants also have relatively little glycogen stores, so dextrose containing solutions must be added to their resuscitation fluids (D5LR). The Shriner's Burns Institute-Galveston Branch has developed the resuscitation formula 5000 cc/m² BSA burn/24 h for resuscitation and 2000 cc/m² Total BSA maintenance fluids using Ringers lactate solution; again one half of the resuscitation fluid is given in the first 8 h and the remainder in the subsequent 16 h. Monitor blood sugars and replace as necessary to keep serum glucose between 60 and 180 gm/dl. Subsequent fluid losses are replaced at 3750 cc/m² BSA remaining open at any time and 1500 cc/m² total BSA for maintenance fluids.

The elderly and people with underlying cardiopulmonary dysfunction need aggressive monitoring with Swan-Ganz catheters to follow volume status. Inhalation injuries commonly require additional fluids to overcome additional evaporative losses from the respiratory tract, commonly as much as twice the estimated needs to resuscitate a similar patient without the respiratory component. In addition to the cutaneous manifestations of an electrical burn injury, there is commonly a component of muscle injury with the release of nephrotoxic substances such as myoglobin. A positive urine dipstick for heme without visualization of intact red cells on microscopic exam points to diagnosis of this complication. To aid in clearance of myoglobin, additional fluids, as well as to replace losses induced by diuretics and mannitol (an osmotic diuretic and free radical scavenger), may be needed with alkalinization of the urine. The formulas above include the use primarily of Lactated Ringers solution; however, in the setting of acute renal failure that results from inadequate resuscitation, the added potassium load becomes potentially dangerous and normal saline should be substituted.

Despite all attempts to control the edema formation postinjury, its occurrence is inevitable. Risk of associated complications need to be constantly monitored. Delayed airway compromise can occur as edema of the glottis forms, both from inhalation injury and the above-mentioned capillary leak. Previously soft compartments in burned extremities can develop elevated intracompartmental pressures and decreased tissue perfusion (compartment syndrome) requiring escharotomies at a later time as resuscitation proceeds.

Several common electrolyte abnormalities occur during the initial postburn period and must be monitored and corrected. Calcium, magnesium and phosphorus are found to be low quite frequently, likely due to wound and renal losses from lowered levels of circulating albumin initially and subsequent altered bone metabolism. Changes in antidiuretic hormone (ADH) levels cause the body to think it is volume depleted, so the stimulation of thirst follows, leading to the ingestion of large amounts of free water. Unmonitored, this results in hyponatremia. Hypernatremia and hyperchloremia will result from overzealous use of normal saline (hypertonic) solutions. Hypokalemia results from ongoing renal losses, while hyperkalemia follows tissue loss and release of this intracellular ion as well as from renal failure.

It cannot be overemphasized that any fluid resuscitation formula is only a guideline and not a guarantee of adequate resuscitation. The principles of critical care, correction of any metabolic acidosis by improving tissue perfusion and good clinical judgment should be the ultimate endpoints of resuscitation.

Assessment, Operative Planning and Surgery for Burn Wound Closure

Peter Dziewulski, Juan P. Barret

4

INTRODUCTION

The burn wound causes both local and systemic effects mediated by the host responses of inflammation, regeneration, and repair. Initial physiological derangement can give rise to shifts in fluids, electrolytes and proteins within body compartments necessitating formal fluid resuscitation in large burns. Other gross metabolic, endocrine, hematological and immunological disturbances can also occur in these patients. The severity of burn injury depends on the etiology of the injury, the percentage body surface area of skin damage and the depth of the burn.

Burn Care, edited by Steven E. Wolf and David N. Herndon. © 1999 Landes Bioscience

The aim of burn wound management is to achieve early sound and durable healing. The management of the burn wound is only one part of the management of the burn patient as a whole.

ANATOMY

Depth of burn injury is divided into partial and full thickness skin loss, with partial thickness burns being divided into superficial and deep types (Fig. 4.1). This classification quantifies the amount of tissue damage into anatomical terms.

1. Erythema (1st degree burns)—involving the epidermis only, usually with no blistering although desquamation can occur later on.
2. Partial thickness (2nd degree burns)—involves epidermis and varying portion of dermis.
3. Superficial if sparing of significant proportion of hair follicles, sebaceous and sweat glands and substantial portion of dermis.
4. Deep if destruction of large proportion of hair follicles, sebaceous and substantial portion of dermis.
5. Full thickness (3rd degree burns)—destruction of epidermis, dermis and all adnexal structures.

PATHOPHYSIOLOGY

The initial local effect of a burn injury can be divided histologically into three differential zones of tissue damage and blood flow.

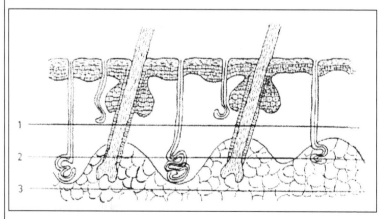

Fig. 4.1. Depth of burn wound: 1) Superficial partial thickness burn—most adnexal structures intact; 2) Deep partial thickness burn—only deep adnexal structures intact; 3) Full thickness burn—all structures damaged.

1. Zone of necrosis—tissue necrosis centrally due to destruction of tissue by injury.
2. Zone of ischemia—surrounds zones of necrosis and can progress and lead to a clinically apparent increase in the area of skin necrosis or depth of injury.
3. Zone of inflammation (hyperemia)—surrounds zone of ischemia and is manifested by increased vascular permeability with extravasation of fluid from the intravascular to the interstitial space leading to edema. The extravasation of water, electrolytes and macromolecules is immediate and can be generalized in larger burns. It continues for 24-48 h and if left untreated can lead to hypovolemic shock.

ESCHAR

The necrotic tissue resulting from a burn is known as eschar. It separates slowly from underlying viable tissue and is a good substrate for microorganisms. If left untreated it becomes colonized, contaminated and eventually infected. Infection attracts white blood cells that can digest the interface and cause separation of the eschar from the underlying viable tissue. Topical antimicrobial agents increase the time to eschar separation.

ASSESSMENT OF THE BURN WOUND

The burn wound must be assessed clinically before a treatment plan can be formulated. The following must be determined; the depth of the burn wound, the size of the burn and the anatomical site of injury.

1) Depth of burn determined by clinical wound inspection and the pinprick test (Table 4.1)
2) Size of the burn determined as percent of total body surface area (%TBSA) using
   a) Wallace's "Rule of Nines" (Fig. 4.2)—useful for initial rapid estimation
   b) Lund and Browder Chart (Fig. 4.3)—for a more precise estimation
   c) Patient's palm ~ 1% of their body surface area—useful for children and smaller burns

Note: Children have larger heads and smaller limbs in terms of body surface area compared to adults.

3) Anatomical Site—important functional and aesthetic areas include; hands, feet, face, eyelids, perineum, genitalia, and joints. These areas need special attention to optimize wound healing and prevent cosmetic and functional problems secondary to hypertrophic scaring.

Table 4.1. Clinical determination of burn depth

Depth of Burn	Clinical Appearance
1) Partial Thickness	Blistered
	Pink and moist underneath blisters
	Wound blanches under pressure
	Demonstrates capillary refill
	Sensation intact
2) Deep Dermal	Some blistering
	Wound moist or dry
	Wound white or fixed staining (red)
	No blanching or capillary refill
	Sensation diminished
3) Full-Thickness	No Blisters
	Wound dry
	Leathery appearance to eschar—feels hard
	Charring
	Fixed staining and hemorrhage areas

Fig. 4.2. Wallace's "Rule of Nines" for estimation of burn size.

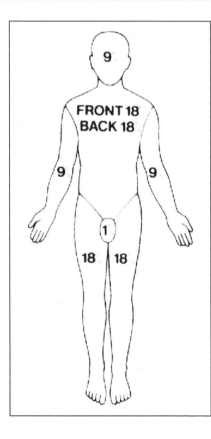

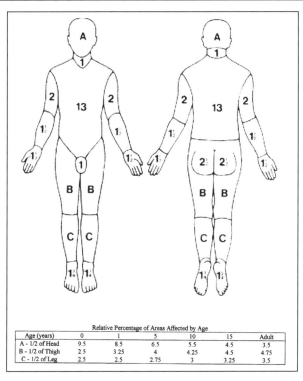

Relative Percentage of Areas Affected by Age						
Age (years)	0	1	5	10	15	Adult
A - 1/2 of Head	9.5	8.5	6.5	5.5	4.5	3.5
B - 1/2 of Thigh	2.5	3.25	4	4.25	4.5	4.75
C - 1/2 of Leg	2.5	2.5	2.75	3	3.25	3.5

Fig. 4.3. Estimation of burn size—Lund and Browder Chart.

INITIAL MANAGEMENT OF THE BURN WOUND

Resuscitation, smoke inhalation and other injuries must be dealt with initially. Maintenance of the airways, breathing and establishing venous access are paramount and are discussed in other chapters. Following assessment of the burn wound the following practical procedure may be required:

1) First Aid—cooling the burn wound soon after the injury (within 30 minutes) is beneficial in removing heat from the wound and limiting tissue damage. It can also reduce early edema and protein extravasation. Care must be taken, as prolonged or excessive cooling can be detrimental. Irrigating the wound in a drench shower for a least 20 minutes is essential in chemical injury.

2) Burn Blister—management is controversial with evidence of blister fluid having both beneficial and deleterious effects. In general they should be removed if large, over joints and produce functional impairment. Small intact blisters can be left in situ to act as a biological dressing.

3) Escharotomies—required if circumferential full thickness burns of chest, limbs or digits are present. In limbs/digits such burns impair circulation and cause distal ischemia. Circumferential full-thickness chest burns can restrict chest wall excursion and impair ventilation. Such burns require mid-axial escharotomies performed either at bedside or in the operating room. A scalpel or electrocautery device can be used to incise through the full thickness burns down to bulging fat. The incisions should extend into adjacent nonburned or less deeply burned tissue. Since the wounds are full thickness, minimal analgesia or anesthesia is required, but extension into less damaged tissue can be very painful.

The decision to perform escharotomy is a clinical one. If you think that a wound may need an escharotomy-then do it! This is particularly relevant if an excision of the clearly full-thickness wound will be done later. An escharotomy incision will only improve outcome without risk of harm in that situation. Waiting for signs of distal ischemia or absent pulses is too late!

Mixed depth full thickness/deep partial thickness injuries producing a similar clinical picture can be treated with topical collagenase although this is not really a substitute for formal escharotomies.

BURN WOUND HEALING

The amount of anatomical tissue destruction and the size of the injury are important determinants of wound healing.

1) Erythema (1st degree burns) usually resolves without any untoward effect within a few days.

2) Superficial partial thickness (2nd degree burns) wounds heal spontaneously by re-epithelialization from epidermal remnants within two weeks and leave few or no scars.

3) Deep partial thickness (2nd degree burns) wounds heal by a mixture of granulation, wound contraction and epithelialization from epidermal remnants and the wound edge. If left to heal spontaneously these wounds take 2-4 weeks or longer to heal and are associated with a high incidence of disfiguring hypertrophic scarring and scar contracture. These wounds often need skin grafting.

4) Full thickness wounds (3rd degree burns) require surgical intervention and split thickness skin grafting. This invariably leads to hypertrophic scarring particularly at the edges of the grafts (marginal hypertrophy). If left to heal spontaneously these wounds granulate, contract and epithelialize from the wound margins. This process is prolonged, leaves the wound susceptible to invasive infection, and leads to significant functional and esthetic deformity.

5) Burn wounds that require skin grafts have a higher incidence of scar hypertrophy if the grafting is performed after 14 days of injury and the wound has no viable dermal elements. Burn wounds that are not going

to heal within two weeks should be debrided and covered with autologous split skin grafts to minimize hypertrophic scarring.

TREATMENT PLANNING

Once the size, site, and depth of the burn wound have been estimated and initial urgent measures have been undertaken, a plan of action must be formulated for further management of the wound. This management plan will include conservative and surgical options depending on the individual patient and the type and site of the wound. In the discussion below our preferred options will be given followed by other alternatives. In general our institution pursues early aggressive surgical intervention in deeper injury to limit the duration of burn illness and reduce associated morbidity and mortality.

Treatment planning depends on the assessment of the following factors:
- Patient's general condition and co-morbid factors
- Patient age
- Burn depth
- Burn size
- Anatomical distribution of injury

MANAGEMENT OF SUPERFICIAL PARTIAL THICKNESS WOUNDS

The aim of management of these types of wounds is to promote rapid spontaneous re-epithelialization with the minimum number of painful dressing changes, and to prevent infection which can convert the injury to a deeper one that requires skin grafting.

SMALL/MEDIUM SIZED SUPERFICIAL PARTIAL THICKNESS WOUND
(< 40% TBSA)
Preferred method
Biobrane®
For patients presenting within 24 h of their injury. After admission and stabilization under sedation or anesthesia the burn blisters are cleaned, debrided and all burned epithelium is removed. Biobrane® is applied to the wound in a circumferential fashion around the limb or trunk so that it is tight and closely adherent to the wound. The Biobrane® is secured by stapling it to itself. Care is taken not to staple the Biobrane® to the patient as this can cause granulomas and the staples are painful to remove. The Biobrane® is then wrapped with a standard dressing of Polysporin/Mycostatin impregnated rolled gauze covered by elastic bandages. The dressings are removed at 24 h to inspect the wound. Oral antibiotics with staphylococcal coverage are given for seven days. If the Biobrane® is adherent after the first day, no further dressings are required. As re-epithelialization occurs in 10-14 days the Biobrane® spontaneously separates from the healed wound.

If wound infection supervenes, the Biobrane® rapidly becomes nonadherent and can trap any exudate produced by the wound. For this reason Biobrane® is not used in patients presenting more than 24-36 h following their injury and in larger wounds (> 40% TBSA). Biobrane® is also relatively expensive compared to common topical antimicrobials.

ALTERNATIVE METHODS
Topical antimicrobials

Topical Silvadene (1% Silver Sulfadiazine) is the usual alternative for these wounds. After cleaning the wound and debridement of the blisters, Silvadene is applied topically to the wound which is then covered with a rolled gauze and elasticized bandage. The Silvadene dressings are changed once or twice daily until re-epithelialization occurs and the wound is healed. This method requires frequent dressing changes, which can be a painful. It is the method of choice for patients presenting late after injury with a colonized wound.

Biological dressings

Biological dressings such as allograft skin, xenograft skin (porcine), human amnion can all be used in a similar fashion to Biobrane® to physiologically close the wound while re-epithelialization occurs. The problems associated with the use of these products include availability, collection, storage, and transmission of infection control and cost.

Other dressings

Conventional dressings such as Vaseline gauze or silicone sheet (Mepitel®) can be used to cover the wound while re-epithelialization takes place. After application, these dressings need frequent changes, which can be painful. These types of dressing are useful for small burns (less than 5% TBSA).

Synthetic dressings such as Duoderm®, Omniderm® Tegaderm® and hydrocolloids have all been used with some success to dress such wounds. Other semi-synthetic biological dressings such as Dermagraft TC® are also being evaluated for use in this type of wound.

Exposure

After cleaning and debridement, wounds are left open in a warm dry environment to crust over. The coagulum formed separates as re-epithelialization proceeds underneath. Advantages of this method are comfort and no need for dressing changes. Disadvantages of this method include prolonged inpatient treatment, specialized ward and nursing requirements and higher infection rates. This technique is now not commonly used apart from the treatment of specialized areas such as the face, genitalia and perineum.

LARGE SUPERFICIAL PARTIAL THICKNESS INJURY (> 40% TBSA)
Preferred treatment
Allograft

These uncommon injuries are more prone to contamination and infection and can have a high morbidity. Best results are achieved if allograft is applied within 24 h of the injury. Under anesthesia the wound is cleaned and all blisters and nonadherent epidermis removed. Allograft split skin grafts meshed 2:1 are placed over the open dermal wound and secured with staples. It is important not to open up the mesh on the allograft as this can lead to desiccation, infection and deepening of the underlying wound. A standard graft dressing is applied. If the burn is thought to be a little deeper, a mid-dermal burn. The burn can be debrided with a dermatome at a depth of 10-15/1000 inch and allograft applied as above. This wound should then go on to heal spontaneously without incorporation or rejection of the allograft into the wound.

ALTERNATIVE METHODS
Other biological or semi-biological dressings

Xenograft skin can be used in a similar fashion to the allograft, but does not usually adhere as well, leaving the wound open to desiccation, infection and pain.

Biobrane® can be used in the same way as for smaller injuries. There is a higher rate of wound infection which can lead to loss of the Biobrane® and deepening of the burn wound.

Topical antimicrobials

Topical antimicrobials such as silver sulfadiazine can be used for this type of wound in a similar manner to that described above. It is the treatment of choice for wounds that present late and are colonized, as by definition the wounds should heal spontaneously. The dressing changes can be painful and are an ordeal for the patient. There is a high incidence of wound sepsis, which can lead to deepening of the burn wound, which may then necessitate skin grafting.

Other dressing

Simple nonbiological dressings such as Vaseline gauze or silicone sheets (Mepitel®) can be used to dress the large partial thickness wound. These dressings can be medicated with an antimicrobial agent. The dressings are covered with rolled gauze, bulky absorbent pads and elasticized crepe bandages.

The dressings are left intact for three to five days unless wound exudate seeps through the dressing. The dressing changes can be very painful and often the patient needs a general anesthetic for the procedure. There is a high incidence of invasive wound sepsis and deepening of the burn wound that often necessitates surgery. This technique is not recommended for larger burns.

MANAGEMENT OF DEEP PARTIAL THICKNESS INJURY (SMALL AND LARGE)

This type of burn has a significant morbidity in terms of time to healing, infective complications and subsequent scarring. Conservative management leading to spontaneous healing usually involves prolonged and painful dressing changes and the resultant scar is invariably hypertrophic leading to cosmetic and functional debility. Thus an early surgical approach that tries to preserve dermis and achieve prompt wound healing is preferred.

PREFERRED TREATMENT
Total wound excision and grafting

Burns that are deemed to be deep partial thickness in nature are best tangentially excised and the wound covered with autologous split skin grafts. The grafts usually require meshing and the amount of wound that can be closed with autograft depends on the donor sites available and the mesh ratio used. Cosmetically and functionally sensitive areas such as the face and hands need thicker sheet autograft for wound closure. If the burn size is large (20%) or if donor sites are scarce, then temporary wound closure with allograft, xenograft or other biological or semi-biological dressings may be required to close the rest of the wound while the donor sites heal. Standard graft dressings are applied. The grafted areas can be inspected five days later. Early inspection of the wound is recommended if there was late presentation or colonization of the excised burn wound. This type of total wound excision can be done in one stage if enough surgeons are available or can be done in two or three stages within the first five days following the burn. Patients with large burns need to return to the operating room for further grafting when their donor sites are healed. This is usually done on a weekly basis.

ALTERNATIVES
Serial wound excision and grafting

This method is employed for larger burns where donor sites are scarce. The surgical technique is similar to that given above but the amount of burn wound excised is the amount that can be covered by meshed split skin grafts from the available donor sites. Unexcised areas are treated with topical antimicrobials until donor sites have healed and can be reharvested, usually 7-14 days later. The unhealed areas of burn wound are susceptible to invasive wound infection before they are excised and this treatment method has a higher morbidity and mortality compared to early excision. The use of the topical antimicrobial flamacerium (silver sulfadiazine and cerium nitrate) has been reported as decreasing episodes of invasive wound infection, morbidity and mortality with this method of treatment.

Topical antimicrobials

The wounds can be treated with daily or twice daily applications of silver sulfadiazine until wound healing is achieved. This may take up to 4-6 weeks and involve the patient in prolonged and painful periods of dressing changes. There is a higher incidence of invasive wound infection using this method with associated deepening of the wound. Once healed there is a much higher incidence of hypertrophic scarring which can be a bother functionally and cosmetically disabling. This method is usually reserved for patients who are thought to be unfit for surgical intervention and for smaller burns in functionally and cosmetically unimportant areas.

FULL THICKNESS INJURY

Full thickness burns will not heal spontaneously unless very small and invariably require skin grafting. The necrotic tissue usually requires excision and the resultant wound requires closure to reduce the risks of invasive infection and systemic sepsis. Prompt excision and wound closure reduces morbidity and mortality inpatients with such injuries.

1) Small Full Thickness Injury (< 10% TBSA)
Preferred method
Excision and autografting

By definition full thickness injuries will not heal spontaneously and require wound closure with split thickness autografts. On presentation it is usually best to excise these wounds in a tangential fashion and obtain wound closure with split thickness autograft. Meshed autograft is used if larger areas need closure, whereas sheet autograft is used for functionally and cosmetically sensitive areas such as the hands and face. Grafts are secured to the wounds by staples or absorbable sutures and are dressed in the standard fashion. Grafts and wounds are inspected on the second day if the initial wound was infected or heavily colonized or on the fifth day if not.

Alternative Treatments
Topical antimicrobials

Inpatients who are elderly or unfit for surgical intervention, conservative management with topical antimicrobials can be used. The antimicrobial agent—usually silver sulphadiazine—is applied once/twice daily until the burn eschar separates and a granulating wound is present. This usually takes approximately three to four weeks to occur and sometimes longer. This granulating wound can then be covered with autograft to achieve wound closure. In certain cases small wounds less than 5 cm diameter can be left to heal spontaneously by wound contraction and epithelialization from the wound margins.

This method of treatment usually results in a higher incidence of invasive wound sepsis, a longer inpatient stay in the burn unit and a longer time to wound healing. It is not recommended except in the special circumstances given above.

2) Medium/Large Full Thickness Injuries (> 10% TBSA)
Preferred treatment
Total burn wound excision and auto/allografting

The treatment of choice for medium and large full thickness injuries is total excision of the burn wound and physiologic wound closure with split skin autograft, allograft and/or synthetic skin substitutes. This early aggressive surgical approach has been shown to improve mortality in certain patient groups with such burns. It is a major surgical undertaking to do this in one sitting with the larger burns (greater 40% TBSA) and needs a coordinated approach from the surgical and anesthetic teams. The timing of surgery postinjury is critical as blood loss in the 24 h postburn has been shown to be half that of surgery after this time (Table 4.2). In centers when numerous surgeons and anesthetists are not available, total wound excision can be staged over two to three operations removing the wound within five days of the injury. The type of wound excision depends on

Table 4.2. Estimated approximate blood loss given in ml per cm$_2$ burn excised in patients >30% TBSA Burn

Day PostInjury	Estimated Blood Loss (ml/cm^2)
0-1	0.4
1-2	0.6
2-16	0.75
>16	0.5

To estimate blood requirements preoperatively the burn size in cm^2 should be estimated. A calculation can then be made if the time postinjury is shown. From Herndon DN et al. Early burn wound excision significantly reduces blood loss. Ann Surg 1990; 211:753-762.

the state of the burn wound. Those patients presenting immediately following their injury usually have an uncolonized wound, which can be excised in a tangential fashion with a skin graft knife. Those patients presenting late a few days after injury will have a colonized or infected wound. Attempts to preserve subcutaneous fat in these cases usually fail and can lead to invasive systemic sepsis; therefore fascial excision is usually preferred in these circumstances.

Wound closure is performed with meshed split thickness skin autograft and allograft if donor sites are insufficient. In large and massive burns special techniques such as overlay grafting are used to cover large wound areas with widely meshed autograft. After total wound excision the whole wound must be physiologically closed with auto- or allograft or a synthetic skin substitute like Integra®.

In large burns where wound closure cannot be achieved primarily with autograft, the patient returns to the operating room when the donor sites are ready for reharvesting at which time allograft is changed and further autograft is applied. This is usually done in stages on a weekly basis until the whole wound is closed with autograft.

ALTERNATIVE METHODS

Serial excision and autografting

This surgical approach has been described above for deep partial thickness burns and entails excision of as much of the wound that can be covered with available autograft. The unexcised areas of burn are treated with topical antimicrobials until the donor sites are ready to be reharvested. This method of treatment has a higher morbidity and mortality in larger injuries and has generally been abandoned.

Topical antimicrobials and autografting of a granulating wound

This approach is again similar to the one described above for deep partial thickness injury. The wound is dressed on a daily or twice daily basis with a topical antimicrobial until spontaneous separation of the eschar occurs leaving a granulating wound. This is then closed with split skin autograft. This technique has a high incidence of invasive wound infection and systemic sepsis and in larger burns is associated with a high mortality. It is only suitable for smaller burns inpatients who are unfit for surgical debridement of the burn wound. It is not recommended for younger, fit patients with larger injuries.

MIXED DEPTH INJURY

Although the descriptions above have alluded to specific depths of burn, in clinical practice most burns are mixed depth with areas of superficial partial, deep partial and full thickness injury in adjacent area. Treatment of such wound depends on the mixture of each component part of the injury, as one will usually predominate. In general superficial partial thickness areas should be left to epithelialize while the areas of deeper injury require excision and wound closure.

SURGICAL PLANNING—ANATOMICAL FACTORS

Prior to commencing any operation, the surgeon must have a plan as to which donor sites are going to be used, which anatomical areas are to be debrided, and the technique used for debridement. It is essential to have an idea of how much autograft is required, which areas are priorities for autograft coverage, the required mesh ratios and where the harvested graft is going.

In smaller burns where donor sites and available graft is plentiful, the focus is to minimize donor site morbidity and to maximize functional and cosmetic outcome. Care is used when choosing donor sites, preferentially taking cosmetically hidden areas such as the upper thighs and scalp. Sheet grafts are preferred. It is probably unnecessary to use meshed grafts in burns less than 30% TBSA.

In major burns (< 60% TBSA), priority goes to covering large areas with available autograft in the smallest number of operations to maximize survival. In these size burns, the number of operations required is estimated to be one operation for every 10% TBSA burned. The sequence of areas to be autografted is variable depending on the surgeon. In general, our practice is to cover the posterior trunk, anterior trunk, lower limbs, upper limbs, and head and neck in order. This sequence maximizes the area covered with autograft early in the course and allows for earlier ambulation. Areas not covered with autograft have allograft placed, which is removed when autograft is available at subsequent operations.

MANAGEMENT AND GRAFTING OF ANATOMICAL AREAS

In general sheet grafts should be used whenever possible, however this not practicable in burns over 30% TBSA. The following considerations need to be taken into account when grafting each anatomical area especially when mesh grafts are used as contracture can occur in the line of the interstices.

TRUNK/BREAST

In general mesh graft interstices on the trunk should be placed horizontally. Care should be taken to preserve the breast or breast bud, especially in females, and to place enough skin with minimal mesh expansion into the inframammary folds and the sterna area to try and reduce subsequent breast deformity. The umbilicus should be preserved if possible.

BUTTOCKS/PERINEUM/GENITALIA

The buttocks are difficult to manage and skin graft take is poor. They are all-prone to fecal soiling and shearing and can be the site of repeated bouts of invasive wound sepsis. It is often worth autografting them in the first operation, but graft take can be disappointing. If the grafts fail it is then best to leave the area for a time when the patient can be nursed prone while the grafts take. This is usually done after all other areas are healed. It is not usually necessary to perform a colostomy to prevent fecal soiling.

The perineum and genitalia are usually managed conservatively with grafting of any unhealed areas later on in the course of surgical treatment.

LOWER LIMB/HIPS/KNEES/ANKLES/FEET

Mesh graft interstices on the lower limbs should run longitudinally along the line of the limb except at the joints. At both knee and ankle joints graft expansion should be minimized if possible and the direction of the interstices should be the same as the axis of rotation of the joint i.e. perpendicular to the longitudinal axis of the limb.

The skin on the sole of the foot is glabrous skin and is very thick and specialized. It will commonly re-epithelialize despite what initially seems a full thickness injury. The sole of the foot is best treated conservatively until it is apparent that spontaneous re-epithelialization will not occur. In contrast the skin on the dorsal aspect of the foot is very thin and often requires grafting. It is important not to use widely meshed skin in this area as any significant hypertrophic scarring can cause difficulties with weight bearing ambulation and fitting of shoes.

UPPER LIMB/AXILLA/ELBOW

The same principles apply to the upper limb as described above. Mesh interstices should run longitudinally on the upper limb apart from the axilla and elbow where the interstices should be parallel to the axis of rotation of the joint. It is important not to widely expand the mesh over the joints.

HANDS

Great attention to detail must be paid to the hand to achieve optimal functional results. The volar aspect of the hand is covered with specialized glabrous skin, which usually heals and it is best to avoid grafting it if possible. The dorsal skin is thin and usually requires grafting in deep burns. In general, sheet graft is preferable to mesh graft and is best secured with catgut sutures. There is some debate as to which way the grafts should be applied to the hand along the longitudinal axis of the hand or perpendicular to it. There is no good evidence to suggest one way is better than the other.

The key to functional success is early mobilization of the hand. Initially after grafting the hand is dressed and splinted in the position of safety with the metacarpophalangeal joints flexed at 70-90°, the interphalangeal joints at 180°, the wrist in neutral or slightly extended and the thumb flexed and adducted at the metacarpophalangeal joint. The grafts are inspected at five days and, if stable, mobilization can be started. If sheet grafts are used they can be exposed with no dressing during mobilization during the day with splintage at night.

Inpatients with large burns, repeated application of allograft may be required until it is time to autograft the hands. It can be very difficult to maintain the position of safety of the hand during this period with splintage alone especially in children under two years of age. In these cases K-wires through the metacarpophalangeal and interphalangeal joints may be required to maintain the safe position of the hand.

Face/Neck/Eyelids

The face and neck are areas that are both cosmetically and functionally important. Deep burns of the face are usually treated conservatively with either topical antimicrobials or repeated applications of allograft until a viable wound bed is present. Occasionally early excision of full thickness facial burns is performed and allograft applied to prepare the wound bed. Conservative treatment tends to preserve viable tissue and is preferred. Further application of allograft may be required before donor sites are available to graft the face. Sheet allograft should be used and placed on the facial wound in cosmetic units (Fig. 4.3).

Medium to thick sheet split skin autograft should be used for the face and applied in cosmetic units to place marginal scars in natural skin crease lines. If available, donor sites should be above the neck for optimum color and texture match. The scalp is an excellent donor site for grafts destined for the face. To get suitable sheet grafts, dermocleisis with a solution of epinephrine should be employed and a powered dermatome with a four-inch guard should be used to get grafts of maximum width.

The eyelids require special attention to prevent corneal injury. Early excision and closure of eyelid burns reduces the incidence of corneal injury secondary to exposure and should be a priority. In the short term temporary tarsorrhaphies (suturing the upper and lower lids together) can be performed to protect the corneas. When applying autograft to the eyelids thick split thickness graft should be used and overcorrection should be performed putting more skin in than seems to be needed as contraction can lead to corneal exposure. Throughout the course of the burn injury the corneas should protected by regular application of eye ointment.

Fig. 4.3. Estimation of burn size—
Lund and Browder Chart

SURGERY

GENERAL CONSIDERATIONS

The key to surgical intervention in the burn patient is good preoperative planning in terms of optimal treatment method (see above), prioritization of areas requiring autografting and the type of skin graft or skin substitute required. It is best to have the shortest surgical time possible to limit blood loss and hypothermia. In larger injuries this requires a team of burn surgeons who are experienced in this type of surgery. Experienced anesthetists are required as these patients present a challenge in blood volume replacement. An operating room team of nurses and technicians who have worked in such cases is also invaluable. It is vital to have blood cross-matched and ready in the operating room before starting any significant burn wound debridement. A guide to blood requirements is given in Table 4.2. Perioperative antibiotics are usually required, the choice of which and duration of treatment are guided by the resident microbiological flora.

TEMPERATURE

The environmental temperature in the operating room must be kept at about 30°C to limit hypothermia and can be achieved by heaters over the operating table. In addition to the routine hemodynamic parameters measured during surgery, the patient's temperature during the procedure and following and the base deficit on repeated blood gas analysis are useful guides to the patient's condition and volume status. A persistent fall in the patient's temperature to below 35°C is a bad prognostic sign and should signal the prompt termination of surgery.

PREPARATION OF PATIENTS

Once anesthetized, preparation and skin cleaning of the patient is very important. In the operating room and under heaters maintaining the environmental temperature, all dressings are removed and body is cleaned with warm aqueous povidone-iodine and the scalp is shaved if burnt or if required for donor site harvest. Any loose eschar or tissue including previously applied allograft skin is removed. The areas are then washed down with warm water (37°C) from a self-retracting hose system. It is important to clean with warm fluids to reduce patient heat loss. Once cleaned the patient is lifted or log-rolled and all soiled drapes are removed and replaced by a foam pad with sterile drapes with a shoulder roll to keep the neck extended.

INSTRUMENTS

The following equipment and instruments are essential for the performance of burn surgery.

Operating table

Burn surgery can be performed on a standard operating table, but the preference at our institution is a specially designed table incorporating a lip at the edge and a drainage hole so that cleaning agents, blood etc., do not run off the table onto the floor and can be disposed of via the drainage hole and tubing to a drain.

Knives

A variety of knives are required for the excision. Standard surgical 15 and 10 blades are required for sharp excision. Tangential and full thickness excision requires skin graft knives such as the Braithwaite, Watson or Goulian knives (Fig. 4.4). The first two skin graft knives are similar and are used for excising large areas on the trunk and limbs. The Goulian knife is smaller and useful for excision of more delicate areas such as the hand and face.

Dermatomes

Skin can be harvested using the skin graft knives mentioned above although it is technically difficult to get consistent, uniform thickness large split skin grafts with these knives. Most burn surgeons use electric or air driven dermatomes such as the Zimmer or Padgett to harvest skin grafts particularly if large amounts from difficult areas are required. The powered dermatomes can be fitted with guards with widths of 2, 3 and 4 inches to harvest grafts or different widths.

Meshers

These are essential if large areas of wound require covering. There are essentially two types of machine that can mesh grafts. One type produces a fixed mesh ratio (2:1, 4:1 etc.) (Brennen Mesher) and if different ratios are required additional machines are used. The other type relies on dermacarriers or boards to produce the mesh ratio and thus one machine can produce grafts of differing mesh ratios using different boards (Zimmer Mesher).

Staplers

Once harvested and applied to the wound (meshed or sheet), grafts require securing to the wound. They can be secured with dressings, sutures or staples.

Fig. 4.4. Examples of skin grafting knives.
a) Goulain knife; b) Watson modification of the Braithwaite knife.

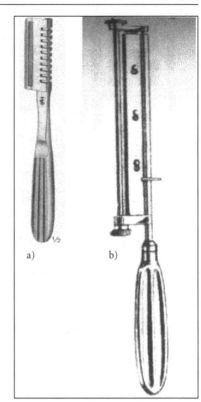

a)   b)

Dressings alone used to secure grafts leave them susceptible to shear. Therefore most surgeons secure grafts with skin staples. Grafts on cosmetically important areas such as the face tend to be secured with sutures, which are usually absorbable.

Tourniquets

Tourniquets can be used to limit blood loss when excising limb burns. It is very useful if the tourniquets can be sterilized so that if the whole limb is burnt the upper part can be excised before application of the sterile tourniquet without contamination of the operative field. If burns are excised under tourniquet it can be difficult to determine the exact depth of excision, as there is no bleeding. If the tourniquets are removed completely, bleeding can be profuse due to reactive hyperemia. A useful technique is to deflate the tourniquet briefly and apply epinephrine soaks to the wound, then reinflate the tourniquet after elevation. This limits blood loss, identifies bleeding vessels in need of hemostasis, and also help in determining depth of excision by inspection of the wound to see if it bled while the tourniquet was deflated. To further limit blood loss, skin grafts are then applied to the excised wounds, a compressive dressing is applied and the limb is elevated prior to deflation of the tourniquet.

Electrocautery

An electrocautery is essential during burn surgery. In larger burns two, three or even four may be required. Electrocautery is used for hemostasis and can also be used for full thickness or fascial burn wound excision. Placement of the grounding plates may be a problem. The soles of the feet can be a useful contact area and multiple large sterile contact plate coated in contact gel can be placed onto open wounds or grafted areas as a temporary measure. It is wise to leave a contact plate attached to the sole postoperatively in case further hemostasis on the ward is required.

Dermocleisis

Infusion of a weak epinephrine solution (1:1,000,000) under burn eschar can reduce the blood loss when the wound is excised. Similar infusion subcutaneously under donor sites (dermocleisis) reduces blood loss and makes skin graft harvesting easier in difficult sites like the scalp, scrotum, chest wall etc.

Adjuncts for hemostasis

In addition to the above, other adjuncts such as hot saline soaks or weak epinephrine solutions (1:400,000) applied topically to the excised burn wound reduce bleeding by stimulating coagulation. Topical thrombin (4-20%) may also be sprayed onto the wound to help with hemostasis.

TECHNIQUES OF WOUND EXCISION

The technique used to excise the burn wound depends on the factors described above. In partial thickness wounds an attempt is made to preserve viable dermis, whereas in full thickness injury all necrotic and infected tissue must be removed leaving a viable wound bed of either fat, fascia or muscle. In general most areas are excised with a hand skin graft knife or powered dermatome. Sharp excision with a knife or electrocautery is reserved for areas of functional cosmetic importance such as the hand and face.

TANGENTIAL

This technique described by Janzekovic in the 1970s requires repeated shaving of deep partial thickness burns until a viable dermal bed is reached, which is manifested clinically by punctate bleeding from the dermal wound bed. The excision is performed using serial passes of a skin graft knife such as the Braithwaite, Watson or Goulian or dermatome set at a depth 5-10/1,000 inch until punctate dermal bleeding is achieved. The more numerous the bleeding vessels in the wound bed, the more superficial the wound. Hemostasis is obtained with hot soaks and electrocautery and the wound is ready for grafting.

FULL THICKNESS

A hand knife such as the Watson or powered dermatome is set at 15-30/1,000 inch and serial passes are made excising the full thickness wound. Excision is aided by traction on the excised eschar as it passes through the knife or dermatome.

Adequate excision is signaled by a viable bleeding wound bed, which is usually fat. The viability of fat can be difficult to determine but in general viable fat is yellow and bleeds. Red fat is dead fat, and discoloration of the fat, punctate hemorrhages, and thrombosed vessels in the wound bed are all indicative of inadequate excision and necessitate further wound excision. After hemostasis the wound is ready for grafting.

Full thickness excision can also be achieved using sharp excision with a knife or with electrocautery. The plane of excision runs between viable and nonviable tissue, and an attempt is made to preserve viable subdermal structures and fat. This is used where contour preservation is important such as the face or where subcutaneous structures such as the dorsal veins in the hand require preservation.

Fascial

This technique is reserved for burns extending down through the fat into muscle, where the patient presents late with a large infected wound and inpatients with life-threatening invasive fungal infections. It involves surgical excision of the full thickness of the integument including the subcutaneous fat down to fascia. This is done with electrocautery and offers excellent control of blood loss and a wound bed of fascia, which is an excellent bed for graft take.

Unfortunately fascial excision is mutilating and leaves a permanent contour defect, which is near impossible to reconstruct. Lymphatic channels are excised in this technique and peripheral lymphedema can be a problem later on.

Avulsion

In some wounds, particularly deeper ones and those treated conservatively, the necrotic eschar can be avulsed from the underlying viable tissue with minimal blood loss. This is achieved by applying a heavy pair of tissue forceps to the eschar and pulling. This technique is usually used in conjunction with fascial or full thickness excision.

Amputation

Occasionally primary amputation must be considered in management of the burn wound. It is usually reserved for high voltage electrical injuries or very deep thermal injuries with extensive muscle involvement and rhabdomyolysis which is life threatening. In general, limb salvage is attempted if possible with preservation of length to try and maximize function. Amputation in these cases is reserved for patients who have an ischemic limb or refractory invasive infection following repeated debridement. In other circumstances amputation is undertaken only if all other measures to preserve a useful functioning limb have failed.

Wound Closure

Following wound excision it is vital to obtain wound closure. Wound closure is permanent with autologous split skin grafts or temporary using allograft or skin substitutes. Physiological closure of the burn wound reduces invasive infection, evaporative water loss, heat loss, pain and promotes wound healing. Temporary skin substitutes are used to achieve physiological wound closure following excision until donor sites have regenerated and are ready for harvesting. These temporary substitutes can be biological. Semibiological skin substitutes can leave in situ aspects of the skin on a permanent basis such as the dermal portion of Integra® (see below), but in general all these coverings buy time while the donor sites heal.

AUTOGRAFT

In general autologous split skin grafts are the gold standard for resurfacing burns. However they have limitations and attempts are being made to resolve some of these by the development of skin substitutes. Split skin grafts can be harvested either as split thickness or full thickness grafts. Full thickness grafts tend not to be used for acute burns, as the donor sites requires closure, do not regenerate and are limited. These grafts also require stringent wound conditions to ensure take. Full thickness skin grafts are extremely useful for postburn reconstruction.

Split skin grafts take more easily, and are the mainstay for wound closure. Split skin grafts can be harvested either with a hand knife or with a powered dermatome (see above). Skin grafts can be used as sheet grafts or can be meshed.

ALLOGRAFT SKIN (HOMOGRAFT)

Of all the materials used for temporary wound closure allograft skin is the most important and its extensive use has been a key factor in improvement in the mortality associated with extensive burns.

Allograft skin is usually harvested from cadaveric donors after appropriate donor selection and screening for communicable disease, and consent from relatives has been obtained. Strict exclusion criteria are applied to ensure safety for transplantation. Exclusion criteria include any history, physical signs or laboratory investigation of infection or sepsis, intravenous drug use, neoplasia, hepatitis, syphilis, slow virus infection, AIDS or HIV, autoimmune disease. Any positive serologies, evidence of serious illness, death of unknown cause, or toxic substances within the tissue are also exclusion criteria. Donor age is usually between 16 and 75 years. Skin from refrigerated cadaveric donors should be retrieved within 24 h.

Harvested skin can be either stored fresh in nutrient media at 4°C for up to a week. If not used the skin is cryopreserved by freezing it in cryoprotectant media containing glycerol to –196°C in liquid nitrogen. Such cryopreserved skin retains 85% viability of its cells at one year. It is important when thawing cryopreserved skin to rapidly rewarm it to preserve cell viability. Both fresh and cryopreserved skin obviously have viable cells within them. Nonviable allograft skin can also be produced either by preserving it within higher concentrations of glycerol or freeze-drying it. Freeze-dried skin can also be ethylene oxide gas sterilized.

In order of preference of allograft take on the excised burn wound, fresh allograft is by far the best followed by cryopreserved, glycerolized, then freeze-dried. When dealing with a sizable wound, the use if viable allograft (fresh or cryopreserved) is far preferable to nonviable (glycerolized and freeze dried). Nonviable skin can be useful in the management of smaller wounds when there is concern about transmission of infectious agents.

Allograft skin is usually harvested, collected, screened, processed, and distributed by a regional tissue bank. Allograft is analogous to blood, and it is important to use this vital resource responsibly. When ordering allograft from the tissue bank it is important to state the type (viable, nonviable, fresh cryopreserved) and amount of allograft required. The amount can be estimated by determining the body surface area and burn size in cm^2.

Allograft skin can also be obtained from living donors, usually parents or relatives of burned children. It is usually harvested immediately prior to its use on the burn victim and is used fresh. In view of the reliable supplies of good quality allograft skin provided by tissue banks, this method is used infrequently.

Allograft skin can be used either as sheet or meshed graft. It is mainly used meshed 2:1, and care is taken not to expand the interstices to prevent desiccation, infection and necrosis of the underlying wound. Meshing the allograft allows any hematoma and seroma drainage.

Sheet allograft tends to be used to cover cosmetic areas such as the face as even with unexpanded mesh granulation tissue can grow through the interstices and leave a permanent pattern.

XENOGRAFTS AND OTHER BIOLOGICAL DRESSINGS

Skin from different species can be used for temporary physiological wound closure. Porcine skin is commonly used and is commercially available. Its main use is as a biological dressing for partial thickness wounds. For full-thickness injury it is not clinically as useful or versatile as allograft and is not generally used for this indication.

Other biological dressings that have been used mainly on partial thickness wounds are substances like human placenta and potato skins, which adhere to the wound, and promote re-epithelialization.

SKIN SUBSTITUTES

Semibiological and synthetic skin replacements are continuously being improved as investigators try to provide the ideal wound healing environment for partial thickness injuries, recreate skin by dermal replacement in full-thickness burns, and attempt to restore epithelial cover by tissue culture techniques. There are numerous products available and can be differentiated to those that provide temporary wound cover while the underlying wound re-epithializes or is ready autografting (i.e., Biobrane®, Dermagraft TC®) and those that close the wound and help reconstitute part of the resultant skin (Integra®).

BIOBRANE®

Biobrane® is a bilayered material made up of a nylon mesh impregnated with porcine collagen which has an outer layer of rubberized silicone sheet attached to it. The outer silicone layer is permeable to gases but not to fluids and bacteria and thus acts like an epidermal layer. Biobrane® can be used for either partial or full thickness burns. In partial thickness burns Biobrane® is applied to a clean viable burn wound and adheres to it allowing rapid re-epithelialization and decreased pain. After excision of full-thickness wounds, application of Biobrane® can close the wound temporarily giving donor sites a chance to heal. In both situations Biobrane® is very susceptible to infection. Purulent exudate can rapidly accumulate under the Biobrane® and can spread so adherence is lost under the whole sheet. This can lead to invasive wound infection and deepening of the wound. It is vital to apply the Biobrane® to the wound within 24 h of the injury and a concurrent course of an oral cephalosporin is usually given. Its use in full-thickness injuries is not as successful as partial thickness injury due to infective problems.

DERMAGRAFT TC®

Dermagraft TC® is a bilayered, temporary skin substitute, which contains biologically active wound healing factors that are in contact with the burn when applied in addition to an external synthetic barrier. The active wound healing factors are fibronectin, type I collagen, tenascin, glycosaminoglycans and a variety of growth factors including transforming growth factor β. This product has been used for immediate closure of clean mid-dermal to indeterminate burn wounds. It is applied in a similar fashion to Biobrane® to a viable clean wound bed and following adherence promotes re-epithelialization. Recent clinical studies have been promising. It has no role in management of the full-thickness burn.

INTEGRA®

Integra® is an acellular bilaminar device that is designed to provide permanent wound closure that replaces dermis. It is made up of a disposable upper layer of silastic that can control evaporative water loss and acts as a barrier to microorganisms and is analogous to the epidermis. The lower layer is a crosslinked matrix of bovine collagen and chondroitin-6-sulfate, which is incorporated into the wound and becomes a 'neodermis'.

This technology is used to replace dermis in full-thickness burns in an attempt to modulate postburn hypertrophic scarring. After excision of the burn the Integra® is applied to the wound in a similar fashion to autograft (Fig. 4.5). Care is taken to avoid wrinkles or pleats in the Integra® and it is secured to the wound with either skin staples or sutures. Nonshear dressings are then applied and 0.5% silver nitrate soaked dressings are applied to the covered areas on a regular basis to try and limit contamination, colonization and infection of the Integra® covered wounds. The Integra® should be inspected daily during this time. Any collections occurring under the matrix should be aspirated and sent for microbiological culture. If any purulent material appears under the Integra® or if it becomes nonadherent, then it should be removed, the underlying wound cultured and the Integra® replaced with allograft skin.

The collagen/chondroitin-6-sulfate matrix is vascularized by host cells over the next three weeks or so and the artificial dermis is gradually replaced with a 'neodermis' which is pink and flat. No granulation tissue should be seen. When the 'neodermis' looks vascularized and has a healthy pink color, the silastic covering can be removed and very thin epidermal autografts (2-4/1000 inch), containing epidermis only can be harvested and applied. This provides epidermal cover

Fig. 4.5. Stages in use of Integra® (Modified from Physicians Training Manual, Integra Lifesciences Corporation)

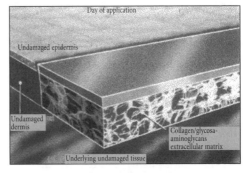

a) Application of Integra® to excised full thickness wound

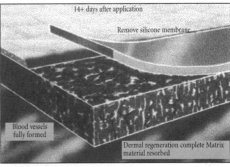

b) Removal of siliacone layer once matrix vascularized

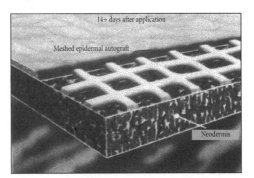

c) Application of epidermal graft onto 'neodermis'

for the 'neodermis' and produces permanent wound closure (Fig. 4.6?). The grafts are susceptible to loss at this stage and 0.5% silver nitrate soaks are applied over a nonshear dressing.

Integra® has been extensively studied and has produced encouraging results both in single center studies and in a multi-centered randomized controlled trial. Studies have reported less hypertrophic scarring with a much more pliable resultant scar and a reduced requirement for secondary reconstructive procedures.

ALLODERM®

De-epidermalized de-cellularized sterile human dermis (Alloderm®) can be used as a dermal replacement both acute care and for postburn reconstruction. In acute cases after excision and preparation of the wound bed. Alloderm® can be applied to the wound with a thin (epidermal) split skin graft applied over it. This bilayered construct is then secured with staples or sutures and is essentially treated as a skin graft. This technique is susceptible to epidermal graft loss due to either desiccation or infection, as the dermal portion of the sandwich must be revascularized first. Its success in the management of acute burns has been variable but, it has been successful in postburn reconstruction following contracture release. It also has been useful in soft tissue augmentation.

CULTURED EPITHELIAL AUTOGRAFT (CEA)

Using tissue culture techniques, epidermal cells (keratinocytes) can be grown in a laboratory and then used to assist wound closure. From a 1 cm² biopsy enough cells can be cultured in approximately 3-4 weeks to cover 1 m² body surface area. These cells can be cultured commercially for patients with large burn injuries however the cost is significant.

This technique only produces the epidermal layer for wound closure and although there have been many reports of successful use of CEA to close burn wounds a number of problems limit their use. The lag time of 3 weeks from biopsy to production of adequate quantities allows wound colonization and granulation tissue to develop leading to low take rates compare to split skin grafts. Once applied the grafts are very fragile and often-prolonged immobilization of the patient is required. Even after successful take the grafted areas remain fragile and blister easily due to poor and delayed basement membrane formation.

Attempts to overcome some of these problems have been to graft the CEA onto an allograft dermal bed as described by Cuono in 1986. Initially after wound excision, allograft is used for temporary wound closure while CEA are produced. When ready the epidermal portion of the engrafted allograft is removed using a dermatome or dermabrasion leaving a viable dermal allograft bed behind onto which the CEA are applied.

This technique has been reported as having better CEA take with improved basement membrane formation and less fragility and blistering.

In general the use of CEA should be reserved for patients with massive burns (> 90%) with extremely limited donor sites or major burns where donor sites are limited, difficult to harvest and cosmetically and functionally important (face, hands feet, genitalia). A recent review of patients at our institution surviving massive burn injury showed that patients treated with CEA had a longer hospital stay, required more operations and had a higher treatment cost compared to a comparative group of patients treated with conventional techniques.

4

SKIN GRAFT TAKE

By definition a graft is completely removed from its donor site, loses its blood supply and requires revascularization when applied to the wound bed. Split skin grafts take on wound beds by adherence, plasmatic imbibition and revascularization.

When a split skin graft is applied to a wound bed, rapid adherence is a good sign implying that the graft will take. Adherence is due to fibrin bonds, which are weak at first and can be disrupted by shear, hematoma or seroma. If serous fluid starts to leak through mesh interstices or fenestration's immediately after graft application and the graft is adherent, the good take is ensured.

Over the first 48 h the graft survives by plasmatic imbibition, that is, absorption of fluid into the graft due to accumulation of osmotically active metabolites and denatured matrix proteins. This fluid may contribute to cell nutrition and may keep vascular channels within the graft open until it is revascularized. Thin grafts survive this process better than thicker ones.

The graft is revascularized over a period of 3-4 days with vessel anastomoses between the wound bed vasculature and existing vessels within the graft (inosculation) and by direct fibrovascular ingrowth from the wound bed into the graft matrix forming new vascular channels.

Full-thickness grafts require a rich blood supply from the wound bed to reestablish blood flow within the dermal plexus of vessels. They get the majority of their revascularization from wound edges and are best on freshly excised wounds. They do not take well on contaminated or granulating wound beds. In the initial stages graft revascularization can be prevented or disrupted by graft shear, hematoma or seroma formation. Graft shear can be minimized by nonshear dressings, pressure dressings, exposure or graft quilting. Hematoma can be minimized by meticulous hemostasis following wound excision. Mesh grafting or fenestration will allow drainage of hematoma or seroma.

Adherence and subsequent take depend on the wound bed, thus freshly excised wounds take graft well with fascia better than fat. Fresh granulating wounds also take grafts well but chronic granulating wounds and contaminated wounds have poorer graft takes due to proteolytic enzymes in the wound that can be produced by both bacteria and cells within the wound itself. In chronic granulating wounds it is not uncommon to see 'ghosting' of skin where initial graft take is good but then the grafts slowly 'dissolve' over a period of days. They can be salvaged by wound care with topical antimicrobials.

GRAFT MATURATION

Following take the graft goes through a number of stages to achieve maturation. Initially there is epithelial hyperplasia and thickening which leads to scaling and desquamation. The epithelial appendages such as sweat and sebaceous glands do not survive grafting but can regenerate in thicker grafts. The grafts are dry and require moisturizing until these functions return. Hair follicles lie in deeper parts of the dermis and in the hyperdermis and are not transplanted in most split skin grafts. They are transplanted in full-thickness grafts and care must be taken in selecting donor sites so as not to transplant hair to a nonhair bearing area. Grafts tend to be re-innervated over a period of time with sensation developing within a month but continued improvement can occur for several years.

Pigmentation of grafts can be troublesome, particularly inpatients with dark skin. Grafts can be hypo- or hyperpigmented and it is difficult to predict which. In general, grafts harvested from the lower half of the body tend to be paler and can become yellow if placed above the clavicle.

The main problem with grafts is that of hypertrophic scarring and contraction. All grafts will be surrounded by a marginal hypertrophic scar. Interstices in mesh grafts will develop hypertrophic scarring and in widely meshed graft will give a 'crocodile skin' appearance.

The wound bed contracts and this is inhibited to a certain degree by the skin graft. The greatest amount of inhibition of wound contraction occurs with grafts in the following order: full-thickness, thick split thickness, thin split thickness, meshed. The amount of wound contraction depends on the proportion of dermal thickness within the graft. Thus areas where there is no dermis, such as at the margin of grafts and in grafts interstices, hypertrophic scarring and wound contraction are inevitable.

Wound contraction around mobile areas and anatomical landmarks can lead to contractures resulting in deformity and impairment of function.

Special Grafting Techniques

In general most grafts are applied and secured in the straightforward fashion given above. However in certain instances special grafting techniques are required to graft difficult or large areas.

Meshing

Grafts are meshed using machines, which essentially cut holes in the skin allowing it to be stretched to cover a larger area than that harvested. The grafts can be meshed at varying ratios, 1:1, 1.5:1, 2:1, 3:1, 4:1, 6:1, 9:1 using different machines. In practice, grafts meshed with an expansion ration more than 3:1 need protection as the wound bed that lies in the interstices (holes) of the graft is prone to desiccation. The wound bed can undergo desiccation and necrosis with subsequent graft loss and deepening of the underlying wound. Therefore special techniques are used to protect widely meshed grafts. Once the graft has taken and the interstices re-epithelialize, hypertrophic scarring in the interstices can be significant with a 'crocodile skin' appearance. This is more pronounced with widely meshed grafts; thus they are reserved for large burns. Mesh ratios of greater than 4:1 are not frequently used. In addition to expanding the area covered by a graft, meshing allows drainage of any underlying hematoma or seroma. Sheet grafts give a better cosmetic appearance but are more susceptible to loss secondary to hematoma or seroma. Sheet grafts are used in cosmetically and functionally important areas such as the face and hands.

FENESTRATION AND QUILTING
Fenestration (cutting multiple small holes in the sheet graft) allows drainage of any hematoma or seroma. The fenestrated areas can leave scars and this technique is best used for areas such as hands that are more functionally than cosmetically important. Quilting of sheet grafts (suturing the graft at multiple sites to resemble a quilt) prevents accumulation of hematoma or seroma under large areas of graft. Quilting is also useful in securing grafts in cosmetically important areas such as the face that are difficult to dress.

BOLSTERS
Tie over bolster dressings are used to secure grafts to difficult or mobile areas. In the acute phase of the burn illness they are used for securing grafts to the back, buttocks, shoulders, axillae or any other similar areas to prevent movement and shearing of the graft. In these cases large bolsters are usually required using gauze dressings for the bolster to apply pressure and 0 silk sutures through the surrounding skin or tissue to tie the dressing on with.

In reconstructive cases smaller bolsters are used to secure full-thickness or thick split skin grafts into areas that have undergone surgical release. In these cases, provaflavine wool or sterile foam sponge can be used as the bolster with 2/0 or 4/0 silk tie over sutures.

OVERLAY TECHNIQUE
This technique is the mainstay for covering large areas of open wound with small amounts of autologous split skin graft. It is useful inpatients with large burns and scarce donor sites. Described by Alexander in 1981, it involves harvesting autograft from available areas and meshing it 4:1. It is placed on the wound and maximally expanded to cover as large an area as possible. This is then overlaid with unexpanded 2:1 meshed fresh or cryopreserved allograft applied at 90° to the autograft in a sandwich pattern (Fig. 4.6). It is important not to expand the allograft as this protects the underlying autograft interstices from desiccation and infection.

The grafted areas are dressed and looked after with standard graft care protocols. Both autograft and allograft adhere and take to the wound. As epithelial migration across the autograft interstices occurs, the overlying autograft becomes loose and detaches leaving a re-epithelialized area underneath. This is known as creeping substitution. This process can take 2-3 weeks before the whole grafted area has epithelialized. Greater expansion ratios for the mesh autograft can be used (6:1, 9:1), but re-epithelialization takes longer and the resultant scarring and appearance tend to be worse.

GRAFT DRESSINGS

The successful take of skin grafts does not solely rely on their application. As already mentioned, wound preparation and hemostasis are vital. The positioning of grafts is also of vital importance in minimizing functional and cosmetic deformity and is discussed below.

Securing the graft and dressing it are important in minimizing loss through shear, hematoma, seroma and infection.

Our traditional preferred graft dressing is gauze impregnated with a Polysporin and mycostatin ointment. The dressings are applied so that the grafts are compressed against the wound. They are then covered with a rolled gauze dressing followed by a bulky gauze dressing to soak up any wound exudate. An elasticized crepe bandage is then applied. Care must be taken not to put circumferential dressings on too tightly on limbs as they can cause distal ischemia, particularly if they

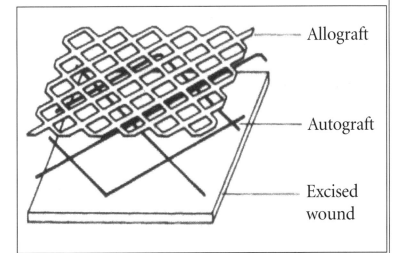

Allograft

Autograft

Excised wound

Fig. 4.6. Diagram representing overlay technique with widely meshed autograft overlayed with meshed allograft (From Alexander UW et al. Treatment of severe burns with widely meshed skin autografts and meshed skin allograft overlay. J Trauma 1981; 21:434.)

dry out and cause constriction. In the same way dressings on the trunk can impair chest wall excursion and inhibit respiration. In children under two who use the diaphragm to breathe, circumferential dressings around the abdomen must not be too tight.

GRAFT CARE

Removal of the dressings and graft inspection are usually performed on the fifth day after grafting. If an extensive area has been grafted then sedation or an anesthetic is required. Any staples used to secure the graft can be removed at this time. A good graft take is indicated by the graft looking pink and being adherent to the underlying wound bed. In meshed grafts there may be evidence of epithelialization of interstices. The graft is usually redressed with a similar but lighter graft dressing and mobilization can commence. Dressings are then done on an alternate day basis until the graft stabilizes and all interstices are closed. At this time the graft can be left exposed and moisturizing cream applied.

During the phase of graft healing there are often crusts and scabs that surround the graft. It is important that these are gently removed, as they can be reservoirs for bacterial proliferation.

If a contaminated or chronic wound has been grafted and there are concerns about infection or hematoma, early dressing change and graft inspection are recommended at 48 h. Great care must be taken when removing dressings in order not to disturb or remove the graft from the underlying wound bed. If the grafted wound looks contaminated or infected at this stage with purulent exudate and graft lysis or 'ghosting' then topical antimicrobial agents can be applied to the wound depending on which organisms have been cultured or are suspected.

DONOR SITES

A donor site is in essence a superficial partial thickness skin wound and should heal within 7 days depending on the thickness of the graft harvested. Care of the donor site is equally as important as the grafted area. Most donor sites will invariably heal, but slow healing or subsequent hypertrophic scarring can be a major problem.

DONOR SITE HEALING

Split thickness donor sites heal by epithelialization from epithelial appendages such as the hair follicles, sweat and sebaceous glands. The thicker the graft taken or if the same site is harvested repeatedly then the number of epidermal appendages is reduced with slower healing and a higher rate of hypertrophic scar formation.

Donor site healing is also dependent on other factors such as age, depth of harvest, wound management and blood supply to the donor site. In larger burns with limited donor sites that require repeated harvesting, recombinant human growth hormone (0.2 mg/kg/day) has been shown to increase donor site healing by up to 25%.

CHOICE OF DONOR SITE

Choice of donor site is important especially inpatients with smaller burns where scarring and deformity should be minimized. In young females with small burns requiring grafting donor sites should be hidden and skin should be harvested from either the buttock or the upper inner aspect of the thighs. In young males the upper outer aspect of the thigh can be used in addition to the above. The scalp is also an attractive donor site, as subsequent hair growth completely hides the scars. Inpatients with larger burns, choice of donor sites is limited and skin grafts should be harvested from any available site.

DONOR SITE DRESSINGS

Immediately following harvesting, epinephrine (1:400,000) soaked dressings are applied topically to the wound to reduce bleeding. Marcaine (0.25%) and epinephrine (1:200,000) can be applied topically to reduce postoperative donor site pain.

The choice of donor site dressings depends on the size and site of the donor area. For small areas, dressings like OpSite or Biobrane are useful as are Alginate dressings. These can be covered by rolled gauze, a bulky gauze dressing and elasticized crepe or, in the case of OpSite, be left exposed. When used for large areas these dressings are prone to infective complications which can lead to conversion of the donor site wound to a deeper one.

The choice for larger donor areas is scarlet red gauze covered by rolled gauze, a bulky gauze dressing and elasticized crepe. The outer dressings are there to collect any blood or exudate and are removed after 6 h exposing the scarlet red gauze which is then dried out using external heaters. These scarlet red gauze dressing are left exposed until the donor sites heal usually within 5-7 days if growth hormone is being used.

DONOR SITE CARE

Vaseline is applied to the scarlet red to soften up the dressing prior to removal, as removing dry dressings tends to damage the healed wound surface underneath. Once donor sites are healed, moisturizing lotion is applied to prevent drying and scaling until the patient returns to the operating room for further surgery. If the donor sites become infected, then topical agents guided by microbiological surveillance are required until healing is achieved. Occasionally a donor site can convert to become a full thickness wound and then requires split skin grafting to achieve wound healing. This is obviously a disastrous complication in a large burn and must be strenuously avoided.

SURGICAL COMPLICATIONS

AIRWAY

The airway in burn patients undergoing surgery is always at risk particularly if they have had an upper airway burn. Repeated turning and movement of the patient and surgery on the head and neck area all increase the risks of endotracheal tube displacement. Vigilance is essential at all times and the burn surgeon must be well versed in the emergency surgical airways.

BLEEDING

Perioperative bleeding is unavoidable to a certain degree. Intraoperative measures to reduce bleeding such as subeschar infusion of epinephrine solutions, limb tourniquets, topical application of epinephrine to both excised wounds and donor sites and topical thrombin are all used routinely. Electrocautery is used to coagulate sizable vessels individually although care must be used in order not to leave behind a charred wound bed—grafts don't take on charcoal! Application of split skin graft has a hemostatic effect due to tissue thromboplastin activation. This coupled with a firm dressing usually stops most bleeding. Persistent bleeding that continues despite repacking and dressing postoperatively with collection of clots in the bed must be taken seriously. It necessitates removal of the dressing, inspection of the graft, removal of any hematoma and hemostasis of any major bleeding either with electrocautery or underunning with a catgut suture.

GRAFT SHEAR

Graft shear is a serious complication that can lead to total loss of the graft necessitating further surgery. It is entirely avoidable by preoperative planning, careful application of dressings, judicious use of bolsters and general care when moving or transferring the patient. The sites most prone to graft shear are those over joints and posterior surfaces. Sites over joints are prone to shear during movement of the joint and this can be minimized by using bulky dressings or splints. Care is required with splints in the acute stage as these can contribute to shear above and below the joint and can also cause pressure areas. Shear of posterior grafts can be minimized by planning surgery with minimal turning of the patients and the use of bolsters.

If a large burn on the back requires grafting the sequence of surgery is to have the patient supine initially, harvest graft and débride any anterior burns. The patient is then positioned prone; the burn excised followed by grafting and bolster dressings. The patient's wound is then turned into a supine position and the anterior surfaces grafted prior to finishing. Great care is taken in transferring the patient back to his/her bed.

INFECTION

Infection of grafted areas postoperatively can lead to graft loss. If a contaminated or chronic wound has been grafted or if there are any suspicions of wound infection then the dressing should be removed at 48 h postoperatively and the graft inspected. If invasive wound infection is suspected, then biopsy of the wound for quantitative microbiology and systemic antibiotics are required.

The bacteria that are usually responsible for such problems are the grampositive organisms such as *Staphylococcus aureus* and Group A Streptococci, although gram negative organisms can also lead to graft loss.

If the wound looks as if it is frankly infected or if there is graft lysis or 'ghosting' with melting away of the graft, topical antimicrobial agents can be used in an attempt to salvage the situation. The mainstays of treatment are gauze dressings soaked in either 0.5% silver nitrate solution or 0.025% hypochlorite solution. At these concentrations, the solutions are bactericidal but do not have a toxic effect on human cells. Mupirocin ointment is very effective against gram positive organisms; however resistance has been reported. Dressings can be changed once or twice daily, more often if invasive infection is suspected. If invasive infection is confirmed by quantitative microbiological examination and signs of systemic sepsis are present, re-excision of the infected tissue should be considered.

SUMMARY

After assessment of the patient, the size, nature and anatomical distribution of the burn wound, a plan must be made. The key to success is to have a well-defined treatment plan and if that involves surgery a surgical plan is essential. As with all types of surgical endeavors, it is wise to have a plan, a backup plan in case the first one fails and finally a lifeboat plan to turn to if all else fails.

SELECTED REFERENCES

1. Alexander JW et al. Treatment of severe burns with widely meshed skin autograft and meshed skin allograft overlay. J Trauma 1981; 21:433.
2. Burke JF, Bandoc CC, Quinby WC. Primary burn excision and immediate grafting as a method for shortening illness. J Trauma 1974; 14:389.
3. Cuono C, Langdon R, McGuire J. Use of cultured epidermal autografts and dermal allografts as skin replacement after burn injury. Lancet 1986; II:1123.
4. Deitch EA et al. Hypertrophic burn scars: Analysis of variables. J Trauma 1983; 23:895.
5. Desai MH, Rutan RL, Herndon DN. Conservative treatment of scald burns is superior to early excision. J Burn Care Rehabil 1991; 12:482.
6. Dziewulski P. Burn wound healing. Burns 1992; 18:466.
7. Engrav LH et al. Early excision and grafting versus nonoperative treatment of burns of indeterminant depth: A randomized prospective study. J Trauma 1983; 23:1001.
8. Heimbach D et al. Artificial dermis for major burns. Ann Surg. 1988; 208:313.
9. Heimbach DM. Early burn excision and grafting. Surg Clin North Am 1987; 67:93.
10. Herndon DN et al. Early burn wound excision significantly reduces blood loss Ann Surg 1990; 211:753.

11.   Herndon DM, Parks DH. Comparison of serial debridement and autografting and early massive excision with cadaver skin overlay in the treatment of large burns in children. J Trauma 1986; 26:149.

12.   Herndon DN et al. A comparison of conservative versus early excision therapies in severely burned patients. Ann Surg. 989; 209:547.

13.   Janzekovic Z. A new concept in the early excision and immediate grafting of burns. J Trauma 1970; 10:1103.

14.   McHugh TP et al. Therapeutic effect of Biobrane in partial and full thickness thermal injury. Surgery 1986; 100:661.

15.   Muller MJ et al. Modern treatment of a burn wound. In: Herndon DN ed. Total Burn Care WB Saunders Co, 1996; 1136.

16.   O'Connor NE et al. Grafting of burns with cultured epithelium prepared from autologous epidermal cells. Lancet 1981; 1:75.

17.   Sherman ST et al. Growth hormone enhances re-epithelialization of human split thickness skin graft donor site. Surg Forum 1989; 40:37.

Anesthesia for Burn Patients

Arjav J. Shah

5

I. INTRODUCTION

Thermal injury produces predictable pathophysiologic responses. These responses must be considered when formulating a plan of management of anesthesia for a burn patient. Airway management, circulatory stabilization, and pulmonary support are essential.

II. PULMONARY CONSIDERATIONS are primarily related to inhalation injury

   A. RISK FACTORS

      1. Burns sustained in closed space

      2. Burns from petroleum products

Burn Care, edited by Steven E. Wolf and David N. Herndon. © 1999 Landes Bioscience

        3. Head trauma

        4. Impaired mental status

   B. INHALATION INJURY is a serious comorbidity in burned patients

      1. In the absence of a cutaneous burn, the mortality rate of patients with:

        Inhalation injury is less than 10%. With a burn, the mortality rate of such patients doubles.

        The injury is the result of toxic chemical products of combustion

        a. Plastics: Hydrogen cyanide poisons mitochondrial cytochrome oxidase, causing tissue asphyxia.

        b. Cotton and synthetic fibers: Aldehydes damage respiratory mucosa and impair ciliary function.

        c. Wood: This and other carbon-containing compounds can produce carbon monoxide (see below).

   C. THREE DISTINCT MANIFESTATIONS OF INHALATION INJURY

      1. Carbon Monoxide (CO) Intoxication

COHb, %	signs and symptoms
0-10	none (angina possible in patients with CAD)
10-20	slight headache, exercise-induced angina, dyspnea on vigorous exertion
20-30	throbbing headache, dyspnea on moderate exertion
30-40	severe headache, N/V, weakness, visual complaints, impaired judgment
40-50	syncope, tachycardia, tachypnea, dyspnea at rest
50-60	coma, convulsions, Cheyne-Stokes respirations
>70	death

        a. Carboxyhemoglobin level should be determined by ABG. CO binds well to hemoglobin so that oxygen cannot be transported, causing hypoxemia; there is also a leftward shift of the oxyhemoglobin dissociation curve. Carboxyhemoglobin absorbs light at the same wavelength as oxyhemoglobin (660 nm) so pulse oximetry readings may be unaffected or even falsely elevated.

        b. The elimination halftime of carbon monoxide is 4 h and can be reduced to 40 minutes with administration of 100% oxygen, which is the mainstay of treatment of CO intoxication.

      2. Upper Airway (Inhalation) Injury is rarely an immediate cause of hypoxemia as onset is usually delayed 24-36 h postburn.

        a. Signs and symptoms

          1) Inflammation of oropharyngeal mucosa.

          2) Facial burns and singed nasal hair.

          3) Hoarseness, stridor, wheezing, rales.

          4) Unexplained hypoxemia.

          5) Carbonaceous sputum production is the most specific sign.

          6) Even in the absence of the above, certain details in the patient history can be suspicious for inhalation injury; for example, a patient may have been trapped in a smoke-filled room.

    b. Evaluation

        1) Chest x-ray is insensitive.

        2) Fiberoptic bronchoscopy

           a) Signs of injury include mucosal erythema, edema, blisters, ulcers, hemorrhage, and soot particles.

           b) Bronchoscopy is typically performed by the anesthesiologist if patient is undergoing surgery. Endotracheal intubation can also be performed over bronchoscope.

    c. If there is a reasonable suspicion of upper airway injury, endotracheal intubation should be done early, because delayed intubation will be difficult to achieve once upper airway edema has developed, leading to a potentially fatal hypoxemia.

        1) Awake direct laryngoscopy has the advantage of requiring little equipment, but requires a great amount of patient cooperation. Furthermore, this technique does not allow visual assessment of the trachea for evidence of inhalation injury.

        2) Cricothyrotomy in experienced hands is an effective airway management technique, but is probably best reserved as a last resort.

        3) Fiberoptic bronchoscopy affords the physician a means to visually assess the upper airway as well as intubate the trachea.

           a) Whenever possible, bronchoscopy is performed with the patient breathing spontaneously.

           b) Sedation with agents such as morphine, midazolam, and/or ketamine should be provided (refer to Pain Management for recommended dosages).

           c) Suggested method for awake fiberoptic nasotracheal intubation.

              • Monitoring should minimally include pulse oximetry, blood pressure, heart rate, and respiratory rate.

              • Administration of the antisialagogue, glycopyrrolate, 5 mg/kg IV, optimizes visualization; sedation as mentioned previously.

              • Select the appropriate sized endotracheal tube (for children, tube size = [age+16] /4), and a lubricated bronchoscope that will fit through the ETT.

              • Supplies should include suction, phenylephrine 0.25% topical nasal drops, rubber nasal airways of varying sizes, lubricant (e.g., lidocaine, Surgilube), extra ETT connectors that will fit into the nasal airways, three 5 ml syringes of saline flush, and three 5 cc syringes of lidocaine, 2% (max. 4 mg/kg).

              • The nasal route is chosen over oral because it is better tolerated by awake patients and there is less angulation for passage of the bronchoscope to the glottis.

5

- All patients should receive 100% oxygen during the procedure.
- After topicalization of both nares, a nasal airway is inserted into the nare not to be intubated. An ETT connector is inserted into the airway, so that the oxygen source can be attached to it, allowing the patient to receive 100% oxygen without interfering with the bronchoscopy.
- The ETT is inserted into the free nare to just above the glottis. The bronchoscope is then inserted through the ETT.
- When the glottis is visualized, 2% lidocaine is sprayed onto the vocal cords via the bronchoscope sideport.
- The bronchoscope may then be gently passed through the vocal cords to the level of the carina, at which point the ETT may be advanced.

4. Pulmonary Parenchymal Injury appears to be the result of secondary changes in the bronchial and pulmonary vasculature. With the exception of steam, direct thermal injury very rarely occurs below the vocal cords.

   a. Mechanisms of such injury probably include inflammatory mediators like complement, interleukins, and cytokines. The inflammatory response may be secondary to the original burn injury or superimposed sepsis.

   b. The clinical picture of the patient with a secondary lung injury manifests as respiratory failure from the adult respiratory distress syndrome.

   c. If a inhalation injury is present the incidence of respiratory failure in the burned patient increases from 5-73%.

III. CARDIOVASCULAR CONSIDERATIONS

A. HYPOVOLEMIA is related primarily to the loss of plasma and interstitial fluid through burned skin and abnormally permeable vasculature.

   1. Blood volume decreases and edema forms most rapidly during the first 8 h postburn.

   2. Hourly urine output with a Foley catheter is the most readily available index of volume replacement. Adults: 0.5-1 cc/kg/h; kids: 1-2 cc/kg/h.

   3. *Hematocrit is a poor indicator of volume status.*

B. HEMODYNAMIC PARAMETERS

   1. Cardiac output: CO is decreased during the initial burn period. Contractility is reduced, probably secondary to inflammatory mediators as well as an attenuated response to catecholamines. After the first 24-48 h, the circulatory system enters a hyperdynamic state, where heart rate and blood pressure are increased. CO is usually twice normal.

2. Systemic vascular resistance: Coincident with the initial decrease in CO, SVR is increased. SVR is markedly low during the hyperdynamic state.

IV. ADDITIONAL PHYSIOLOGIC CONSIDERATIONS

A. HYPERMETABOLISM increases with the extent of the burn injury
1. Probably secondary to inflammatory mediators
2. Calories tend to be diverted away from wound healing; it is therefore recommended to begin enteral nutrition as soon as possible.
3. Hypermetabolism increases production of CO_2 *and consumption of O_2.*
4. Below-normal ambient temperatures increase metabolic rate; a warm operating room is mandatory.

B. HEMATOLOGIC
1. Red blood cells have a shortened half-life, but maintain their normal oxygen-carrying capacity.
2. Disseminated intravascular coagulation is the most extreme form of coagulopathy encountered in burned patients—fortunately, it is rare. After the acute burn period, prophylaxis for deep venous thrombosis should be employed, as there is a significant decrease in levels of proteins C and S, as well as antithrombin III.

C. RENAL FUNCTION varies with the time since the original burn injury.
1. Etiologies of early renal insufficiency in burned patients
   a. hypovolemia
   b. mediators of vasoconstriction, including catecholamines and the renin-angiotensin system
   c. myoglobin, nephrotoxic medications
2. During the hyperdynamic state, glomerular filtration rate is elevated. Certain drugs may be cleared more rapidly than expected, leading to lower than desired serum drug levels. Tubular resorptive function, however, may be diminished. Predicting accurate drug doses in individual patients is therefore difficult and best managed by measuring serum drug levels (e.g., aminoglycosides) or titrating a drug to the desired effect.

PHARMACOKINETICS AND PHARMACODYNAMICS IN BURN PATIENTS

I. GENERAL CONSIDERATIONS

A. INCREASED extracellular volume and volume of distribution.
B. ALTERATIONS in plasma protein composition, especially hypoalbuminemia and increased levels of acute phase proteins.
C. THE CONCLUSION then is that normal doses of anesthetic medications may result excessively high or low active, unbound amount of drug.

II. MUSCLE RELAXANTS

A. DEPOLARIZING AGENTS—SUCCINYLCHOLINE
1. Marked hyperkalemia severe enough to cause cardiac arrest is possible if succinylcholine is used in burn patients

2. Although there is some controversy regarding the postburn interval during which succinylcholine is contraindicated, it is reasonable to completely avoid the use of succinylcholine in burn patients.

B. NONDEPOLARIZING AGENTS

1. Reduced sensitivity of these agents in burn patients is felt to be secondary to postburn proliferation of extrajunctional nicotinic acetylcholine receptors.

2. Therefore, increased doses of nondepolarizing agents may be required; however, unless required to facilitate mechanical ventilation, their use is unnecessary in burn patients.

III. SEDATIVES AND ANALGESICS

A. ALTHOUGH burn patients clearly require increased doses of sedatives and analgesics, pharmacokinetics cannot completely explain this phenomenon.

B. THE DOSES of sedatives and analgesics must be titrated to effect; but the following serves as a useful starting point:

Agent	Recommended Dosages
morphine sulfate	0.03-0.1 mg/kg IV
midazolam	0.03-0.1 mg/kg IV
scopolomine	0.4-1 mg po or 0.2-0.6 mg IV/IM
propofol	0.5-1 mg/kg IV
ketamine	0.5-1 mg/kg IV or 2.5-5 mg/kg IM

PREOPERATIVE ANESTHETIC ASSESSMENT OF BURN PATIENTS

I. HISTORY

A. CHARACTERISTICS OF THE BURN INJURY

1. **Time of injury** must be known as blood loss varies not only with local infections but also with the time elapsed since the occurrence of the burn:

Surgical Procedure	Predicted Blood Loss
< 24 h since burn injury	0.45 ml/cm^2 burn area
1-3 days since burn injury	0.70 ml/cm^2 burn area
> 4 days since burn injury	0.90 ml/cm^2 burn area
infected burn wounds	1.0-1.25 ml/cm^2 burn area

2. Environment in which the injury occurred has both hemodynamic and pulmonary implications, e.g., a person trapped in an enclosed, smoke-filled room is likely to have an inhalation injury, with a subsequent need for airway protection and increased fluid requirements.

3. Burn source will determine the extent of injury.

a. Electrical injuries may produce far more tissue destruction than is visually apparent, leading to myoglobinemia, myoglobinuria, and possible pigment nephropathy (acute renal failure).

b. Chemical burns may have systemic toxicity (e.g., hydrogen cyanide), or cause pulmonary damage by unsuspected inhalation of fumes (e.g., sulfuric acid).

B. CHARACTERISTICS OF THE PATIENT

1. Age can have profound implications for long-term prognosis as well as the individual's ability to compensate for the physiologic stresses associated with a burn injury. In general, the extremes in age (i.e., the very young, very old), tend to be the most critically ill for a given burn injury.
2. Coexisting medical problems

II. PHYSICAL EXAMINATION

A. CHECK FOR HEAD AND NECK BURNS, SINGED NASAL HAIRS, HOARSENESS, as these are signs that supraglottic edema may develop or is already present.

B. CARBONACEOUS SPUTUM, WHEEZES, OR DIMINISHED BREATH SOUNDS are signs of possible inhalation injury.

C. ABDOMINAL DISTENSION may indicate an ileus, which increases the risk of aspiration of gastric contents during anesthetic induction.

D. SEARCH for sites suitable for placement of invasive lines and other monitoring equipment.

III. LABORATORY AND RADIOGRAPHIC EVALUATION

A. COMPLETE BLOOD COUNT (CBC)

B. ARTERIAL BLOOD GAS, particularly for burns >30% TBSA and in suspected inhalation injury. Remember that pulse oximetry measurements are unaffected even in patients hypoxic from carbon monoxide intoxication.

C. CHEST RADIOGRAPH should be obtained in any burn >30% TBSA and in suspected inhalation injury. Evidence of ARDS, infiltrates, or effusions is sought to anticipate potential problems with intraoperative oxygenation.

IV. PREOPERATIVE ORDERS

A. ADULTS

1. NPO after midnight—make certain that a maintenance rate of intravenous fluids is administered during fasting.
2. Premedications will depend on the patient's preoperative condition—e.g., patients who are already intubated with continuous sedation probably do not require premedication. If premedications are indicated:
   a. Midazolam (Versed) 2-5 mg IV on call to the operating room.
   b. Glycopyrrolate (Robinul) 0.2 mg IV, on call to the operating room, is useful if fiberoptic bronchoscopy is planned.
3. Type and cross blood components based on predicted blood loss.

B. CHILDREN

1. NPO after midnight (0400 for infants), with maintenance intravenous fluids during fasting.

2. Premedications are generally recommended for children to lessen the anxiety of surgery and being separated from parents.

   a. Acetaminophen (Tylenol) 15 mg/kg po up to 1000 mg on call to the operating room.

   b. Midazolam (Versed) 0.5 mg/kg po up to 20 mg on call to the operating room.

   c. Scopolomine 0.4-1.0 mg po, on call to the operating room, is not only useful as an antisialagogue, but is also an effective and inexpensive sedative in children.

3. Type and cross whole blood based on predicted blood loss.

V. INTRAMUSCULAR KETAMINE ADMINISTRATION IN CHILDREN

A. INTRAMUSCULAR MEDICATIONS, as a routine form of analgesia and sedation, produce highly unpredictable drug plasma levels and are therefore best avoided. For children, IM injections can be physically and psychologically traumatic ("needlephobia").

B. INTRAMUSCULAR KETAMINE, however, is useful as a premedication and for brief procedures where intravenous access is unavailable (e.g., outpatient facial moulage sessions).

C. BIOJECT™ NEEDLE-FREE MEDICATION INJECTOR can be used to inject a local anesthetic prior to injecting ketamine with a standard needle or inject ketamine directly.

D. SELECTING THE CORRECT BIOJECT™ SYRINGE

Patient weight (kg)	Injection site	Syringe
Less than or equal to 7	thigh/gluteal	brown/#3
Greater than 7, less than 23	deltoid	brown/#3
Greater than 7, less than 23	thigh/gluteal	blue/#4
Greater than 23	deltoid	blue/#4

E. RECOMMENDED DOSING

1. Local anesthesia–$NaHCO_3$, 0.1 ml and lidocaine (2%), 0.9 ml.

2. Ketamine–1-2 mg/kg IM on transport to OR; 5-10 mg/kg IM for procedures outside of the operating suite (e.g., facial moulage)

INTRAOPERATIVE MONITORING

I. INTRAOPERATIVE MONITORING of a burned patient is comparable to that of any critically ill patient undergoing major surgery.

II. MINIMUM STANDARDS of the American Society of Anesthesiologists.

A. THE CONTINUOUS PRESENCE OF A QUALIFIED ANESTHETIST

B. CONTINUOUS F_iO_2 MEASUREMENT

C. PULSE OXIMETRY

D. VENTILATORY MONITORS

1. Observing chest excursion, auscultation of breath sounds.

2. End-tidal carbon dioxide analysis.

3. Disconnect alarms during mechanical ventilation.

    E. CONTINUOUS ELECTROCARDIOGRAPHY—either with standard adhesive gel electrodes or staples/alligator clips

    F. ARTERIAL BLOOD PRESSURE AND HEART RATE determination at least every five minutes.

    G. CONTINUOUS BODY TEMPERATURE MEASUREMENT (nasopharyngeal, esophageal, axillary, rectal, urinary bladder)

III. **ADDITIONAL MONITORING MODALITIES**

    A. CARDIOVASCULAR MONITORING can be supplemented if detection of sudden hemodynamic alterations is required.

      1. An arterial line can provide a beat-to-beat record of BP and provide access to obtain repeated blood samples for ABGs and other tests.

      2. A central venous line, in otherwise healthy patients, can correlate directionally and quantitatively with changes in LVEDP.

      3. Pulmonary arterial catheters, however, better estimate the determinants of cardiac output in critically ill patients, and also allow calculation of DO_2, VO_2, and numerous other hemodynamic parameters. PA catheter complications must be weighed against benefits of invasive monitoring.

Recommended sites for placement of CVP and PA catheters (most to least desirable)

Left Subclavian Vein
Right Subclavian Vein
Right Internal Jugular Vein
Femoral Veins

---

      4. All lines should be rewired three days after insertion and new sites found six days after the original insertion.

    B. FOLEY CATHETER

IV. **GUIDELINES FOR INSERTION OF CENTRAL VENOUS AND INTRAARTERIAL CATHETERS**

    A. CHOOSING THE APPROPRIATE SIZE CENTRAL VENOUS CATHETER

Age or Size	Catheter Size
< 4 years old	5.3 French
> 4 years old	6 French
> 50 kg with expected large blood loss	8 French

    B. CHOOSING THE APPROPRIATE SIZE ARTERIAL CATHETER

Size	Artery	Catheter Size and Length
< 5 kg	Radial	2.5 French/5 cm
> 5 kg	Radial	3 French/5 cm
< 5 kg	Femoral	2.5 French/8 cm
> 5 kg	Femoral	3 French/8 cm

INDUCTION AND MAINTENANCE OF ANESTHESIA IN BURN PATIENTS

I. **GENERAL ANESTHESIA IS THE TECHNIQUE OF CHOICE IN ACUTELY BURNED PATIENTS**

A. INDUCTION

1. Evaluation of the airway plays a key role in the technique to be used.
   a. In patients with facial burns who do not have airway obstruction, consider awake intubation.
   b. If inhalation injury is suspected, awake fiberoptic intubation is recommended, usually by the nasal route, which is better tolerated.
2. Preoperative hemodynamics will determine the induction agent(s) selected. The following list is not all-inclusive—one goal of any anesthetic technique for acutely burned patients is to maintain hemodynamic stability.
   a. Ketamine
      1) Has sympathomimetic properties, and not only increases heart rate and blood pressure, but also preserves hypoxic and hypercapnic ventilatory drive and reduces airway resistance.
      2) In critically ill patients with no intrinsic sympathetic reserve, ketamine can act as a myocardial depressant.
      3) It is the only nonopioid induction agent that is analgesic.
      4) The unpleasant hallucinations experienced postoperatively can be attenuated with midazolam.
   b. Propofol
      1) Has the advantage of being an antiemetic and having a rapid and thorough elimination.
      2) Compared to ketamine, propofol at induction doses produces apnea and hypotension.
   c. Volatile Agents
      1) Mask induction with nitrous oxide and halothane/ isoflurane is typically used in pediatric patients who have intravenous access prior to surgery.
      2) Volatile anesthetics all produce dose-dependent myocardial depression and vasodilatation.
      3) Hypoxic pulmonary vasoconstriction is blunted, and can result in detrimental ventilation/perfusion mismatching.
      4) Despite the above concerns, unlike the altered pharmacokinetics and dynamics of IV agents, volatile anesthetics tend to have more predictable wash-in and washout times.
   d. Opioids
      1) In general, the intraoperative use of opioids is not advised, especially with the availability of the ketamine and its analgesic properties. If used, MSO_4 to a maximum of 0.1 mg/kg IV may reduce the amount of volatile agent(s) required.

5

B. MUSCLE RELAXANTS
  1. Succinylcholine is well-known to cause hyperkalemia, and can lead to cardiac arrest if the preoperative K > 5.0.
     a. The greatest risk of hyperkalemia appears to be between 10 and 50 days postburn.
     b. These zones, however, are poorly defined.
     c. The safest recommendation is to avoid the use of succinylcholine in burn patients.
  2. Nondepolarizing relaxants are acceptable for muscle relaxation in burn patients, although higher doses than in other patients are required.
  3. With the exception of patients who need facilitation of mechanical ventilation, the routine use of muscle relaxants in acutely burned patients is unnecessary and therefore not recommended.

C. ANESTHESIA is typically maintained with any of the previously mentioned induction agents along with nitrous oxide and oxygen.

D. TYPICAL ANESTHETIC TECHNIQUES FOR ACUTELY BURNED PATIENTS
  1. Adults should preferably have intravenous access prior to induction of anesthesia.
     a. In a hemodynamically stable patient, propofol can be followed by mask induction with isoflurane to allow endotracheal intubation. Anesthesia would be maintained with oxygen, nitrous oxide and isoflurane.
     b. In an unstable patient, induction may be done with ketamine and topical lidocaine on the vocal cords prior to intubation. Oxygen, nitrous oxide, and ketamine would be the maintenance agents.
  2. Children should also have intravenous access prior to induction of anesthesia, but often initial induction with a volatile agent to permit placement of an intravenous catheter may be necessary.
     a. Induction techniques in children with intravenous access are essentially identical to those for adults. Inhalation induction, as previously described, is a frequently used technique in children.

PAIN MANAGEMENT

  I. **PATIENT DISCOMFORT** is an obvious result of untreated pain, but it can also lead to subsequent noncompliance with other therapies, as well as a distrust of the managing physician(s).

 II. **ADVERSE PHYSIOLOGIC CONSEQUENCES OF PAIN**

Organ System	Clinical Effect
Respiratory increased skeletal muscle tension decreased total lung compliance	hypoxemia, hypercapnia ventilation-perfusion mismatching atelectasis, pneumonia

Cardiovascular	
increased myocardial work	dysrhythmias, angina, myocardial infarction, congestive heart failure

Endocrine	
increased ACTH	protein catabolism, lipolysis
increased cortisol	hyperglycemia
increased glucagon	
increased epinephrine	
decreased insulin	
decreased testosterone	decreased protein anabolism
decreased insulin	
increased aldosterone	salt and water retention
increased antidiuretic hormone	
increased cortisol	congestive heart failure
increased catecholamines	vasoconstriction
increased angiotensin II	increased myocardial contractility
	increased heart rate

Coagulation	
increased platelet adhesion	increased incidence of thromboembolism
diminished fibrinolysis	
activation of coagulation cascade	

Immunologic	
lymphopenia	decreased immune function
depression of reticuloendothelial system	
leukocytosis	
reduced killer T-cell cytotoxicity	

Gastrointestinal	
increased sphincter tone	ileus
decreased smooth muscle tone	

Genitourinary	
increased sphincter tone	urinary retention
decreased smooth muscle tone	

III. **BECAUSE PAIN FROM BURNS CAN BE CONSTANT,** continuous
therapeutic levels of analgesia must be maintained. The severity of burn
pain justifies the use of intravenous narcotics and sedative/hypnotic
agents. As in other aspects of burn management, the concept of titrating
therapy to desired effect is practiced.
   A. ADULTS (UNIVERSITY OF TEXAS—BLOCKER BURN UNIT)
      1. Morphine sulfate (MSO_4) may be effective in doses as little as 1 mg or
         as large as 15 mg. The extent of the burn injury and other comorbidi-
         ties (e.g., an intubated/mechanically ventilated patient) will deter-
         mine the most effective dose and frequency of administration.
      2. Midazolam (Versed), although lacking analgesic properties, comple-
         ments narcotics, especially during dressing changes and for intubated
         patients. Doses in the range of 0.025-0.1 mg/kg are effective and should
         be in small (0.5-1 mg) increments.

B. CHILDREN (SHRINERS BURN INSTITUTE, GALVESTON) A comprehensive written protocol is available at SBI, and the following summarizes the salient points:

1. If the patient complains of pain, then the patient has pain.
2. Background analgesia All patients receive acetaminophen, 15 mg/kg po q4h.
   a. (Patient > 3 years old) If more background analgesia is required, then give MSO_4, 0.3 mg/kg po q4h.
   b. (Patient < 3 years old) If more background analgesia is required, then give MSO_4, 0.1 mg/kg po q4h or 0.03 mg/kg IV q4h.

Procedure/Event *(may be used for both adults and children)*	*Recommended Therapies (in* *order of preference)*
Dressing changes and staple removal (pretub)	1. MSO_4, 0.3 mg/kg po and Versed, 0.5 mg/kg po 2. MSO_4, 0.03 mg/kg IV and Versed 0.03 mg/kg IV 3. ketamine, 0.5-2 mg/kg IV* 4. propofol, 0.5-1 mg/kg IV* 5. nitrous oxide, 50%, by patient-controlled face mask*
Rehabilitation therapy	1. MSO_4, 0.1-0.3 mg/kg po 2. MSO_4, 0.03 mg/kg IV.
Immediate 24 h postoperative period	1. MSO_4, 0.3 mg/kg po and Versed, 0.5 mg/kg po q3-4h or alternate each every 3-4h 2. MSO_4, 0.03 mg/kg IV and Versed 0.03 mg/kg IV q2-4h or alternate each every 2-4h 3. or patients > 5 years, morphine patient-controlled analgesia (PCA)- *continuous infusions are not recommended* (see attached guidelines)
Postoperative period for reconstructive surgery patients	1. Vicodin (hydrocodone 5 mg/acetaminophen 500 mg† 2. Lortab elixir (5 ml contains hydrocodone
2.5 mg/acetaminophen 167 mg) † *Anesthesiology team should be notified	†hydrocodone, 0.1-0.2 mg/kg po q4-6h

Patient-controlled analgesia-suggested pediatric guidelines

PCA Parameters	MSO_4, 1 mg/ml
PCA dose	0.05 mg/kg
Lockout interval	6-15 minutes
4-h Limit	0.2-0.3 mg/kg

Nutrition in Burn Patients

Victor M. Perez

INTRODUCTION

6

The response to injury, known as hypermetabolism, occurs most dramatically following severe burn. Increases in oxygen consumption, metabolic rate, urinary nitrogen excretion, lipolysis and weight loss are directly proportional to the size of the burn.[1] This response can be as high as 200% of the normal metabolic rate, and returns to normal only with the complete closure of the burn wound.[2] There is debate regarding the pathogenesis of this hypermetabolic state, but the general consensus is that inflammation associated with the burn wound, heightened cortisolemia, and the increased adrenergic activity seen in these patients are all important factors.

Because the metabolic rate is so high, energy requirements are immense. These requirements are met by mobilization of carbohydrate, fat, and protein stores. Since the demands are prolonged, these energy stores are quickly depleted, leading to loss of active muscle tissue and malnutrition. This malnutrition is associated with functional impairment of many organs, delayed and abnormal wound healing, decreased immunocompetence, and altered cellular membrane active transport functions. Malnutrition in burns can be subverted to some extent by delivery of adequate exogenous nutritional support. The goals of nutrition support are to maintain and improve organ function, prevent protein-calorie malnutrition, and improve outcomes.

Supporting the burn patient with adequate energy sources is paramount to good outcome. Important topics in this regard are:
1. calculation of the caloric needs,
2. composition of the nutritional supplements and
3. means by which these nutrients are delivered.

Burn Care, edited by Steven E. Wolf and David N. Herndon. © 1999 Landes Bioscience

CALCULATING CALORIC NEEDS

Caloric requirements in adult burn patients are calculated using the Curreri formula, which calls for 25 kcal/kg/day plus 40 kcal/% TBSA burned/day.[1] This formula provides for maintenance needs, plus the additional caloric needs of the burn wounds. As an example, a 100 kg man with a 50% TBSA burn would require 2500 kcal for maintenance needs plus an additional 2000 kcal for burn related metabolism. Therefore, he would require 4500 kcal/day that would be delivered throughout the hospital course until the wounds were healed.

In children, formulas based on body surface area are more appropriate[3,4] because of the greater body surface area per kilogram. We recommend the following formulas depending in the child age (Table 6.1). The formulas change with age based on the body surface area alterations that occur with growth.

DIETARY COMPOSITION

6

The composition of the nutritional supplement is also important. The optimal dietary composition contains 1-2 gm/kg/day of protein, which provides a calorie to nitrogen ratio at around 100:1 with the above suggested caloric intakes. This amount of protein will provide for the synthetic needs of the patient, thus sparing to some extent the proteolysis occurring in the active muscle tissue.

Some amino acids are conditionally essential for these critical patients. Glutamine is an important fuel for rapidly dividing cells such as enterocytes, lymphocytes and macrophages. Recently, it has been demonstrated that supplemental glutamine prevents deterioration in gut permeability and preserves mucosal structure avoiding bacterial translocation in animal models of injury. Arginine is an amino-acid which has been associated with accelerated wound healing, and supplemental amounts up to approximately 2% of the total calories is recommended. These amino acids are present in most enteral formulas, and it remains to be determined whether further supplementation above these concentrations is of benefit.

Table 6.1. Formula for caloric calculations in children used at SBI

Age group	Maintenance fluids	Resuscitation fluids (burn wound needs)
Infants (0-12 mos.)	2100 kcal/TBSA/24 h	1000 kcal/TBSA burned/24 h
Children (1-12 years)	1800 kcal/TBSA/24 h	1300 kcal/TBSA burned/24 h
Adolescents (12-18 years)	1500 kcal/TBSA/24 h	1500 kcal/TBSA burned/24 h

*TBSA expressed in m2

Nonprotein calories can be given either as carbohydrate or as fat. Carbohydrates have the advantage of stimulating endogenous insulin production, which may have beneficial effects on muscle and the burn wounds as an anabolic hormone. In addition, fatty liver is commonly seen after severe burns, which may be related to diet. It has been shown recently that almost all of the fat deposited in the liver is derived from peripheral lipolysis and not from de novo synthesis of fatty acids in the liver from dietary carbohydrates. In fact, the likely cause for fatty infiltration is relative inefficiency of hepatic transport of delivered fat. For this reason, we prefer to use a carbohydrate based feeding in order to decrease the amount of fat that the liver must handle. Currently we use Vivonex TEN® as our standard tube feeding which contains mainly carbohydrates and virtually no fat.

A number of vitamins and trace materials (vitamins A, C, E, zinc, folic acid and iron) are added because of their significant functions: free radical scavengers, enhancing the immune response, and accelerating wound healing. See Table 6.2 for supplemental recommendations at Shriners Burns Hospital.

DIETARY DELIVERY

The diet may be delivered in two forms, either enterally through enteric tubes, or parenterally through intravenous catheters. Parenteral nutrition may be given in isotonic solutions through peripheral catheters or with hypertonic solutions in central catheters. In general, the caloric demands of burn patients prohibit the use of peripheral parenteral nutrition. In addition, total parenteral nutrition (TPN)

Table 6.2. SBI vitamin and mineral supplementation

0-12 years of age

       Liquid or Chewable Multivitamin 1 dose q.d.
       Ascorbic acid 250 mg q.d.
       Folic acid 1 mg q. m.w.f.
       Vitamin A
            < 2 years, 2500 IU
            2-12 years, 5000 IU
            Zinc sulfate
            < 2 years, 55 mg q.d.
            2-12 years, 110 mg q.d.
            Vitamin E 5 mg q.d.

12 years or older
       Adult Multivitamins q.d.
       Folic acid 1 mg q. m.w.f.
       Vitamin A 10000 IU q.d.
       Zinc sulfate 200 mg q.d.
       Vitamin E 10 mg q.d.

6

delivered through a central vein has been associated with increased complications (i.e. sepsis, thrombophlebitis, death) and currently is almost abandoned in our hospitals. Herndon and others showed that in 30 burn patients randomized to receive either TPN or enteral feedings (milk) mortality was 40% higher in the TPN group, indicating that TPN increased mortality in these patients. TPN is reserved only for those patients who cannot tolerate enteral feedings.[5,6]

In burn patients as well as in most of the critical care patients, enteral feedings are recommended over parenteral feedings, other advantages are:

1. More physiologic and less costly
2. Maintains gut structure and function, may help prevent the translocation of bacteria and/or toxins[7]
3. Blunts the hypermetabolic response to injury
4. Associated with decreased incidence of sepsis.

Enteral feeding has been associated with some complications, however, which can be disastrous. Careful attention to detail is important in order to avoid their presence. In general these complications can be divided into:

1. Mechanical complications (aspiration pneumonia, sinusitis, nasoalar, esophageal and gastric mucosal irritation and erosion, tube lumen obstruction)
2. GI complications (diarrhea, fecal impaction)
3. Metabolic complications (dehydration, hyperglycemia, hyper- or hyponatremia, hyper or hypophosphatemia, hypercapnia, hyper or hypokalemia)

Although gastric ileus is somewhat common, the small intestinal component is rarely seen, therefore the gastrointestinal tract past the pylorus can be used for administration of feedings. We recommend early feeding through nasoduodenal tubes. Most of our patients begin feedings within 6 h after burn, at a low rate (10-30 cc/h) and advancing as tolerated to meet caloric needs while reducing IV fluids accordingly. Tube feedings are continued throughout the hospital course at calculated rates until the wounds are healed.

All of our patients receive both nasogastric and a nasoduodenal tubes. The gastric tube is initially used to decompress the stomach. Then after the first burn wound excision it is used to provide a low rate of feeding to the stomach (30 cc/h) as a buffer, decreasing the incidence of peptic ulcer disease and erosive gastritis. It is also used to check gastric residuals every hour, so as to avoid gastric distention with its risk of aspiration. Gastric pH is checked hourly with the addition of antacids (Maalox, Mylanta) to maintain pH > 4.5. Nasoduodenal tubes are placed alongside the nasogastric tube to deliver most of the tube feedings. The feeding through this tube is continuous at a rate to meet the caloric needs. Nasoduodenal tubes are notoriously difficult to place. See Table 6.3 for suggestions in successful placement.

Many commercial feeding solutions are available, although whole bovine milk is a viable alternative. Milk is nutritionally balanced, inexpensive, easily available, and well tolerated. Potassium requirements are met, but sodium (25 mEq/L) needs to be supplemented. Infants under one year of age, are normally fed with

Table 6.3. Tips helpful in the placement of nasoduodenal tubes

Right lateral decubitus position for 2 h
Use of prokinetic medications such as
    • Metoclopramide
    • Cisapride
    • Erythromycin
Use of bedside fluoroscopy
Use of endoscopy
Always check for adequate position with radiological studies.

commercial infant formulas to meet calculated caloric needs. As mentioned previously, our standard feeding is Vivonex TEN® (1 kcal/cc and .038 gm protein/cc). We start as a 1/2 strength dilution to decrease osmotic diarrhea. The rate and concentration are advanced to meet the caloric needs as tolerated.

Diarrhea is a common problem in tube fed patients. Diarrhea is generally defined by the volume of output, with > 1500 cc (30 cc/kg)/day as diagnostic. The reasons for diarrhea are multiple and include altered gut flora associated with antibiotic use, continuous feedings, and the osmolarity of the feedings. Measures that should be taken when diarrhea is encountered include the following:

1. Check for *Clostridium difficile colitis* by examining the stool for toxin and treating with oral flagyl or vancomycin.
2. Include bulk in the tube feedings by adding psyllium (Metamucil®)
3. Add Bacid® to alter the microflora
4. Decrease the osmolarity of the feedings by adding water to the formula. The infused volume must increase to meet the calculated caloric demands.

TRANSITIONING TO REGULAR DIET

Burn patients should be given a regular diet as soon as it is tolerated. The transition from tube feedings to regular PO intake is slow and may take several days to weeks. The following steps are useful in achieving this goal:

1. Reduce tube feedings accordingly, as the PO intake increases (the sum should be 100% of the goal assessed)
2. Consider only nocturnal tube feedings with a daytime regular diet.
3. When the PO intake is 50% of the goal, begin a 3 days trial of PO only.

Oral fluid administration should be controlled. Burn patients are susceptible to hyponatremia if oral fluid intake is uncontrolled. At our hospitals, we follow guidelines for juice/soda intake (see Table 6.4). The general concept is to give only fluids that have caloric value, avoiding the excessive amount of free water in order to minimize the presence of hyponatremia.

Frequent assessment of the burn patient is needed to ensure that enteral nutrition support is being tolerated and that nutritional goals are met. Body weight, fluid intake and output, serum electrolytes, blood glucose, BUN, creatinine, cal-

Table 6.4. Recommendations for juice/soda intake in pediatric acute burns

Age	Juice	Soda	Time period
0-1 year	0	0	24 h
1-4 years	60 cc/8h (180cc)	0	24 h
5-10 years	100 cc/8 h (300cc)	60 cc/8 h (180cc)	24 h

cium, phosphorus and magnesium are monitored daily, prealbumin and liver enzymes twice weekly, and 24 h total urinary urea nitrogen weekly. These laboratory tests are important to give an objective assessment of metabolic homeostasis expected to be achieved with the nutritional support. Improved serum protein tests and nitrogen balance indicate an adequate protein caloric state.

SUMMARY

The hypermetabolic response in burn patients can be as high as 200% the normal metabolic rate. The goals of adequate nutritional support are to maintain and improve organ function, prevent protein-calorie malnutrition, and improve outcomes in general. The optimal dietary composition contains protein at about 1-2 gm/kg/day, with a calorie to nitrogen ratio around 100:1. Fatty liver is common after severe burns. For this reason we prefer to use carbohydrate-based feedings, excluding the use of excessive lipids. Enteral administration of feedings is recommended over parenteral feedings because it is more physiologic, less costly, maintains gut function and has less severe complications. Frequent assessment of the burn patient is required to ensure that nutritional goals are met. Burn patients should be given regular diet as soon as it is tolerated.

REFERENCES
1. Herndon DN, Curreri PW. Metabolic response to thermal injury and its nutritional support. CUTIS 1978; 22 (4):501-506, 514.
2. Yarborough MF, Herndon DN, Curreri PW. Nutritional management of the severely injured patient; (1) Thermal injury. Comtep Surg 1978; 13:15-20.
3. Hildreth MA, Herndon DN, Desai MH, Duke MA. Reassessing caloric requirements in pediatric burn patients. J Burn Care Rehabil 1988; 9(6): 616-618.
4. Hildreth MA, Herndon DN, Desai MH, Broemeling LD. Caloric requirements of patients with burns under one year of age. J Burn Care Rehabil 1993; 14:108-112.
5. Waymack JP, Herndon DN. Nutritional support of the burned patient. World J Surg 1992; 16:80-86.
6. Herndon DN, Barrow RE, Stein M, Linares H, Rutan TC, Rutan RL, Abston S. Increased mortality with intravenous supplemental feeding in severely burned patients. J Burn Care Rehabil 1989; 10(4):309-313.
7. Herndon DN, Morris SE, Coffey JA Jr, Milhoan RA, Barrow RE, Traber DL, Townsend CM. The effect of mucosal blood flow on enteric translocation of microorganism in coetaneous thermal injury. Prog in Clin Biol Res 1989; 308:201-206.

Infections in Burns

Peter I. Ramzy

INTRODUCTION

Septic morbidity in severely burned patients poses an enormous challenge to even the most experienced critical care physician. Many features unique to burn patients make diagnosis and management of infection especially difficult. Burn injury represents the most extreme endpoint along the spectrum of traumatic injury and as such is associated with profound alterations in host defense mechanisms and immune function. These derangements predispose thermally injured patients to local and systemic invasion by microbial pathogens.

Many of the clinical signs and symptoms used to diagnose infection in other settings are unreliable in the burn intensive care unit since they are often present even in the absence of true underlying infection. Advances in critical care such as earlier resuscitation and support of the hypermetabolic response have decreased burn mortality, but infections are still pervasive in severely burned patients and account for significant morbidity and mortality.

With regard to burn wound infection, the cornerstone of management continues to be aggressive early debridement of devitalized and infected tissue. Unfortunately, burn patients are rapidly colonized by nosocomial pathogens and foci of invasive infection must be identified and treated quickly with appropriate antimicrobial therapy. In addition to the burn wound, other potential foci for invasive infection include the tracheobronchial tree, the lungs, the gastrointestinal tract, central venous catheters, and the urinary tract.

Once an infection is disseminated hematogenously and becomes established in a burn patient, it is very difficult to eradicate, even with large doses of broad-spectrum antimicrobial therapy. Traditional thinking would argue for beginning broad-spectrum coverage at the first signs of infection and then narrowing the coverage as results of cultures come back. While this is clearly true for many critically ill patients, burns represent a unique situation, which may merit more aggressive management.

Burn Care, edited by Steven E. Wolf and David N. Herndon. © 1999 Landes Bioscience

The role of systemic antimicrobial therapy in the treatment of infection in burn patients is still very controversial. New emerging strains of multiresistant organisms represent an ominous threat in the burn unit and monotherapy with conventional antimicrobials may be inadequate for some infections. Development of newer and more potent agents targeted at these pathogens holds some promise for the future. In the meantime, treatment with two or more agents is becoming necessary in the management of these gram-negative invasive infections.

CHANGING SCOPE OF INFECTIOUS MORBIDITY IN BURNS

Before the advent of early excision and grafting and the development of topical antimicrobial agents, burn wound sepsis invariably resulted in the death of severely burned patients. Near total burn wound excision early in the hospital course has led to a precipitous decline in mortality.[1] This is due at least in part to a concomitant reduction in the incidence of burn wound sepsis. In addition to early excision and closure of the burn wound, topical antimicrobials have made a significant impact on septic morbidity from invasive burn wound infection. While great strides have been made in the area of burn wound infection, pulmonary infection has taken over as the primary cause of septic mortality in burn patients. Nosocomial pneumonias in the setting of inhalation injury and a large cutaneous burn are associated with mortality as high as 60%.[2] Inevitably, a downward spiral of progressive pulmonary insufficiency ensues, as pneumonia leads to prolonged ventilatory dependence, iatrogenic barotrauma, and respiratory failure.

In addition to pneumonia, fungal infections are becoming more commonplace in the burn intensive care unit. While systemic candidiasis has been around for some time, angioinvasive infections with Fusarium and Aspergillus are being seen more frequently. While burn patients used to die from inadequate resuscitation and burn wound sepsis, they now die from inhalation injury, pneumonia, and rampant fungal septicemia. Antifungal chemotherapy has also emerged as an important modality for managing complicated fungal infection in thermally injured patients

BURN-INDUCED IMMUNOSUPPRESSION

Thermal injury is associated with a state of generalized immunosuppression which is characterized by an impairment of host defense mechanisms and defects in humoral and cell-mediated immunity. There are several specific alterations in host defense which are intrinsic to the burn injury itself and which predispose these patients to microbial invasion. Superimposed on these intrinsic alterations are extrinsic factors unrelated to the burn injury which increase the likelihood of invasive infection.

The most important intrinsic factor is breach of the mechanical barrier provided by the skin. While there is a normal resident skin flora, invasive infection is rare through an intact epithelial barrier. The skin has bacteriostatic properties that normally limit the degree of colonization. The local microenvironment is not supportive for growth of microbial pathogens. This changes drastically with a severe burn injury. The burn wound provides a warm and moist microenvironment in which bacterial proliferation is fostered. Microbial growth is rapid as once nonpathogenic organisms are now allowed to flourish. It is important to realize that the most important intrinsic factor is breach of the mechanical skin barrier, since this has implications for the overall approach to infection control. It is the fundamental and primary defect. Antimicrobial therapy and wound care can be viewed as temporizing measures to stave off infection until the primary defect is repaired. This is what makes early excision and closure of the burn wound so important.

In addition to breaching the skin barrier, burn injury also results in transient mesenteric vasoconstriction, which leads to intestinal ischemia. Mesenteric ischemia following thermal injury is associated with a loss of gut mucosal integrity, which then predisposes patients to bacterial translocation from the gastrointestinal tract.

Patients with large cutaneous flame burns often have an associated smoke inhalation injury. Another significant intrinsic alteration is impairment of the mucociliary clearance mechanism following smoke inhalation. This predisposes patients to microbial invasion of the tracheobronchial tree as the bacterial load increases secondary to inadequate clearance of secretions and cellular debris by the mucociliary escalator. In addition to these alterations in host defense, there are specific defects in humoral and cell-mediated immunity which occur following severe burn injury. The most important is impaired function of natural killer cells. Dysfunction of natural killer cells has been demonstrated in several studies.[3] In addition, the generalized immunosuppression of burn injury is also characterized by specific alterations in B and T cell function.

Extrinsic factors synergize with the intrinsic factors described above to produce the picture of a patient who is profoundly susceptible to invasive infection. Intubation and mechanical ventilation increase the risk of colonization of the tracheobronchial tree. It is important to recognize that the burn intensive care unit is a reservoir of potential microbial pathogens. Tracheostomies represent a similar hazard and have been shown to increase the risk of colonization and nosocomial pneumonia. Immobilization is another extrinsic factor associated with the development of nosocomial pneumonia. Indwelling Foley catheters predispose patients to the development of urinary tract infection. Prolonged central venous catheterization is associated with an increased risk of sepsis. In general, extrinsic and iatrogenic risk factors should be minimized in order to decrease the chance of opportunistic infection in a patient who is already prone to infection secondary to factors which are intrinsic to the injury.

DIAGNOSIS AND MANAGEMENT OF SPECIFIC INFECTIONS

BURN WOUND INFECTION

The diagnosis and management of burn wound infection is based on early identification of an infected wound. Clinically, burn wound infection is most often recognized based on gross appearance or conversion of a partial thickness to a full thickness wound. Once there is clinical suspicion of invasive burn wound sepsis, it is imperative to obtain quantitative wound cultures. Generally, wound cultures growing organisms at greater than 1×10^5 organisms/gm of tissue are considered indicative of a wound at significant risk for invasive sepsis. It is important to realize, however, that histologic confirmation of actual tissue invasion by the microbial pathogens is the only way to clearly establish the diagnosis of invasive burn wound sepsis. The most common pathogens include methicillin-sensitive and methicillin-resistant *Staphylococcus* species and *Pseudomonas aeruginosa*.

Topical antimicrobial agents play an important role in decreasing the incidence of burn wound infection. The astute clinician must be cognizant, however, that antimicrobial therapy is not a substitute for aggressive debridement of grossly infected and devitalized tissue. Excision of all infected tissue continues to be the mainstay of treatment. Nonetheless, topical antimicrobial agents are useful and it is important to be familiar with them. There are several commonly used agents which include silver sulfadiazine, mafenide acetate, and silver nitrate. In addition, sodium hypochlorite or Dakins solution is often helpful in certain situations.

Silver sulfadiazine is advantageous in that it is painless on application. Unfortunately it does not penetrate through eschar very well, which makes it inadequate for deep partial thickness and full thickness burns. In sharp contrast, mafenide acetate is associated with much better penetration but causes pain upon application and may cause a metabolic acidosis secondary to inhibition of carbonic anhydrase. Silver nitrate provides broad-spectrum coverage but fails to penetrate. Sodium hypochlorite in low concentration provides excellent bactericidal activity and does not impair wound healing. In higher concentrations, it may impair wound healing, however. With the exception of transient exposure for procedures, povidone-iodine should generally be avoided since it is associated with impaired wound healing and inhibition of fibroblasts and also can cause thyroid and immune dysfunction. Other topical agents include Bactroban, Bacitracin, Polymyxin B, and Mycostatin. Bactroban provides excellent staphylococcal coverage; however cost may be prohibitive. Bacitracin is useful for minor wounds, and is most often combined with Neomycin and Polymyxin into a triple antibiotic ointment. Polymyxin is petroleum based and thus keeps grafts moist. Mycostatin may be combined with either Polymyxin or Silvadene in order to extend the coverage of these agents. Tables 7.1 and 7.2 summarize the topical agents.

Table 7.1. Topical antimicrobials

Topical Agents	Advantages	Disadvantages
Silver Sulfadiazine	Painless	Lack of penetration
Mafenide Acetate	Penetrates	Painful, Carbonic anhydrase inhibitor
Silver Nitrate	Broad spectrum	Limited penetration
Sodium Hypochlorite	Broad spectrum	Impairs wound healing in high doses

Table 7.2. Other topical agents

Bacitracin	Gram-positive coverage	Minimal Often combined with polymyxin and neomycin into triple ointment
Polymyxin B	Petroleum-based Keeps grafts moist	Often combined with mycostatin into "Polymyco"
Polymyco (Polymyxin and mycostatin)	Extended coverage	
Bactroban	Staphylococcal coverage	Very expensive Useful for ghosted grafts
Silvamyco (Silvadene and mycostatin)	Extended coverage	

CATHETER RELATED INFECTIONS

Central line sepsis is associated with prolonged indwelling central venous catheters. Meticulous sterile technique is essential during line placement to avoid introduction of potential pathogens. All areas should be carefully prepped and draped with Betadine or Hibiclens solution and the physician gowned and gloved appropriately prior to insertion. Central line sepsis may be primary in which the central line is the original focus of infection. It also may be secondary, in which case, the catheter tip is seeded and serves as a nidus for continued shedding of microorganisms into the blood stream. Signs of erythema or inflammation around the insertion site should alert the clinician to the potential for a line infection. However it is important to realize that there may be significant infection of the catheter tip even when skin surrounding the insertion site appears normal. Central lines can be associated with the development of both gram negative and gram positive sepsis. The key concept to recognize is that central lines represent an avascular foreign body and as such are prone to microbial seeding. There is significant controversy with regard to the frequency of line changes necessary to avoid catheter-related infection. It is the author's preference that central venous catheters be changed over a wire by the Seldinger method every 3-5 days. More frequent line changes may actually increase the risk of central line sepsis. Once a catheter-related infection is suspected, the central venous line should be promptly removed and the tip cultured. Systemic antimicrobial therapy can be initiated for a short time, but generally once the source of infection has been removed the patient should improve quickly.

URINARY TRACT INFECTION

Urinary tract infections can generally be divided into upper and lower urinary tract infection. True pyelonephritis is very rare in thermally injured patients; however, lower urinary tract infection can occur as a result of a chronic indwelling Foley catheter. The diagnosis should be suspected when there are greater than 1×10^5 organisms cultured from a urine specimen. Also urinalysis may reveal white cells and cellular debris associated with active infection. The most common organisms are gram negative pathogens such as *Escherichia coli*. The appropriate treatment consists of a 7-10 day course of an antimicrobial with good gram negative coverage. Fluoroquinolones such as ciprofloxacin are often very effective for uncomplicated cases. If there is suspicion of an ascending infection, then more aggressive treatment with prolonged systemic antimicrobials is warranted.

TRACHEOBRONCHITIS

Smoke inhalation injury is a chemical tracheobronchitis that results from the inhalation of the incomplete products of combustion and is often found in association with severe burn injury. Inhalation injury impairs the mucociliary transport mechanism and predisposes patients to colonization of the tracheobronchial tree by microorganisms. In addition, direct cellular injury to the respiratory epithelium results in the formation of extensive fibrinous casts composed of inflammatory exudate and sloughed cells. Increased bronchial blood flow leads to increased airway edema. As necrotic debris accumulates and airway edema is increased, patients become susceptible to postobstructive atelectasis and pneumonia. There is no specific treatment for tracheobronchitis other than aggressive pulmonary toilet and supportive measures. It is important to realize, however, that an upper respiratory infection can quickly turn into a lower respiratory infection with significant mortality.

PNEUMONIA

The diagnosis of pneumonia in severely burned patients is exceedingly problematic. During the acute phase of injury these patients demonstrate a hypermetabolic response characterized by increased basal metabolic rate and resetting of their hypothalamic temperature setpoint. Increased levels of catecholamines result in a hyperdynamic circulation. For these reasons, many of the usual signs and symptoms of pneumonia are unreliable in the severely burned. Fever, leukocytosis, tachypnea, and tachycardia may all be present even in the absence of an infection. Sputum examination is rarely helpful since specimens are often contaminated with oropharyngeal flora. More invasive sampling techniques such as bronchoalveolar lavage have been advocated; however, these, have also been shown to be less than ideal for establishing a diagnosis of pneumonia. Radiographic findings can be helpful if they reveal lobar consolidation. Unfortunately, concomitant inhalation injury and changes in pulmonary vascular permeability more often result in diffuse nonspecific radiographic changes consistent with noncardiogenic pulmonary edema. Pneumonias can result from descending infection of the tracheobronchial tree or from hematogenous dissemination of microbial pathogens. Inhalation injury is associated with descending infection and has clearly been shown to increase the incidence and the mortality of nosocomial pneumonia in the burn population. Generally, patients with a significant inhalation injury and a pneumonia develop atelectasis, ventilation-perfusion mismatch, arterial hypoxia, and respiratory failure. Prolonged mechanical ventilation leads to inevitable barotrauma and further worsening of pulmonary status in these patients. While bronchoalveolar lavage has been shown to correlate better with the presence of tracheobronchitis than with radiographic evidence of true pneumonia, it is the best available tool.[4] For this reason, a positive lavage in the appropriate clinical context mandates aggressive intervention. These nosocomial pneumonias are generally gram negative infections and systemic antimicrobial therapy with multiple agents is generally required until the infection resolves clinically. Amikacin and piperacillin or ceftazidime are generally recommended for serious infections, but antibiotics should be selected on the basis of susceptibility patterns in each hospital. Once cultures are returned, antimicrobial coverage may be narrowed appropriately.

INVASIVE FUNGAL INFECTIONS

Invasive fungal infections are occurring more frequently in the burn population today. There should be a high index of suspicion for invasive fungal sepsis anytime there is a severely burned patient who presents with a septic picture, but has negative blood cultures and is unresponsive to antibiotic therapy. Systemic candidiasis is a known complication of thermal injury and is most likely directly related to generalized immunosuppression and broad-spectrum antimicrobial therapy. Treatment with intravenous amphotericin B is the mainstay of treatment. More recently, angioinvasive infections with *Fusarium*, *Aspergillus*, and *Mucor* have been seen. These fungi have a predilection for endothelial invasion and thus can spread quickly leading to rampant septicemia. Treatment generally consists of itraconazole as first line therapy and fluconazole, or amphotericin B in selected cases. Unfortunately, many fungi are rapidly becoming resistant to amphotericin B, making other agents necessary. These infections are often fatal since they result in widespread dissemination and extensive direct tissue invasion.

SEPSIS

Sepsis may result from seeding of the bloodstream from the burn wound, the respiratory tract, the gastrointestinal tract, the urinary tract, and central venous catheters. The burn wound and the lungs account for the vast majority of cases. It is important to differentiate bacteremia from septicemia. Bacteremia refers to the presence of bacteria in the blood stream and may occur transiently after burn wound manipulation or excision. This transient bacteremia generally resolves and is not associated with any significant morbidity. Septicemia, however, implies a widespread response at the tissue level to bacteria or their products and toxins.

Traditionally sepsis is categorized as gram positive or gram negative. Gram negative sepsis is by far the most predominant in severely burned patients. The diagnosis of sepsis is a clinical diagnosis. Laboratory studies are supportive. A patient who is adequately resuscitated and becomes hemodynamically unstable should alert the clinician to the possibility of either active bleeding or the development of septic shock. The five cardinal signs of sepsis are hyperventilation, thrombocytopenia, hyperglycemia, obtundation, and hypothermia. Leukocytosis and fever are also important, but must be interpreted with caution in this setting. Patients who develop florid sepsis and progress to septic shock will manifest decreased systemic vascular resistance and hypotension. In these cases, inotropic support is needed in addition to systemic antimicrobial therapy. Blood cultures are helpful if they are positive, but unfortunately they are often negative even in a critically septic patient.

THE DILEMMA OF SYSTEMIC ANTIMICROBIAL THERAPY IN BURNS

AGGRESSIVE CHEMOPROPHYLAXIS VERSUS CONSERVATIVE MANAGEMENT

The use of systemic antimicrobial chemoprophylaxis in severely burned patients is a subject of much controversy. Conventional wisdom holds that topical antimicrobial therapy and aggressive wound care are sufficient for severely burned patients in the absence of significant signs of infection. Proponents of this philosophy maintain that only after clinical suspicion of an infection exists, should systemic antimicrobial therapy be initiated. At this point, appropriate cultures are drawn and coverage is adjusted. Proponents of conservative management further hold that injudicious use of antimicrobials selects for multiple resistant organisms and predisposes patients to superinfection. Unfortunately, this strategy may be somewhat inappropriate in patients with massive burns. Because of the generalized immunosuppression and the derangements in host defense that occur following burns, these patients are already at substantial risk for invasive infection. The question then becomes not "will this patient become infected?" but "when will this patient become infected?" Clearly, once disseminated infection has occurred, antimicrobial therapy is much less efficacious. Nonetheless, caution must be exercised with over aggressive antibiotic use since these agents are often nephrotoxic and burn patients may already have marginal renal status secondary to

Table 7.3. Cardinal signs of sepsis

Clinical	Laboratory
Hypothermia	Thrombocytopenia
Hyperventilation	Hyperglycemia
Obtundation	

inadequate or delayed resuscitation. Proponents of aggressive antimicrobial chemoprophylaxis would argue that it decreases the incidence of sepsis following massive excision and appears to reduce mortality. In addition, bacterial surveillance cultures can usually be used to discern the pathogens a patient is most likely to be infected with ahead of time. While neither aggressive antimicrobial chemoprophylaxis nor conservative management has been shown to be superior, either approach is valid, provided the clinician is prepared to frequently reevaluate the patient and has the appropriate resources in place to guide empiric antimicrobial selection. Some would propose using burn size as a guideline for determining the need for empiric coverage. In general, when a septic picture emerges in a patient with a massive burn, aggressive treatment is mandated. In our institution, we routinely begin empiric therapy with vancomycin, imipenem, and levofloxacin. Antimicrobial coverage is then adjusted as appropriate, based on culture and sensitivities.

REFERENCES

1. Herndon DN, Parks DH. Comparison of serial debridement and autografting and early massive excision with cadaver skin overlay in the treatment of large burns in children. J Trauma 1986; 26:149-52.
2. Shirani KZ, Pruitt BA, Mason AD Jr. The influence of inhalation injury and pneumonia on burn mortality. Ann Surg 1987; 20:82.
3. Stein MD, Gamble DN, Klimpel KD et al. Natural killer cell defects resulting from thermal injury. Cell Immunol 1984; 86:551-556
4. Ramzy PI, Herndon DN, Wolf SE et al. Correlation of bronchial lavage with radiographic evidence of pneumonia in severe burns [abstract 117]. In Proceedings of the American Burn Association, Chicago: J Burn Care Rehabil 1998; 19(1):S193

Multiple Organ Failure

Doraid Jarrar, Steven E. Wolf

INTRODUCTION

Major burns are relatively common injuries that require multidisciplinary treatment for patient survival and recovery. Statistics indicate that one million people are burned every year in the United States. Of these, 60,000-80,000 require admission to a specialized burn center with 5,000 associated deaths each year. Many of these deaths are due to "sepsis" and multiple organ failure.

Early aggressive resuscitation regimens have improved survival dramatically over the past four decades. With the advent of vigorous fluid resuscitation, irreversible burn shock has been replaced by sepsis and subsequent multiple organ failure as the leading cause of death associated with burns. In our pediatric burn population with burns over 80% total body surface area (TBSA), 17.5% of the children developed sepsis defined by bacteremia.[1] The mortality rate in the whole group was 33%, most of which succumbed to multiple organ failure. Some of the patients who died were bacteremic and "septic", but the majority were not. These findings highlight the observation that the development of multiple organ failure is often associated with infectious sepsis, but it is by no means required to develop this syndrome. What is required is an inflammatory focus, which in severe burns is the massive skin injury that requires inflammation to heal. It has been postulated that the progression of patients to multiple organ failure exists in a continuum with the systemic inflammatory response syndrome (SIRS).[2] Nearly all burn patients meet the criteria for SIRS as defined by the consensus conference of the American College of Chest Physicians and the Society of Critical Care Medicine[3] (Fig. 8.1). It is therefore not surprising that multiple organ failure is common in burned patients.

Burn Care, edited by Steven E. Wolf and David N. Herndon. © 1999 Landes Bioscience

Fig. 8.1. Multiple organ failure prevention. All severe burn patients have SIRS by definition (tachycardia, hyperpyrexia, tachypnea). Efforts of clinicians caring for these patients

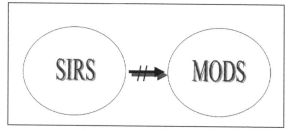

are directed at prevention of the progression to MODS (multiple organ failure syndrome).

ETIOLOGY AND PATHOPHYSIOLOGY

The progression from the systemic inflammatory response syndrome to multiple organ failure is not well explained, although some of the responsible mechanisms in some patients are recognized. Most of these are found in patients with inflammation from infectious sources. In the burn patient, these infectious sources most likely emanate from invasive wound infection or from lung infections (pneumonias). As organisms proliferate out of control, endotoxins are liberated from gram-negative bacterial walls and exotoxins from gram-positive and gram-negative bacteria are released. Their release causes the initiation of a cascade of inflammatory mediators that can result, if unchecked, in organ damage and progression toward organ failure. Occasionally, failure of the gut barrier with penetration of organisms into the systemic circulation may incite a similar reaction. However, this phenomena has only been demonstrated in animal models, and it remains to be seen if this is a cause of human disease.

Inflammation from the presence of necrotic tissue and open wounds can incite a similar inflammatory mediator response to that seen with endotoxin. The mechanism by which this occurs, however, is not well understood. Regardless, it is known that a cascade of systemic events is set in motion either by invasive organisms or from open wounds that initiates the systemic inflammatory response syndrome which may progress to multiple organ failure. Evidence from animal studies and clinical trials suggests that these events converge to a common pathway, which results in the activation of several cascade systems. Those circulating mediators can, if secreted in excessive amounts, damage organs distal from their site of origin. Among these mediators are endotoxin, the arachidonic acid metabolites, cytokines, neutrophils and their adherence molecules, nitric oxide, complement components, and oxygen free radicals (Table 8.1).

ENDOTOXIN

Endotoxin, a component of the wall of gram-negative bacteria, is released upon lysis of bacteria and activates a variety of cells via its receptor CD14. Endotoxemia causes fever, hypotension, and activation of liver cells to release acute phase proteins. It also stimulates monocytes, the predominant source of cytokines, to pro-

---

Table 8.1. Etiology and prevention of multiple organ failure

Factors in the development of multiple organ failure

Endotoxin

> *Burn Wound*
> *Pneumonia*
> *Bacterial Translocation*
> Arachidonic Acid Metabolites
> Cytokines
> Neutrophils and their Adherence Molecules
> Nitric Oxide
> Oxygen Free Radicals

Prevention Measures

> Aggressive Resuscitation
> Early and Complete Burn Wound Excision
> Routine Central Line Changes
> Directed Antimicrobial Therapy
> Pulmonary Toilet
> Continued Infection Surveillance
> Enteral Feedings
> Immunomodulation

8

---

duce and secrete excessive amounts of cytokines. Paradoxically, appropriate antibiotic treatment may initially even increase the levels of circulating endotoxin through lysis of the pathogens.

ARACHIDONIC ACID METABOLITES

Arachidonic acid is the precursor for prostaglandins and thromboxanes through the cyclooxygenase pathway and for the leukotrienes through the lipoxygenase pathway. Prostaglandins (PGE), especially PGE_2, is a powerful endogenous immunosuppressant. Thromboxane A_2 and other metabolites of the cyclooxygenase pathway are potent vasoconstrictors in both the splanchnic and pulmonary microvasculature. Leukotrienes affect vascular tone and increase vascular permeability, contributing to edema formation and pulmonary dysfunction.

CYTOKINES

Cytokines are a group of signaling proteins produced by a variety of cells that are thought to be important for host defense, wound healing and other essential host functions. Although cytokines in low physiologic concentrations preserve homeostasis, excessive production may lead to widespread tissue injury and organ dysfunction. Four of these cytokines, tumor necrosis factor alpha (TNF-α), interleukin 1 beta (IL-1β, interleukin 6 (IL-6) and interleukin 8 (IL-8) have been most strongly associated with sepsis and multiple organ failure. IL-1β and IL-6 are most consistently found to be elevated inpatients with septic episodes.

OXYGEN FREE RADICALS AND NITRIC OXIDE

The effects of the toxic products of oxygen free radical formation are only now being elucidated. From in vitro models and in vivo animal models, we know that tissues that initially were in shock and are then reperfused produce oxygen free radicals that are known to damage a number of cellular metabolism processes. This process occurs throughout the body during burn resuscitation, but the significance of these free radicals in human burn injury is unknown. It was found that free radical scavengers such as superoxide dismutase improve survival in animal models; however, this has not been established in human patients.[4] Oxygen free radicals oxidize membrane lipids, resulting in cellular dysfunction. Endogenous natural antioxidants, such as vitamins C and E, are low in patients with burns, suggesting that therapeutic interventions may be beneficial.[5] Augmenting the effects of the primary endogenous antioxidant glutathione might also lead to improved outcomes.

Nitric oxide, a metabolite of the amino acid arginine, is one of the major mediators of the hypotensive response to sepsis. However, its has complex interactions with other mediators, and further work in determining its role in the pathogenesis of SIRS and multiple organ failure need to be performed before therapies to modify its effects are widely adopted.[6] Inhaled nitric oxide at 5-15 ppm will improve oxygenation and lower pulmonary artery pressures during ARDS, presumably by selectively dilating those pulmonary vessels that flow past open alveoli. This results in an increase in flow to the open airways, allowing for better air exchange and a decrease in pulmonary shunting.

PREVENTION

This brief outline of the proposed mediators of multiple organ failure shows the complexity of the problem. Since different cascade systems are involved in the pathogenesis, it is so far impossible to pinpoint a single mediator that initiates the event. Thus, since the mechanisms of progression are not well known, specific intervention to treat the cause is not possible. Therefore, prevention is likely to be the best solution (Table 8.1).

The great reduction of mortality in our institution from large burns was seen with early excision and an aggressive surgical approach to deep wounds. Early removal of devitalized tissue prevents wound infections and decreases the inflammation associated with the wound. In addition, it eliminates small-colonized foci which are a frequent source of transient bacteremia. Those transient bacteremias during surgical manipulations of the burn wound may prime immune cells to react in an exaggerated fashion to subsequent insults, leading to whole body inflammation and remote organ damage. We recommend complete early excision of clearly full-thickness wounds within 48 h of the injury.

Oxidative damage from reperfusion after low flow states make early aggressive fluid resuscitation imperative. This is particularly important during the initial phases of treatment and operative excision with its attendant blood losses. Furthermore, the volume of fluid may not be as important as the timeliness with which it is given. In the study of children with greater than 80% TBSA burns, it was found that one of the most important contributors to survival was the time required to start intravenous resuscitation, regardless of the initial volume given.[1]

Topical and systemic antimicrobial therapy have significantly diminished the incidence of invasive burn wound sepsis. Perioperative antibiotics clearly benefit patients with injuries greater than 30% TBSA burns. Vigilant and scheduled replacement of intravascular devices will minimize the incidence of catheter-related sepsis. We recommend changes of indwelling catheters every three days. The first can be done over a wire using sterile Seldinger technique, but the second change requires a new site. This protocol should be kept as long as intravenous access is required. Where possible, peripheral veins should be used for cannulation, even through burned tissue. The saphenous vein, however, should be avoided because of the high incidence of thrombophlebitis.

Pneumonia, which contributes significantly to mortality in burned patients, should be vigilantly anticipated and aggressively treated. Every attempt should be made to wean patients as early as possible from the ventilator in order to reduce the risk of ventilator associated nosocomial pneumonia. Furthermore, early ambulation is an effective means of preventing respiratory complications. With sufficient analgesics, even patients on continuous ventilatory support can be out of bed and in a chair.

Blood cultures may be necessary to identify specific bacteria if a source cannot be identified. This is particularly true for the operating room, where transient bacteriemia and endotoxemia are common. For ongoing evidence of inflammation outside of intraoperative fluid shifts and transient hypotension, common sources are the wound and tracheobronchial trees, and efforts to identify causative organisms for sepsis should be concentrated there. Weekly cultures from the burn wound should guide specific perioperative antibiotic coverage.

The gastrointestinal tract is a natural reservoir for bacteria. Starvation and hypovolemia shunt blood from the splanchnic bed and promote mucosal atrophy and failure of the gut barrier.[7] Early enteral feeding reduces septic morbidity and prevents failure of the gut barrier.[8] In our institution, patients are fed immediately via a nasogastric tube with Vivonex TEN®, although other enteral feedings may suffice, including milk. Early enteral feedings are tolerated in burn patients and preserve the mucosal integrity and may reduce the magnitude of the hypermetabolic response to injury. Support of the gut goes along with carefully monitored hemodynamics since sufficient splanchnic blood flow is essential to prevent translocation of bacteria.[9]

Specific immunomodulation to prevent the onset of multiple organ failure does not yet exist. Clinical trials with antibodies against endotoxin have not proven efficacy, safety and cost-effectiveness.[10-12] Although, animal studies have shown that pretreatment with monoclonal antibodies against tumor-necrosis factor alpha (TNFα) increases survival, clinical results were disappointing.[13]

ORGAN FAILURE

Even with the best efforts at prevention, the presence of the systemic inflammatory syndrome that is ubiquitous in burn patients may progress to organ failure. The general development begins either in the renal or pulmonary systems and can progress through the liver, gut, hematologic system, and central nervous system. The development of multiple organ failure does not preclude mortality, however, and efforts to support the organs until they heal are justified.

RENAL FAILURE

With the advent of early aggressive resuscitation, the incidence of renal failure coincident with the initial phases of recovery has diminished significantly in severely burned patients. However, a second period of risk for the development of renal failure, 2-14 days after resuscitation, is still present.[14] Renal failure is hallmarked by decreasing urine output, fluid overload, electrolyte abnormalities including metabolic acidosis and hyperkalemia, the development of azotemia, and increased serum creatinine. Treatment is aimed at averting complications associated with the above conditions.

Urine output of 1 cc/kg/h is sufficient. When the output falls below this level, initial efforts should be concentrated on discerning the status of the intravascular volume. Initial fluid boluses should be given and if these go without response, atrial filling and pulmonary artery pressures should be measured with a Swan-Ganz catheter. If it appears to be primary renal dysfunction with an adequate intravascular volume and cardiac output, loop diuretics should be given to maintain urine output (up to 1 mg/kg of lasix every 4 h). Oftentimes in primary renal insufficiency, these measures will fail requiring other treatments.

Fluid overload in burned patients can be alleviated by decreasing the volume of fluid being given. These patients have increased insensible losses from the wounds which can be roughly calculated (see resuscitation chapter). Decreasing the infused volume of intravenous fluids and enteral feedings below the expected insensate losses will alleviate fluid overload problems. Electrolyte abnormalities can be minimized by decreasing potassium administration in the enteral feedings and giving oral bicarbonate solutions such as Bicitra. Almost invariably, severely burned patients require exogenous potassium because of the heightened aldosterone response which results in potassium wasting, therefore hyperkalemia is rare even with some renal insufficiency.

Should the problems listed above overwhelm the conservative measures, some form of dialysis may be necessary. The indications for dialysis are fluid overload or electrolyte abnormalities not amenable to other treatments. We usually begin with peritoneal dialysis through catheters placed in the operating room. We instill one liter of infusate into the peritoneum which is tailored to treat the treat the problem at hand. Hypertonic solutions are used to treat fluid overload, and the concentrations of potassium and bicarbonate are modified to produce the desired results. The dwell time is usually 30 minutes followed by drainage for 30 minutes. This treatment can be repeated in cycles until the problem is resolved. For maintenance, 4-6 such cycles a day with prolonged dwell times (1 h) are usually sufficient during the acute phase.

Occasionally, hemodialysis will be required. Continuous veno-venous hemodialysis is often indicated in these patients because of the fluid shifts that occur. These patients are not stable hemodynamically and therefore we prefer this method. All hemodialysis techniques should be done in conjunction with experienced nephrologists.

After beginning dialysis, renal function may return, especially in those patients that maintain some urine output. Therefore, patients requiring such treatment may not require lifelong dialysis. It is a clinical observation that whatever urine output was present will decrease once dialysis is begun, but it may return in several days to weeks once acute process of closing the burn wound nears completion.

PULMONARY FAILURE

Many of these patients require mechanical ventilation to protect the airway in the initial phases of their injury. We recommend that these patients be extubated as soon as possible after this risk is diminished. A trial of extubation is often warranted in the first few days after injury, and re-intubation in this setting is not a failure. To perform this technique safely, however, requires the involvement of experts in obtaining an airway. At our institutions, these maneuvers are done in conjunction with an experienced anesthesiologist. The goal is extubation as soon as possible to allow the patients to clear their own airways, as they can perform their own pulmonary toilet better than we can through an endotracheal tube or tracheostomy.

The first sign of impending pulmonary failure is a decline in oxygenation. This is best followed by continuous oximetry, and a fall in saturation below 92% is indicative of failure. Increasing concentrations of inspired oxygen will be necessary, and when ventilation begins to fail denoted by increasing respiratory rate and hypercarbia, intubation will be needed. Various maneuvers described in the inhalation injury chapter may then be required.

HEPATIC FAILURE

The development of hepatic failure in burned patients is a very challenging problem that does not have many solutions. The liver functions to synthesize circulating proteins, detoxify the plasma, produce bile, and provide immunologic support. When the liver begins to fail, protein concentrations of the coagulation cascade will fall to critical levels and these patients will become coagulopathic. Toxins will not be cleared from the bloodstream, and concentrations of bilirubin will increase. Complete hepatic failure is not compatible with life, but a gradation of liver failure with some decline of the functions is common. Efforts to prevent hepatic failure are the only effective methods of treatment.

With the development of coagulopathies, treatment should be directed at replacement of factors II, VII, IX, and X until the liver recovers. Albumin replacement may also be required. Attention to obstructive causes of hyperbilirubinemia such as acalculous cholecystitis should be entertained as well. Initial treatment of this condition should be gallbladder drainage which can be done percutaneously.

HEMATOLOGIC FAILURE

Burn patients may become coagulopathic via two mechanisms, either through depletion/impaired synthesis of coagulation factors or through thrombocytopenia. Factors associated with factor depletion are through disseminated intravascular coagulation (DIC) associated with sepsis. This process is also common with coincident head injury. With breakdown of the blood-brain barrier, brain lipids are exposed to the plasma which activates the coagulation cascade. Varying penetrance of this problem will result in differing degrees of coagulopathy. Treatment of DIC should include infusion of fresh frozen plasma and cryoprecipitate to maintain plasma levels of coagulation factors. For DIC induced by brain injury, following the concentration of fibrinogen and repleting levels with cryoprecipitate is the most specific indicator. Impaired synthesis of factors from liver failure is treated as alluded to above.

Thrombocytopenia is common in severe burns from depletion during burn wound excision. Platelet counts of below 50,000 are common and do not require treatment. In general, we withhold platelet transfusions regardless of platelet count in the absence of clinical bleeding. Even in those who are bleeding from the wounds, most of the loss is from open vessels in the excised wound which require surgical control. Only when the bleeding is diffuse and is also noted from the IV sites should consideration for exogenous platelets be given. Patients with severe burns will often have several instances of thrombocytopenia. Our reluctance to give platelets is based on the development of anti-platelet antibodies, which will make platelet transfusions ineffective later when they are truly required.

CENTRAL NERVOUS SYSTEM FAILURE

Obtundation is one of the hallmarks of sepsis, and in burns this is not excepted. The new onset of mental status changes not attributed to sedative medications in a severely burned patient should incite a search for a septic source. Treatment is supportive.

SUMMARY

All burn patients are by definition affected of the systemic inflammatory response syndrome (SIRS), characterized by hyperthermia, increased respiratory rate, and tachycardia. Efforts to prevent the progression to multiple organ failure are chronicled above. Carefully monitored hemodynamics, early excision of burn wound, appropriate antibiotic coverage, early enteral feeding and good respiratory care are so far most promising in the prevention of organ failure and in reducing its morbidity. Once organ failure has developed, efforts at organ-specific support will provide some survivors.

REFERENCES

1. Wolf SE, Rose JK, Desai MH, Mileski J, Barrow RE, Herndon DN. Mortality determinants in massive pediatric burns: An analysis of 103 children with ≥ 80% TBSA burns (≥ 70% full-thickness). Ann Surg 1997; 225:554-569.

2. Bone RC, Grodzin CJ, Balk RA. Sepsis: A new hypothesis for pathogenesis of the disease process. Chest 1997; 112:235-43.

3. Muckart DJ, Bhagwanjee S. American College of Chest Physicians/Society of Critical Care Medicine Consensus Conference definitions of the systemic inflammatory response syndrome and allied disorders in relation to critically injured patients. Crit Care Med 1997 25:1789-95.

4. Rhee P, Waxman K, Clark L, Tominaga G, Soliman MH. Superoxide dismutase polyethylene glycol improves survival in hemorrhagic shock. Ann Surg 1991; 57:747-750.

5. Schiller HJ, Reilly PM, Bulkley GB. Tissue perfusion in critical illnesses. Antioxidant therapy. Crit Care Med 1993; 21:S92-S102.

6. Nava E, Palmer RM, Moncada S. Inhibition of nitric oxide synthesis in septic shock: how much is beneficial. Lancet 1991; 338:1555-1557.

7. Herndon DN, Ziegler ST. Bacterial translocation after thermal injury. Crit Care Med 1993; 21:S50-S54.

8. Moore FA, Moore EE, Jones TN, McCroskey BL, Petersen VM. TEN versus TPN following major abdominal trauma-reduced septic morbidity. J Trauma 1989; 29:916-922.

9. Tokyay R, Zeigler ST, Traber DL, Stothert JC, Loick HM, Heggers JP, Herndon DN. Postburn gastrointestinal vasoconstriction increases bacterial and endotoxin translocation. J Appl Physiol 1993; 74(4):1521-1527.

10. Ziegler EJ, Fisher CJ Jr, Sprung CL, Straube RC, Sadoff JC, Foulke GE, Wortel CH, Fink MP, Dellinger RP, Teng NN et al. Treatment of gram-negative bacteremia and septic shock with HA-1A human monoclonal antibody against endotoxin, A randomized, double blind, placebo-controlled Trial. N Engl J Med 1991; 324:429-436.

11. Greenman RL, Schein RM, Martin MA, Wenzel RP, MacIntyre NR, Emmanuel G, Chmel H, Kohler RB, McCarthy M, Plouffe J et al. A controlled clinical trial of E5 murine monoclonal IgM antibody to endotoxin in the treatment of gram–negative sepsis. JAMA 1991; 266:1097-1102.

12. Wentzel RP. Anti-endotoxin monoclonal antibodies—a second look (editorial comment) N Engl J Med 1992; 326:1151-1153.

13. Tracey KJ, Fong Y, Hesse DG, Manogue KR, Lee AT, Kuo GC, Lowry SF, Cerami A. Anti-cachectin/TNF monoclonal antibodies prevent septic shock during lethal bacteremia. Nature 1987; 330:662-664.

14. Jeschke M, Wolf SE, Barrow RE, Herndon DN. Mortality in burned children with acute renal failure. Arch Surg 1998, 134:752-756.

Inhalation Injury

Marc G. Jeschke

BACKGROUND

Mortality from major burns has decreased in the past 20 years by improved intensive care unit practices, improvement in wound management, and better control of sepsis and hemodynamic disorders. The single most important associated injury with burns that contributes to mortality is smoke inhalation injury. New technologies have increased the capability to diagnose clinically significant inhalation injuries. These studies have demonstrated that 20-30% of all major burns are associated with a concomitant inhalation injury, with a mortality of 25-50% when patients required ventilatory support for more than one week postinjury.[1]

Approximately 80% of fire-related deaths result not from burns but from inhalation of the toxic products of combustion. The upper airway is able to modify the temperature of inspired air such that smoke inhalation does not cause a thermal injury. The exception is the inhalation of high-pressure steam, which has four times the heat-carrying capacity of dry air and can cause direct thermal injury to the airways. Therefore the injurious agent in smoke is not temperature, but instead the toxic chemicals present in smoke. Many of these toxic chemicals may act together to increase mortality. This is especially true of carbon monoxide (CO) and hydrogen cyanide (HCN) where a synergism has been found to increase tissue hypoxia and acidosis and may also decrease cerebral oxygen consumption and metabolism. Other possible contributing toxic substances are hydrogen chloride (produced by polyvinyl chloride degradation), nitrogen oxide, or aldehydes which can result in pulmonary edema, chemical pneumonitis or respiratory irritability.

Lung injury from smoke inhalation is associated with tracheobronchial hyperemic sloughing of ciliated epithelium, formation of copious tracheal exudates, and pulmonary capillary permeability changes resulting in a pulmonary edema. Animal studies showed a progressive increase in lung permeability during the first 6 h following thermal injury.[2] The inhalation of toxic smoke causes the release of thromboxane and other inflammatory mediators which increase pulmonary ar-

Burn Care, edited by Steven E. Wolf and David N. Herndon. © 1999 Landes Bioscience

tery pressure, cause secondary damage to the respiratory epithelium, and release chemotactic factors.[3] Neutrophils subsequently diapedese from the pulmonary microvasculature and release enzymes such as elastase and free oxygen radicals which disrupt endothelial junctions and the epithelial integrity permitting exudate of protein rich plasma to enter the lung.[3] A concomitant reduction in the pulmonary immune function may lead to bacteria growth and pneumonia.[4]

CLINICAL PHASES

The clinical course of patients with inhalation injury is divided into three stages:

FIRST STAGE
Acute pulmonary insufficiency—Patients with severe lung injuries show acute pulmonary insufficiency from 0-36 h after injury with asphyxia, carbon monoxide poisoning, bronchospasm, upper airway obstruction and parenchymal damage.

SECOND STAGE
Pulmonary edema—This second stage occurs in 5-30% of patients, usually from 48-96 h after burn.

THIRD STAGE
Bronchopneumonia—Appears in 15-60% of these patients with a reported mortality of 50-86%. Bronchopneumonia occurs typically 3-10 days after burn injury, is often associated with the expectoration of large mucus casts formed in the tracheobronchial tree. Those pneumonias appearing in the first few days are usually due to penicillin resistant Staphylococcus species, whereas after 3-4 days, the changing flora of the burn wound is reflected in the appearance in the lung of gram negative species, especially Pseudomonas species.

DIAGNOSIS

Early detection of bronchopulmonary injury is critical in improving survival after a suspected inhalation injury.

CLINICAL SIGNS
History of exposure to smoke in closed space (patients who are stuporous or unconscious)
Physical findings: facial burns/singed nasal vibrissae/bronchorrhea/sooty sputum/auscultatory findings (wheezing or rales).
Laboratory findings: hypoxemia and/or elevated levels of carbon monoxide.

Diagnostic Methods

Chest X-ray was showed to be a insensitive method because admission studies are very seldom abnormal and may remain normal as long as seven days postburn.

The standard diagnostic method on every burn patient should be *bronchoscopy* for upper airway injury. Positive findings are: airway edema/inflammation/mucosal necrosis/presence of soot and charring in the airway/tissue sloughing/carbonaceous material in the airway. All patients that have clinical signs of smoke inhalation injury listed above should undergo bronchoscopy either through an endotracheal tube or transnasal with sedation to determine the presence of smoke inhalation injury.

To define parenchymal injury the most specific method is the *133 Xe lung scanning*, which involves intravenous injection of radioactive xenon gas followed by serial chest scintiphotograms. This technique identifies areas of air trapping from small airway partial or total obstruction by demonstrating areas of decreased alveolar gas washout.

Additionally *pulmonary function* tests can be performed and could show an increased resistance and decreased flow in those with abnormal 133 Xe scans.

TREATMENT

General Treatment

The treatment of the inhalation injury should **start immediately** with the administration of 100% oxygen via face mask or nasal cannula. This helps reverse the effects of CO poisoning and aids in its clearance, as 100% oxygen lowers its half-life time from 250 to less than 50 minutes. Maintenance of the airway is critical. If early evidence of upper airway edema is present, early intubation is required because the upper airway edema normally increases over 8-12 h. Prophylactic intubation without good indication however should not be performed. The method of intubation should be that with which the intubator is most familiar; both the nasal and oral routes are appropriate. Occasionally, the injury around the face and neck may be such that the airway is at risk from edema, and the standard intubation techniques with paralysis may not be safe. In those situations, an awake nasotracheal intubation or fiberoptic intubation by the most experienced personnel is preferred.

Table 9.1. Intubation criteria

Criteria	Value
PaO$_2$ (mm Hg)	< 60
PaCO$_2$ (mm Hg)	> 50 (acutely)
P/F ratio	< 200
Respiratory/ventilatory failure	Impending
Upper airway edema	Severe

Several clinical studies have shown that pulmonary edema was not prevented by fluid restriction. Indeed, fluid resuscitation appropriate for the patient's other needs results in no increase in lung water, has no adverse effect on pulmonary histology, and improves survival. Although overhydration could induce pulmonary edema, inadequate hydration increases the severity of pulmonary injury by sequestration of polymorphonuclear cells and leads to increased mortality.[1] In both animal and clinical studies, it was shown that fluid resuscitation is adequate if normal cardiac index or urine output were maintained. This might require 2cc/kg/% TBSA burn more fluid volume than required for an equal size burn without inhalation injury.

Prophylactic antibiotics for inhalation injury are not indicated, but are clearly indicated for documented lung infections. Empiric choices for treatment of pneumonia prior to culture results should include coverage of methicillin-resistant *Staphylococcus aureus* in the first few days postburn (these develop within the first week after burn) and of gram-negative organisms (especially Pseudomonas or Klebsiella) which mostly occur after one week postburn. Systemic antibiotics regimes are based on serially monitored sputum cultures, bronchial washings, or transtracheal aspirates.

PHARMACOLOGICAL MANAGEMENT

The theoretical benefits of corticosteroid therapy include a reduction in mucosal edema, reduced bronchospasm and the maintenance of surfactant function.

Table 9.2. Pharmacological management

Treatment	Time/Dosage
Bronchodilators (Albuterol)	Q 2 h
Nebulized heparin	5.000 to 10.000 units with 3 cc normal saline Q 4 h which alternates with
Nebulized acetylcysteine	20%, 3 cc Q 4 h
Hypertonic saline	Induce effective coughing
Racemic epinephrine	Reduce mucosal edema

Table 9.3. Airway clearance techniques

Criteria	Time/Dosage
Chest physiotherapy	Q 2 h
Cough deep breathing exercise	Q 2 h
Turn patient side to side	Q 2 h
Flow humidification	High
NTS/OTS	As needed
Sputum cultures	Q M-W-F
Bronchoscopy evaluation and lavage	Q OP visit and therapeutically if needed
Ambulation	Early

However, in several animal and clinical studies mortality increased with the administration of corticosteroids and bronchopneumonia showed a more extensive abscess formation. Thus the use of corticosteroids is contraindicated.

In recent studies, the importance of localized heparin treatment of the airway in combination with acetylcysteine and albuterol was shown. In these studies, mortality and ventilator days improved because of these results. These treatments are used routinely on all our patients with inhalation injury (Table 4.2).

Ventilator management (guideline from the American College of Chest physicians): Target ventilator settings should be those designed to elicit an acceptable oxygen saturation at a plateau pressure of less than 35 cm H_2O (clinical conditions that are associated with a decreased chest wall compliance, plateau pressures greater than 35 cm H_2O may be acceptable). To accomplish the goal of limiting plateau pressures, pCO_2s should be permitted to rise (permissive hypercapnia) unless other contraindications exist that demand a more normal PCO_2 or pH.

PEEP is useful in supporting oxygenation. The level of PEEP required should be established by empiric trials and reevaluated on a regular basis. PEEP levels should start at 5 cm H_2O and be increased in 2.5 cm H_2O increments. PEEP trials should be performed to optimize oxygenation and cardiac output. The effectiveness of PEEP is related to surface tension abnormalities and the marked tendency for atelectasis in these patients. Large tidal volumes (12-15 ml/kg) with PEEP may be needed if pressure limited strategies fail to maintain oxygenation. Peak flow rates should be adjusted as needed to satisfy patient inspiratory demands, usually set between 40-100 l/min, depending on expired volume and inspiratory demand.

Typical ventilatory settings would begin with volume controlled ventilation with a volume of 12-15 ml/kg and a rate of 10 breaths/minute and 40% O_2 with 5 cm H_2O positive end expiratory pressure. The rate and tidal volume are then adjusted to maintain a normal arterial pCO_2. If the plateau pressures on these settings are above 35 mm Hg, the tidal volume can be decreased and the rate increased to maintain the same minute ventilation. Rates greater than 20 breaths per minute may not be well tolerated. If this is unsuccessful, a change to pressure controlled ventilation to control the peak pressures may be required. Care must be taken when performing this maneuver to ensure that minute ventilation is maintained the same as the settings with volume control. As the patients' pulmonary compliance changes with progression of the disease, the delivered tidal volumes for the set pressure may change, thus altering minute ventilation and CO_2 removal. Only clinical assessment by arterial blood gases or end tidal CO_2 monitoring and appropriate changes in the ventilator settings will maintain targeted blood CO_2 concentrations. Volume control settings are safer in this respect, but this safety may be sacrificed to control inspiratory pressures.

Oxygenation may also be difficult at this point because the process that is decreasing pulmonary compliance requiring the high pressures to gain the necessary tidal volumes is also increasing the intrapulmonary shunt. As the opening pressure for alveoli increases with decreased compliance, more alveoli are closed, allowing blood to run through their associated capillaries without contact with air to exchange gases. This unoxygenated blood mixes with oxygenated blood from open alveoli, decreasing the oxygen content in the whole. Strategies to increase oxygenation include increasing the fractional inspired content of O_2 (F_iO_2) above 40%. Percent O_2 concentrations above 60% might be toxic because of the increase in reactive oxygen metabolites. Therefore, efforts should be made to keep the F_iO_2 below this level. The next strategy employed should be to increase the PEEP, which should not be set above 15 cm H_2O to avoid barotrauma. If this is not successful, increasing inspiratory times to increase the inspiratory-expiratory ratio of the respiratory cycle might also improve oxygenation. Ratios as high as 3:1 may be required (normal 1:4). In general, alert patients do not tolerate increasing the inspiratory-expiratory ratio, and higher levels of sedation and even paralysis may be necessary. Further measures to improve oxygenation such as inhaled nitric oxide and partial liquid ventilation are experimental, but might be attempted in the presence of a controlled clinical trial.

When an acceptable combination of ventilator settings are reached to provide for adequate ventilation and oxygenation, the process of weaning from the ventilator begins. In general, ventilator weaning should be done by one physician with a defined plan. In terms of oxygenation, F_iO_2 should be decreased first to 40%, then decreasing the inspiratory-expiratory ratio to 1:2, followed by decreasing PEEP to 5 cm H_2O. Ventilation should be addressed by decreasing the set ventilator rate on an SIMV volume control mode with the addition of pressure support for spontaneous breaths, until a machine rate of 4 is reached. At that point, if the spontaneous respiratory mechanics are adequate, the patient may be extubated. The reader is referred to other ICU handbooks for a more in depth discussion of this and alternative weaning techniques.

SUMMARY

Inhalation injury is commonly associated with burns. Mortality from this condition has markedly improved with better ICU techniques and prevention of complications. Recognition of the possibility of inhalation injury and directed treatment will improve outcomes.

Table 9.4. Extubation criteria

Criteria	Value
PaO_2/F_iO_2 (P/F) ratio	> 250
Maximum inspiratory pressure (MIP) (cm H_2O)	> 60
Spontaneous tidal volume (ml/kg)	> 5-7
Spontaneous vital capacity (ml/kg)	> 15-20
Maximum voluntary ventilation	> present twice the minute volume
Audible leak around the ET tube with cuff deflated	

REFERENCES

1. Herndon DN, Curreri PW, Abston S, Rutan TC, Barrow RE. Treatment of burns. Current problems in surgery 1987; (24)6:343-397.
2. Till Go, Johnson KJ, Kunkel R et al. Intravascular activation of compliment and acute lung injury. J Clin Invest 1982; 69:1126-1134.
3. Herndon DN; Traber DL, Pollard P. Pathophysiology of inhalation injury. In: Total Burn Care. WB Saunders Company LTD, 1996; 175-183.
4. Rue LW III, Cioffi WG Jr, Mason AD Jr et al. Improved survival of burned patients with inhalation injury. Arch Surg 1993; 128:772-80.
5. Cioffi WG, DeLemos RA, Coalson JJ et al. Decreased pulmonary damage in primates with inhalation injury treated with high-frequency ventilation. Ann Surg 1993; 218:328-337.

9

Nonthermal Burns

Edgar J. Pierre, Steven E. Wolf

Nonthermal burns differ from thermal injuries in many ways, however the results are similar, soft tissue damage. These nonthermal injuries consist of burns from chemicals and injuries from electrical current. While thermal injury damages tissue by the transfer of heat, chemicals and electricity damage tissue by transfer of potential energy from chemical reactions and transfer of electrical energy respectively. It must be pointed out that thermal injury produced by chemical reactions and heat developed by resistance to electrical current can cause secondary damage in these injuries.

CHEMICAL BURNS

Most chemical burns are accidental from mishandling of household cleaners, although some of the most dramatic presentations involve industrial exposures. In the scope of this chapter, it is impossible to address the many thousands of agents which may be encountered, and for this reason only the most common are reviewed here.

Thermal burns are in general short-term exposures to heat, but chemical injuries may be of longer duration, even for hours in the absence of appropriate treatment. The degree of tissue damage as well as the level of toxicity is determined by the chemical nature of an agent, concentration, and the duration of skin contact.[1] Chemicals cause their injury by protein destruction, with denaturation, oxidation, formation of protein esters, or desiccation of the tissue. In the USA, the composition of most household and industrial chemicals can be obtained from the Poison Control Center in the area, with suggestions for treatment.

Speed is essential in the management of chemical burns. For all chemicals, lavage with copious quantities of clean water should be done immediately after removing all clothing. Dry powders should be brushed from the affected areas before irrigation. Early irrigation dilutes the chemical which is already in contact with the skin, and timeliness increases effectiveness of irrigation. For example, 10 ml of 98% sulfuric acid dissolved in 12 liters of water will decrease the pH to

10

5.0, a range which can still cause injury. If the chemical composition is known (acid or base), monitoring of the spent lavage solution pH will give a good indication of lavage effectiveness and completion. A good rule of thumb is to lavage with 15-20 liters of tap water or more for significant chemical injuries. The lavage site should be kept drained in order to remove the earlier, more concentrated effluent. Care should be taken to drain away from uninjured areas to avoid further exposure.

All patients should be monitored according to the severity of their injuries. They may have metabolic disturbances, usually from pH abnormalities because of exposure to strong acids or caustics. If respiratory difficulty is apparent, oxygen therapy and mechanical ventilation must be instituted. Resuscitation should be guided by the body surface area involved (burn formulas); however, the total fluid needs may be dramatically different from the calculated volumes. Some of these injuries may be more superficial than they appear, particularly in the case of acids, and therefore will require less resuscitation volume. Injuries from bases, however, may penetrate beyond that which is apparent on exam and therefore will require more volume. For this reason, patients with chemical injuries should be observed closely for signs of adequate perfusion, such as urine output. All patients with significant chemical injuries should be monitored with indwelling bladder catheters to accurately measure the outputs.

Operative debridement if indicated should take place as soon as a patient is stable and resuscitated. Following adequate lavage and debridement of those wounds treated nonoperatively, burn wounds are covered with antimicrobial agents or skin substitutes. Once the wounds have stabilized with the indicated treatment, they are taken care of as with any loss of soft tissue. Skin grafting or flap coverage are performed as needed.

SPECIFIC CHEMICALS

ALKALI

Alkalies such as lime, potassium hydroxide, bleach, and sodium hydroxide are among the most common agents involved in chemical injury. Accidental injury frequently occurs in infants and toddlers exploring cleaning cabinets. There are three factors involved in the mechanism of alkali burns: 1) saponification of fat causes the loss of insulation of heat formed in the chemical reaction with tissue; 2) massive extraction of water from cells causes damage because of alkali's hygroscopic nature; and 3) alkalis dissolve and combine with the proteins of the tissues to form alkaline proteinates, which are soluble and contain hydroxide ions. These ions induce further chemical reactions, penetrating deeper into the tissue.[2] Treatment involves immediate removal of the causative agent with lavage of large volumes of fluid, usually water. Attempts to neutralize alkali agents with weak acids are not recommended, because the heat released by neutralization reactions induces further injury. Particularly strong bases should be treated with lavage and consideration of wound debridement in the operating room. Tangential removal of affected areas is performed until the tissues removed are at a normal pH.

Cement

Cement (calcium oxide) burns are frequent, and they are usually work-related. Such a burn is similar to an alkali injury, and the critical substance responsible for the skin damage is the hydroxyl ion.[3] Oftentimes, the agent has been in contact with the skin for prolonged periods, such as underneath the boots of a cement worker who seeks treatment hours after the exposure, or after the cement penetrates clothing and when combined with perspiration induces an exothermic reaction. Treatment consists of removing all clothing and irrigating the affected area with water and soap until all the cement is removed and the effluent has a pH of less than 8. Injuries tend to be deep because of exposure times, and surgical excision and grafting of the resultant eschar may be required.

Acids

Acid injuries are treated initially like any other chemical injury, with removal of all chemicals by disrobing the affected area and copious irrigation. Acids induce protein breakdown by hydrolysis, which results in a hard eschar that does not penetrate as deeply as the alkalis. These agents also induce thermal injury by heat generation with contact of the skin, further causing soft tissue damage. Some acids have added effects, such as calcium chelation by phosphoric and hydrofluoric acid. Common acids causing injuries and their mechanisms of action are listed below in Table 10.1.

Table 10.1. Common acids and their peculiarities

Acid	Uses and Mechanism of Action
Acetic Acid	Glacial acetic acid is the 100% form, the 5% form is known as vinegar, typical acid burn
Chromic Acid	Metal cleaner in a strong sulfuric acid solution, typical acid burn
Dichromate Salts	Corrosive agents, surgical debridement should be entertained (lethal dose 50 mg/kg)
Hydrochloric Acid	Typical acid burn, fumes can cause a pneumonitis
Muriatic Acid	Commercial grade hydrochloric acid
Nitric Acid	Strong acid, can form organo-nitrate compounds
Oxalic Acid	Binds calcium salts, treat like a hydrofluoric acid burn
Phosphoric Acid	Binds calcium salts, treat like a hydrofluoric acid burn
Sulfosalicylic Acid	Typical acid burn, systemic absorption may cause renal and hepatic toxicity
Sulfuric Acid	Typical strong acid burn
Tannic Acid	Typical acid burn, systemic absorption may cause renal and hepatic toxicity
Trichloroacetic Acid	Typical acid burn, systemic absorption may cause renal and hepatic toxicity

10

FORMIC ACID

Formic acid injuries are relatively rare, usually involving an organic acid used for industrial descaling and as a hay preservative.[4] Electrolyte abnormalities are of great concern for patients who have sustained extensive formic acid injuries, with metabolic acidosis, renal failure, intravascular hemolysis, and pulmonary complications (ARDS) common.[5] Acidemia detected by a metabolic acidosis on arterial blood gas analysis should be corrected with intravenous sodium bicarbonate. Hemodialysis may be required when extensive absorption of formic acid has occurred. Mannitol diuresis is required if severe hemolysis occurs after deep injury. A formic acid wound typically has a greenish appearance, and is deeper than what it initially appears to be; it is best treated by surgical excision.

HYDROFLUORIC ACID

Hydrofluoric acid is a toxic substance used widely in both industrial and domestic settings, and is the strongest inorganic acid known. Management of these burns differs from other acid burns in general. Hydrofluoric acid produces dehydration and corrosion of tissue with free hydrogen ions. In addition, the fluoride ion complexes with bivalent cations such as calcium and magnesium to form insoluble salts. Systemic absorption of the fluoride ion then can induce intravascular calcium chelation and hypocalcemia, which causes life-threatening arrhythmias. Beyond initial copious irrigation with clean water, the burned area should be treated immediately with copious 2.5% calcium gluconate gel. These wounds in general are very painful because of the calcium chelation and associated potassium release. This finding can be used to determine the effectiveness of treatment. The gel should be changed at 15-minute intervals until the pain subsides, an indication of removal of the active fluoride ion. If pain relief is incomplete after several applications or symptoms recur, intradermal injections of 10% calcium gluconate (0.5 ml/cm² affected), and/or intra-arterial calcium gluconate into the affected extremity may be required to alleviate symptoms. If the burn is not treated in such a fashion, decalcification of the bone underlying the injury and extension of the soft tissue injury may occur.

All patients with hydrofluoric acid burns should be admitted with electrical cardiogram monitoring, with particular attention to prolongation of the QT interval. Twenty ml of 10% calcium gluconate solution should be added to the first liter of resuscitation fluid,[6] and serum electrolytes must be closely monitored. Any EKG changes require a rapid response by the treatment team with intravenous calcium chloride to maintain heart function. Several grams of calcium may be required in the end until the chemical response has run its course. Serum magnesium and potassium also should be closely monitored and replaced. Speed is the key to effective treatment of this chemical injury.

HYDROCARBONS

The organic solvent properties of hydrocarbons promote cell membrane dissolution and skin necrosis. Symptoms present with erythema and blistering, and the burns are typically superficial and heal spontaneously. If absorbed systemically, toxicity can produce respiratory depression and eventual hepatic injury thought to be associated with benzenes. Ignition of the hydrocarbons on the skin induces a deep full-thickness injury.

ELECTRICAL INJURY

Three to five percent of all admitted burned patients are injured from electrical contact. Electrical injury is unlike other burn injuries as the visible areas of tissue necrosis represent only a small portion of the destroyed tissue. Electrical current enters a part of the body, such as the fingers or hand, and proceeds through tissues with the lowest resistance to current, generally the nerves, blood vessels, and muscles. The skin has a relatively high resistance to electrical current, and is therefore mostly spared. The current then leaves the body at a "grounded" area, typically the foot. Heat generated by the transfer of electrical current and passage of the current itself injures the tissues. During this exchange, the bone is a sink for the generated heat from the surrounding muscle and serves as a source of additional and continued thermal damage in the ensuing moments. Blood vessels transmitting much of the electricity initially remain patent, but may proceed down a path of progressive thrombosis as the cells either die or repair themselves. For these reasons, most of the damaged tissue is not visible.

Injuries are divided into high and low voltage injuries. Low voltage injury is similar to thermal injury without transmission to the deeper tissues and exhibits zones of injury from the surface extending into the tissue.[7] Most household currents (110-220 volts) produce this type of injury, which only causes local damage. The worst of these injuries are those involving the edge of the mouth (oral commissure) sustained by children gnawing on household electrical cords.

The syndrome of high voltage injury consists of varying degrees of cutaneous burn at the entry and exit sites combined with hidden destruction of deep tissue.[8,9] Oftentimes, these patients will also have cutaneous burns associated with ignition of clothing from the discharge of electrical current. Initial evaluation may consist of cardiopulmonary resuscitation from induced ventricular fibrillation; thus if the initial electrocardiogram (ECG) findings are abnormal or there is a history of cardiac arrest associated with the injury, continued cardiac monitoring is necessary along with pharmacological treatment for any dysrhythmias.[10] The most serious derangements occur in the first 24 h after injury. If patients with electrical injuries have no cardiac dysrhythmias on initial ECG or history of cardiac arrest, no further monitoring is necessary.

Patients with electrical injuries are at risk for other injuries associated with being thrown from the electrical jolt, or from falls from heights in an effort to disengage from the electrical current. In addition, the violent tetanic muscular contractions which result from alternating current sources may cause a variety of fractures and dislocations.[11] These patients should be assessed as would any patients

10

with blunt traumatic injuries. Intra-abdominal injuries with bowel disruption are also reported with high-voltage injuries; therefore attention to this possible complication should take place.

The key to managing patients with an electrical injury lies in the treatment of the wound. The most significant injury is within the deep tissue, and subsequent edema formation can cause vascular compromise to any area distal to the injury. Assessment should include circulation to distal vascular beds, as immediate escharotomy and fasciotomy may be required. Should the muscle compartment be extensively injured and necrotic such that the prospects for eventual function are dismal, early amputation may be necessary. We advocate early exploration of affected muscle beds and debridement of devitalized tissues, with attention to the deeper periosteous planes, as this is the area with continued damage from the heated bones. Fasciotomies should be complete, and may require nerve decompressions, such as carpal tunnel and Guyon's canal releases. Tissue that has questionable viability should be left in place, with planned re-exploration in 48 h. Many such re-explorations may be required until the wound is completely debrided.

After the devitalized tissues are removed, closure of the wound becomes paramount. Although skin grafts will suffice as closure for most wounds, flaps may offer a better alternative, particularly with exposed bones and tendons. Even exposed and superficially infected bones and tendons can be salvaged with coverage by vascular tissue. Early involvement by reconstructive surgeons versed in the various methods of wound closure is optimal.

Muscle damage results in release of hemochromogens (myoglobin), which are filtered in the glomeruli and may result in obstructive nephropathy. Therefore, vigorous hydration and infusion of intravenous sodium bicarbonate (5% continuous infusion) and mannitol (25 gms every 6 h for adults) are indicated to solubilize the hemochromogens and maintain urine output if significant amounts are found in the serum. These patients also will require additional intravenous volumes over predicted amounts based on the wound area because most of the wound is deep, and cannot be assessed by standard physical examination. In this situation, urine output should be maintained at 2 cc/kg/h.

DELAYED EFFECTS

Neurological deficits may occur. Serial neurological evaluations should be performed as part of routine examination in order to detect any early or late neuropathology. Central nervous system effects such as cortical encephalopathy, hemiplegia, aphasia, and brain stem dysfunction injury have been reported up to 9 months after injury,[12] and others report delayed peripheral nerve lesions characterized by demyelination with vacuolization and reactive gliosis. Another devastating long term effect is the development of cataracts, which can be delayed for several years. These complications may occur in up to 30% of patients with significant high-voltage injury, and patients should be made aware of their possibility even with the best treatment.

SUMMARY

Chemical and electrical injuries represent a challenge to the treating surgeons, with some deviations from typical burn care as described above. The long-term goals, however, remain the same. Namely, timely intervention to save life and limb, followed by efforts to maximize functional and cosmetic outcome.

REFERENCES

1. Fitzpatrick KT, Moylan JA. Emergency care of chemical burns. Postgrad Med 1985, 78:189-194.
2. Mozingo D, Smith A, McManus W, Pruitt B, Mason A. Chemical burns. J Trauma 1990, 28(5):642-647.
3. Pike J, Patterson A, Aarons MS. Chemistry of cement burns: Pathogenesis and treatment. JCBR 1988, 9:258-260.
4. Sigurdsson J, Bjornsson A, Gudmundsson ST. Formic acid burn local and systemic effects: Report of a case. Burns 1983, 9:358-361.
5. Naik RB, Stephens WP, Wilson DJ et al. Ingestion of formic acid-containing agents: Report of three fatal cases. Postgrad Med J 1980, 56:451-4552.
6. Trevino MA, Herrmann GH, Sprout WL. Treatment of severe hydrofluoric acid exposures. J Occup Med 1983, 25:861-863.
7. Laberge LC, Ballard PA, Daniel RK. Experimental electric burns: Low voltage. Ann Plast Surg 1984; 13:185-190.
8. Robson MC, Hayward PG, Heggers JP. The role of arachidonic acid metabolism in electrical injury. In: Lee RC, Burke JP eds. Electrical Trauma: Pathophysiology and Clinical Management. Cambridge University Press 1992, 179-188.
9. Robson MC, Murphy RC, Heggers JP. A new explanation for the progressive tissue loss in electrical injuries. Plast Recon Surg 1984; 73:431-437.
10. Robson MC, Smith DJ. Care of the thermal injured victim. In: Jurkiewicz MJ, Krizek TJ, Mathes SJ, Ariyan S eds. Plastic Surgery: Principles and Practice. St. Louis: CV Mosby Co. 1990, 1355-1410.
11. Robson MC, Krizek TJ, Wray RC. Care of the thermally injured patient. In: Zuidema GD, Rutherford RB, Ballinger WF, eds. The Management of Trauma. Philadelphia: WB Saunders, 1979: 666-730.
12. Christensen JA, Sherman RT, Balis GA, Waumett JD. Delayed neurologic injury secondary to high voltage injury with recovery. J Trauma 1980; 20:166-168.
13. Monafo WW, Freedman BM. Electrical and lightning injury. In: Bostwick JA ed. The Art and Science of Burn Care. Rockville: Aspen Publishers Inc 1987: 241-254.

10

Burn Reconstruction

Juan P. Barret

The severity of injury and deformity from burns ranges from relatively minor to severe. Nevertheless, even minor disfigurements can have severe psychological and social impact on the victim. The basic concerns are for function, comfort and appearance. Normal and hypertrophic scarring, scar contracture, loss of parts of the body and change in color and texture of injured skin are processes common and unique to all burned patients. The burn surgeon has to prevent and minimize deformity, fight the loss of function and restore normality when possible.

Plastic surgery patients expect the results of surgical treatment to be aesthetically pleasing as well as functionally correct. This is also true for burn patients. More than anyone else, their expectations as to what they want and desire are far beyond the real possibilities of the state of the art techniques available.

As in the acute phase, a realistic approach solves later disappointments and misunderstandings. An informed patient can understand the basis of the problem and ask for reality.

Burn reconstruction starts when the patient is admitted in the acute phase and lasts until the patient's expectations have been reached and/or there is nothing else to offer. However, it is normally a life commitment, and, although there may be no other possibilities at that point, the patient-surgeon relationship still continues (see Table 11.1).

ACUTE MANAGEMENT OF BURNS

Preventing of and minimizing scarring in burn patients starts during the acute phase. Reducing the inflammatory and catabolic response after burn injury by a team approach and early closure of the wound is paramount to control wound healing in these patients. Early excision and grafting of deep partial thickness

---

Burn Care, edited by Steven E. Wolf and David N. Herndon. © 1999 Landes Bioscience

---

Table 11.1. Characteristics of burn reconstructive plastic surgery

---

1. Start at acute period
2. Strong patient-surgeon relationship
3. Development of a "master plan"

Table 11.2. Techniques useful in the acute phase to diminish reconstructive needs

---

1. Use of darts in escharotomies when crossing joints
2. Use sheet grafts when possible
3. Place seams following skin tension lines
4. Place grafts transversely over joints
5. Use aesthetic units to the face and hands with medium thickness split skin grafts
6. Use of splints, face masks and silicone inserts as soon as possible
7. Early pressure therapy
8. Early ambulation and exercise

---

wounds and full thickness wounds is, generally, the only way to control scarring. The final result, though, is always unpredictable, as individual factors are difficult to predict and control.

It is preferable that the surgeon managing the acute injury will be responsible for later reconstruction. If this is not the case, the reconstructive surgeon should be consulted early on so that the needs for reconstruction enter into the plan of the acute care.

Neck, oral and joint splints can prevent deformities. Good planning of face grafts, extensive use of sheet grafts in all locations when possible and the presence of living dermis during burn excision and grafting are of paramount importance. On the other hand, bearing in mind the future reconstructive needs of the patient helps to spare important areas for use as donor sites in the acute phase. Having, for instance, a neck with normal, unscarred skin helps in resurfacing the face with expanded tissue.

Different procedures are important during the acute phase to minimize later reconstruction (see Table 11.2). Grafting the face with medium thickness skin grafts in aesthetic units is of extreme importance to resemble a normal appearance once mature scars in the area are present. Linear escharotomies should be avoided, and darts, which help to break the direction of the incision (see Fig. 11.1) when crossing joints, help to prevent linear hypertrophic scarring. Similarly, only the dermis has to be incised when performing them. Fat does not produce a tight compartment syndrome. If excessive pressure is still present after the escharotomy has been performed, a closed blunt fasciotomy through a small incision should be considered.

Graft seams should follow skin tension lines so that they resemble normal wrinkles or folds. They should be longitudinal in the limbs, and grafts on the

Fig. 11.1. Escharotomy to the ulnar aspect of the right arm. Note that the incision follows a dart shape when crossing the joint in order to avoid linear hypertrophic scarring.

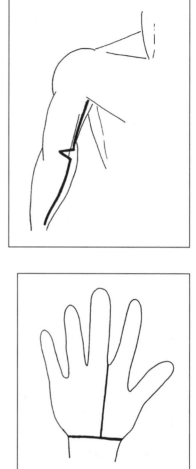

Fig. 11.2. Positioning skin grafts following the longitudinal axis of the hand prevents an unpleasant and troublesome scar over the knuckles. The hand has to be grafted in the functional position to minimize scar contracture and maximize function.

11

joints must be placed transversely, perpendicular to the axis of the limb. This maneuver avoids linear scars extending over and beyond joints.

Medium split thickness skin grafts give a good appearance on grafted hands. It is the author's belief that grafts should be placed following the axis of the limb, with a seam placed between the second and third metacarpal bones (see Fig. 11.2). In this way, the grafts extend from the dorsum of the hand to the fingers, and there is only one longitudinal scar extending to the second web space. Grafting the dorsum of the hand as a complete unit renders an unsightly and unpleasant scar over the knuckles.

Splints, face masks, silicone gel sheets, early pressure therapy, ambulation and skeletal traction and fixation are also of great importance to produce the best result and to avoid future operations.

Burn trauma requires aggressive rehabilitation to prevent debilitating deformities. Burn distribution as well as burn depth is a good predictor of rehabilitation outcome. Prevention of burn deformities includes proper positioning with or without splints, exercise to maintain joint range of motion, maintenance of muscle strength and muscle tone and early mobilization. All the above is also true not only for the acute period but also for the reconstructive period.

Burn patients tend to assume the position of comfort, which is many times responsible for deformities that require reconstructive surgery (see Table 11.3). Positioning in bed is then one of the most important ways to prevent them (see Table 11.4). Exercise reduces edema, maintains joint motion and strength, reduces scars and maintains development. Ambulation can begin as soon as the patient is deemed medically stable with wounds properly dressed and doubly wrapped.

Positioning and splinting affects many problems in the care of burned patients. Splints are used for either immobilization or mobilization by using static and dynamic splints. Initially splints are used at all times except for exercise and immediately postop during the immobilization period. As active range of motion increases and is maintained, protocol changes to night-only splinting. Skeletal traction and fixation are used also on a limited basis to prevent and correct burn scar contracture formation, always tailored to the patient's needs.

Table 11.3. Position of comfort after burn trauma (to be avoided)

1. Neck flexion
2. Shoulder protraction
3. Elbow flexion
4. Metacarpal extension
5. Interphalangeal flexion
6. Wrist flexion
7. Hip flexion
8. Knee flexion
9. Ankle plantar flexion

Table 11.4. Prevention of deformity: positioning in bed

1. Maintain straight alignment of the trunk and neck
2. Neck should be in slight extension
3. Arms should be elevated in the neutral plane or in line with the glenoid at approximately 15-20° of horizontal flexion and 80° of abduction
4. Elbow should be in full extension
5. Hand should be in the intrinsic plus position with the thumb in flexion and abduction
6. Hips should be in extension and abduction
7. Knees should be in full extension
8. Foot should be in neutral position and 90° or greater dorsiflexion

11

TIME OF RECONSTRUCTION

It has been proposed that definitive correction of burn scarring should be delayed for one year or longer after healing. It is certainly true that inaesthetic and ugly scars mature over time and with the effect of pressure and splints many of them do not require surgery once the acute phase of scar maturation has taken place. Patience, many times, is the best tool of the reconstructive surgeon.

Even though the former is in general true, there are certain procedures that must be addressed before the golden period of scar maturation is over. When considering burn reconstruction, there are procedures that are urgent, others that are essential and many that are desirable. It is in the latter that the patient-surgeon relationship, negotiation with the patient and a good rapport is necessary (see Table 11.5).

Urgent procedures are those in which the golden period of scar maturation does not apply, when it is absolutely certain that an operation is needed and noble structures are exposed or are severely damaged. Urgent procedures are to be planned to correct function that are not suitable amenable to treatments, often because time is of the essence. An eyelid release to protect an exposed cornea, correction of distracted or entrapped neurovascular bundles, severe fourth degree contractures and severe microstomia fall into this group. Intense rehabilitation, splinting and pressure therapy are mandatory after correction of these deformities. Normally, skin grafts are necessary, since scars are very immature and flaps may be at risk of complications at this time.

Essential procedures are those in which, although they are not urgent and important structures or the overall health of the patient is not challenged, an early operation may improve the late appearance and the rehabilitation of the patient. At first, the deformity should be addressed nonoperatively. If this approach does not lead to the appropriate results, an operation may be considered. In this section fall all burn scar contractures that do not respond to rehabilitation and hypertrophic scarring and contractures that prevent the patient from eating, bathing, moving, and performing activities of daily living.

Table 11.5. Timing burn reconstructive surgery

---

1. Urgent procedures
   - Exposure of noble structures (e.g., eyelid releases)
   - Entrapment or compression of neurovascular bundles
   - Fourth degree contractures
   - Severe microstomia
2. Essential procedures
   - Reconstruction of function (e.g., limited range of motion)
   - Progressive deformities not correctable by ordinary methods
3. Desirable procedures
   - Reconstruction of passive areas
   - Aesthetics

Finally, we have the desirable reconstructive needs. Most of the problems fall into this category. These are very often aesthetic problems and scar contractures that, although not prominent, produce great discomfort to the patient. Many of the problems disappear in the first two years postburn with appropriate care. These are the problems that benefit most from patience and time. Many important deformities seen a few months postburn, that would require extensive surgery, improve with time, and can be treated with simple or less extensive procedures later on. The author has found that in all desirable reconstructive procedures, it is a good practice to wait until all red and immature scars have disappeared before starting any kind of surgery. Many times an early operation is an unnecessary operation under these circumstances.

Many factors other than scar maturation, however, affect the decision of when to operate on burn scars. Psychological and socioeconomic factors are very important when making a decision. The patient's mood plays an important role, since an unmotivated or depressed patient will not cooperate. Moreover, operating on such a patient may produce discomfort and discouragement, which, eventually, can diminish the patient's compliance and prevent further reconstruction. The social status of the patient is also of great relevance. Emotional support received from friends, family and co-workers are important, as is his economic status. When making a plan, all these particular circumstances need to be taken into account.

PATIENT-SURGEON RELATIONSHIP

Burn patients, among all plastic surgery patients, need more care and a good relationship with their surgeon. The relationship is normally a long lasting one, many times extending for a lifetime. Patients require a surgeon's professional expertise, but also time, a good dose of optimism and compassion. Many times the patient-surgeon relationship starts in the acute phase when the plastic surgeon acts as the primary burn surgeon. Other times, the physician, at some point in the patient's recovery, refers him/her to the reconstructive surgeon. Nevertheless, in both situations, the initial meeting is important. At that time, the patient presents a set of complaints. The reconstructive surgeon will have to evaluate the complaints, the patient's motivation for surgery and the psychological status of the patient. We have to remember, though, that the patient will evaluate the surgeon's attitude and conduct also. As with any other kind of surgery, it is very important to know previous and current medical conditions, allergies, medications, operations and other health history. If the reconstructive surgeon has not been involved in the care of the acute injury, a complete record of the inpatient and outpatient care pertaining to the burn injury should be obtained. Also, direct contact with the referring burn surgeon is very important. The first meeting should be professional, private and unhurried. At this time the surgeon has to determine the patient's motivation and expectations. This is an extremely important point in burn plastic surgery. The patient's expectations are usually unrealistic. They expect to be normal again, and it is the surgeon's responsibility at this point to assess the chief complaints and explain to the patient the real possibilities. The patient has to understand the limitations of surgery and that first function and then cosmesis will be addressed. Although many times at the outset deformities or major problems will be apparent and ready for surgery, it is preferable to have subsequent visits before surgery, when further inquiries can be addressed and preparation for surgery can be done unhurriedly. A photographic workup is extremely important to document the case, assist in definitive preoperative planning and for documentation. Burn reconstructive surgery is normally an elective procedure; however, often different approaches may be considered before surgery. When dealing with long-term scars and burn deformities, different problems may be encountered intraoperatively that might require a complementary technique. These specific issues of burn reconstructive surgery have to be explained in detail to the patient, and the surgeon needs to foresee and include them in the preoperative planning and the informed consent so that unpleasant surprises are not encountered later.

Patients need to be reassured frequently. The reconstructive surgeon needs to know the patient's fears and feelings as the reconstructive plan goes on. Several times a burn reconstruction project involves more than 10 operations, many clinic visits and often a long time to make a final assessment. The latter, in the case of a small child, may be more than 18 years. The patient's feelings and impressions must be addressed continuously, and any trouble, minor disappointment or depression detected early on and treated as needed. The author has found it very helpful to maintain contact with the psychology team that worked with the patient in the acute phase. Patients know, then, that they are available any time help is needed. If this approach is not possible, finding a reliable and affordable source for psychology support for patients is advisable.

Despite our best efforts, however, some patients ask to stop the reconstructive process before all treatments and planned operations are performed. Patients become more realistic as time and surgery go by, and sometimes they decide to cancel future operations. If a good patient-surgeon relationship has been achieved, many times this is just a small "honeymoon" for a patient that has been involved with surgery for the last years. Most of them return to the office to continue the process and achieve all possible reconstruction when their enthusiasm renews.

BURN RECONSTRUCTIVE VISIT: DEVELOPMENT OF A MASTER PLAN

As noted before, a complete record of the acute hospitalization should be obtained when possible. A thorough history and physical examination must be obtained. Quality and color of the skin in the affected areas must be noted: abnormal scars, hyper- or hypopigmentation, contractures, atrophy and open wounds. Function has to be addressed next; all involved joints are examined and range of motion noted. Any scar contracture extending beyond joints has to be defined also. Next, skeletal deformities have to be addressed. Many times scar contractures distort joints and the body maintains an abnormal position to overcome the deformity. This is particularly true in children; the effect of traction on a growing joint and bone can create long term deformities. In children, and in all patients whose injuries were produced in childhood, a complete X-ray workup must be obtained to examine the status of bones and joints. In severe restriction of function, an X-ray must be obtained also to rule out heterotopic calcification.

The needs for physiotherapy, occupational therapy and pressure garments have to be considered at this time. Also, if any of these devices are to be needed after the operation, the patient has to be referred to the rehabilitation department. Finally, an inventory of all possible sites for donor tissue is made.

Once patients have expressed all their chief complaints and a thorough examination of the patient is done, a master plan is developed. All reconstructive possibilities are discussed with the patient, and timing and order of such procedures is outlined. Negotiation is the key point during this period. Many times what is most evident and most unpleasant for a patient is one of the last problems to be addressed by the master plan. All important points and pitfalls are explained to the patient. The importance of addressing all urgent, essential and functional problems first has to be understood by the patient. This is very important, since the patient can be extremely upset when important cosmetic problems are disregarded at the beginning and, on the other hand, other not such serious problems (to them) are addressed first.

On developing a master plan it is important to start the reconstruction with a "winner" for the first procedure. A small and easy operation, with few possible complications and evident and quick improvement to the patient's appearance, such as an excision of a small hypertrophic scar on the face or a simple Z-plasty of an unpleasant scar contracture are important procedures that can show the patients what can be achieved with reconstructive surgery and encourage them to carry on with the master plan. More complex and difficult operations are started later, with an enthusiastic patient, since it normally takes longer for these complex operations to demonstrate definitive benefits.

Finally, it is important to perform as many procedures as possible in the preschool years in children and offer the patient multiple, simultaneous procedures. Time, effort and money are thereby best invested. The essentials of burn reconstruction are summarized in Table 11.6.

PATIENT CARE IN BURN RECONSTRUCTIVE SURGERY

Preoperative, intraoperative and postoperative care of burn reconstructive patients include all techniques and special treatments of general plastic surgery and any state of the art special plastic surgery techniques. The scope of procedures performed in burn reconstructive surgery ranges from split thickness grafts to

Table 11.6. Essentials of burn reconstruction

1	Strong patient-surgeon relationship
2	Psychological support
3	Clarify expectations
4	Explain priorities
5	Note all available donor sites
6	Start with a "winner" (easy and quick operation)
7	As many surgeries as possible in the preschool years
8	Offer multiple, simultaneous procedures
9	Reassure and support the patient

tissue expansion and microsurgery. The reader is referred to other selected readings to find more specific plastic surgery techniques.

As stated previously, a good preoperative plan is essential to avoid later surprises. The plastic surgeon operating on burn patients works most of the time with scarred and injured skin. It is important to handle with extreme care all tissues since vascularization in the area is normally altered. Patients are instructed to stop smoking for at least three weeks before surgery. All meals and drinks containing active vascular drugs need to be tapered, and any medications noted in order to stop all unnecessary drugs. The patient is instructed also to avoid medications, such as aspirin, that may increase intraoperative and postoperative bleeding. Uncontrolled hypertension, cough, nausea and disorders of coagulation need to be known by the surgeon and treated as needed, since they increase the risk of hematoma. It is always advisable that the patients present for surgery with a responsible adult who will take care of them after surgery.

The evening before surgery the patient is instructed to have the skin cleansed with bacteria-reducing soaps and a light dinner is advised. Burn patients have normally hypertrophic scarring, seams and intradermal cysts that are prone to have a high bacterial load. It is advisable, also, to include in the plan perioperative use of antistaphylococcal agents. If a skin flap or introduction of alloplastic material is to be performed, antibiotics should be continued in the postoperative period for at least two more doses. Intraoperatively, large doses of local anesthetics are to be avoided, and the extensive use of electrocoagulation is minimized since it increases the risk of necrosis of the scarred skin. Similarly, the use of subcutaneous epinephrine is limited because of the same risks. All dermal or scar edge bleeding is controlled intraoperatively with topical thrombin (1000 units/ml).

Smooth emergence from general anesthesia free of coughing and vomiting is essential in burn reconstructive surgery, as are controlling high or low blood pressure episodes, nausea and vomiting. Also, hyperactive and anxious patients may benefit from anxiolytic medication to avoid sudden and uncontrolled movements in the immediate postoperative period. Light dressings are applied after surgery, and any high pressure avoided since it can injure burned tissue. Immobilization is kept at a minimum, and passive and active range of motion are started as soon as possible in the postoperative period. It helps to avoid edema formation, congestion and recurrence of contractures. Splints, prostheses and pressure garments have to be used either immediately or early after the operation. Rehabilitation is normally part of the reconstructive master plan, so that it has to be included and started after surgery. Silicone inserts to grafted areas have been found helpful to control the early phase of scar maturation, as they apply gentle and uniform pressure to the wounds and position joints. It is also very important to have good pain control, since having a comfortable and cooperative patient helps positioning, rehabilitation and the success of any operation. Patient-assisted analgesia is the best option if the patient is able to use it. Other than that, hydrocodone and morphine are good alternatives. Anxiolytics should be considered as part of the pain control program, and the addition of anti-itching medications and anti-emetics such as diphenhydramine and droperidol are very helpful. Finally, providing the patient and family an environment that is cozy and relaxing helps them and the burn reconstructive team to cope better with the periodic admissions, decreasing fear and anxiety before every step in the progress of the reconstructive program.

SURGICAL APPROACH TO THE BURN RECONSTRUCTIVE PATIENT

Some progress has been made in burn reconstructive surgery in the last decades, although its impact is not as dramatic as in other areas of plastic surgery. Burn reconstructive surgery for many decades involved incisional or excisional releases of the affected scars and skin autografting. However, nowadays, the first approach should involve local or regional flaps. They provide new and vascularized tissue to the area, they grow in children and render the best functional and cosmetic result. These flaps can be raised either with normal skin or burn scar. Even though it is generally true that burned tissue can be congested, ischemic and necrotic, it can be used as a reliable flap if extreme care is used while raising the flap and if the injured skin is left attached to the underlying tissues. This expands burn reconstruction to new territories and techniques.

When considering the surgical approach to a burned patient, the surgeon has to ask himself what is the patient's primary complaint, what tissues are left, what parts are missing and what sort of donor sites are available. The techniques available for burn reconstruction are summarized in Table 11.7.

The chief complaint or complaints need to be carefully evaluated. If immature scars or an increasing deformity is present and there is not an urgent or essential procedure to be performed, pressure garments and occupational and physical therapy are indicated. If the deformity is stable and there is a need for reconstruction, an inventory of donor sites and priorities are to be performed. At this point, tissue deficiency has to be assessed. If there is no deficiency and local tissues can be easily mobilized, excision and direct closure or Z-plasties can be performed (see Fig. 11.3). On the other hand, if there is a deficiency in tissue, the need for reconstruction of underlying structures needs to be addressed. If the deformity

---

Table 11.7. Techniques available for burn reconstruction

---

1. Without deficiency of tissue
   • Excision and primary closure
   • Z-plasty
2. With deficiency of tissue
   • Simple reconstruction
     - Skin graft
     - Transposition flaps (Z-plasty and modifications)
   • Reconstruction of skin and underlying tissues
     - Axial and random flaps
     - Myocutaneous flaps
     - Tissue expansion
     - Free flaps

---

affects the skin and subcutaneous tissues, skin autografting, Z-plasties, and all the modifications of them, such as trident flaps, are advised (see Fig. 11.4). When reconstruction of underlying structures is necessary, flaps are considered, including direct cutaneous, musculocutaneous, expanded and free flaps. The choice is made then on a patient per patient basis. Many times, composite grafts and bone or cartilage grafts are also necessary in order to perform a complete reconstruction. The use of alloplastic materials in these circumstances is not advisable because of their tendency to extrude.

In summary, even though incisional release and skin autografting is still the technique most used in burn reconstruction, flaps should be used when possible (remember that Z-plasty and its modifications are transposition flaps). The burn reconstruction plan needs to be tailored to the individual patient and the chief complaint since some anatomic areas are best suited to specific techniques.

OVERVIEW OF BURN RECONSTRUCTION

HEAD AND NECK

Burns to the head and neck are still a challenge to the burn team. Residual deformities produce severe distortion with disfigurement and functional limitations. Bridging scars from chin to neck to anterior shoulder results in exaggerated kyphosis with neck flexion and protraction of the shoulders. Prevention of these deformities is very important to minimize later reconstruction. Neck splinting in hyperextension, pressure garments, mouth spreaders and facemasks are an important part of the acute care that affects outcome. Early excision of full thickness burns to the face and skin autografting in aesthetic units is extremely important to produce a natural appearance of the grafted face. Contractures to the eyelids are often urgent procedures that are performed before the rest of the scars are mature. The most frequent deformity is the ectropion, although more severe cases present with distraction of the canthal folds, fusion of part of the eyelids and

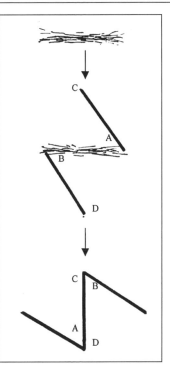

Fig. 11.3. Two-limb transposition flap ("Z-plasty"). Central limb has to be placed following the scar. All limbs must have the same length. Designing the flaps with tip angles of 60° renders the best outcome. The flaps extend the length of the linear contracture by stealing tissue laterally. Therefore, good relaxation of surrounding tissues is an asset.

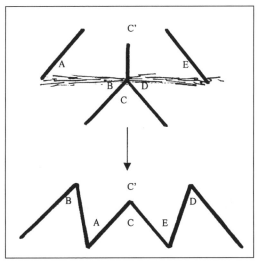

Fig. 11.4. Five-limb transposition flap ("Trident flap"). Note that two Z-plasties and a Y to V advancement flap comprise it. It is very useful when there is not much extra skin laterally to move.

distortion of the lacrimal punctate. Release of upper and lower eyelid contractures has to be performed separately, with undermining of the surrounding tissues. Full thickness grafts are most suitable for lower eyelids where stability is the goal, while split thickness skin autografts are used for upper eyelids to improve mobility. Microstomia is another deformity encountered in facial burns. It can interfere with basic function such as nourishment and speaking. Lip ectropions and deformity of commissures are common. Skin grafts are most suitable for the former, but local flaps are better for the latter problem. Small deformities to the lips, however, can be solved many times with patient-tailored local flaps. The nose is a prominent focus on the face, since it is an aesthetic landmark. Different degrees of deformities can be found in this area. Subtotal destruction of the nose and tip can be restored with a forehead flap, with or without previous expansion. In these situations, support of the nasal tip area needs to be provided, and for that purpose mucocartilaginous flaps from the nasal septum or helical rim composite grafts are of benefit. In less severe deformities, local flaps and composite grafts are the techniques of choice. Other passive deformities include ear deformities. Ear reconstruction in burned patients can be done with rib cartilage grafts. If there is no suitable subcutaneous pocket, a superficial temporalis fascial flap can be used to provide the framework, with a split thickness skin graft on top. Other times, tissue expansion to the retroauricular area can be performed prior to the creation of a rib cartilage framework.

Neck contractures are deformities that affect function and normal living. Generally, they have to be addressed before any passive reconstruction to the face is started. It is also advisable that in the presence of a concomitant lower lip ectropion, a neck release is performed first, and the remainder of the lip ectropion addressed later, if it is still present. Many times the lower lip ectropion is caused by severe neck contracture, and after correction the lip contraction subsides or is minimized. When neck contractures are present and do not respond to physiotherapy, an early operation is advised. Localized bands are best treated with local flaps, but more severe contractures require incisional or excisional release, depending of the extension of the deformity and skin autografting. Silicone inserts and neck splinting are essential to prevent recurrences.

BURN ALOPECIA

One of the areas where the effects of the burn injury are most noticeable is the scalp. Healing of deep partial and full thickness burns very often lead to areas of scalp alopecia. This produces an important psychological impact on the patient since it affects self-esteem and image. Small areas of patchy alopecia can be effectively treated with excision and direct closure; however, tissue expansion is still the gold standard of treatment for burn alopecia. McCauley et al classified burn scalp alopecia in terms of the pattern and the extension (see Table 11.8). This classification has proved very useful in our approach. Patchy burn alopecia extending across the entire scalp or total alopecia are not suitable for reconstruction. On the other hand, alopecia extending to up to 50% of the scalp can be corrected with single expansion and closure, whereas larger areas of alopecia or different concomitant segments of alopecia can be managed with sequential expansion. Many times overinflation of the expander is necessary, and it is important to bear in mind that expanded tissue normally contracts 20%. Care of these patients is similar to any patients undergoing tissue expansion.

UPPER EXTREMITY

Hypertrophic scars and contractures to the upper extremity promote the position of comfort: protraction and adduction of the shoulder, elbow in flexion and the "burned hand position": wrist in flexion, metacarpophalangeal extension, interphalangeal flexion and first metacarpal extension and adduction. Overall appearance of the hand is that of a "claw deformity". Many of these problems can be prevented with splinting and the arm elevated in the neutral plane or in line with the glenoid at approximately 15-20° of horizontal flexion and 80° of abduction, elbow in full extension and hand in the intrinsic plus position with thumb in flexion and abduction.

Linear contractures to the shoulder can be addressed with local flaps. Many times four and five flap Z-plasties are very useful. When the contracture extends to all or nearly all the axilla, incisional release and autografting is preferable, although regional rotational flaps can be used if available. It has to be noted, however, that a contracture of the axilla cannot be released at the same time a neck release is performed since it is not possible to maintain correct neck hyperextension while abducting the shoulders in the postoperative period. The neck needs to be addressed first, followed by the shoulder release, allowing a perfect result in each operation.

Contractures to the elbow normally include flexion deformity, which is best addressed with local Z-plasties or, when not possible, incisional release and autografting. It must be noted, however, that heterotopic calcification has to be ruled out when dealing with limitation of extension.

The most common deformities of the hand are wrist and dorsal contractures **11** with extension, web space contractures and boutonniere deformities. Extension deformity to the wrist and dorsum of the hand normally requires an incisional release and autografting, whereas web space contractures are best reconstructed with local flaps. Sometimes a skin autograft is necessary to add length to the reconstruction of the linear contractures. Boutonniere deformities need reconstruction of the extensor mechanism. If contracture to the palmar surface coexists, a

---

Table 11.8. Classification of burn alopecia (after McCauley et al)

Type 1: Single alopecia segment
    - A, less than 25%
    - B, 25-50%
    - C, 50-75%
    - D, 75%
Type 2: Multiple alopecia segments amenable for tissue expansion
Type 3: Patchy burn alopecia
Type 4: Total alopecia

---

full thickness graft or a cross finger flap is necessary. Extensor tendon destruction or adhesions are normally treated with tenolysis, and, if tendon repair is necessary, a flap must be considered. Finger transfers, thumb lengthening and internal and external fixation are to be considered in severe and selected cases.

One of the most important parts of the reconstruction of the burned hand is the rehabilitation plan. It must be started as soon as the skin coverage is stable. Pressure therapy, web spacers and night splints are necessary to achieve the expected results.

LOWER EXTREMITY

Severe burns to the lower extremity can be a source of morbidity. Deformity to the feet can affect gait. Severe destruction may even prevent standing. A good and durable skin coverage must be supplied to these areas in order to improve weight bearing and gait. Good acute care can prevent some of the deformities to this area. Excision and grafting to all full thickness burns with early ambulation and physical therapy are important to prevent them. When in bed, feet should be in the neutral position and 90° or greater dorsiflexion. Orthopedic shoes and metatarsal bars are helpful in positioning foot burns in infants and small children.

Hip flexion is the position of deformity for burns that extend from the abdomen to the thigh. Bilateral symmetric involvement results in increased lordosis and/or knee flexion. Knee burns, whether anterior or posterior, most often impose knee flexion.

The most common deformity to the foot and ankle occurring in deep burns is equinovarus deformity. It includes ankle in equinus, hind-foot inversion and fore-foot varus and equinus. Intrinsic deformities of the foot occur from extreme extension of the toes from dorsal foot burns. Rocker bottom foot occurs when both anterior and posterior scars are present.

Linear scars to the lower extremity should be treated with local transposition flaps when possible. If wide scar bands extend over and beyond the joints, incisional release and autografting is performed. Equinovarus deformity is first addressed with serial casting of the involved area. When this technique is not effective, release and coverage with local flaps or autografts is advised. Severe and long term deformities benefit from the Ilizarov technique to reverse burn scar contracture.

Intrinsic deformities to the foot include dorsal deformity of the toes and shortening of the transverse and longitudinal axis. These are normally best treated with transverse burn scar releases and skin autografting with extension of the incision to the longitudinal axis if restoration of the normal transverse arch is needed. Web contractures to the toes are approached as in the burned hand. Internal fixation of the toes is sometimes needed when severe subluxation of the metatarsal-phalangeal joint is present.

SUMMARY

Burn patients are an important challenge to the reconstructive surgeon. Reconstruction starts the first day after the initial injury and may last for a lifetime. Proper acute care and prompt rehabilitation diminish later reconstructive problems. A close patient-physician relationship is essential to render the best ultimate outcome. The reconstructive surgeon becomes at the same time friend, counselor and physician. All plastic surgery techniques are applicable to burn reconstruction, but they need to be tailored to the individual. Finally, extreme care on handling tissues and conscientious postoperative care are essential to optimize the results.

Burn survivors deserve all the admiration and respect from all health care professionals involved in their care. A strong commitment from the reconstructive surgeon is essential.

SELECTED READINGS

1. Total Burn Care. Herndon DN, ed. Saunders. London 1996.
2. Patient care in Plastic Surgery. 2nd edition. In: Barrett BM Jr., ed. St. Louis: Mosby 1996.
3. Operative techniques in plastic and reconstructive surgery. Face burns: Acute care and reconstruction. In: Engrav LH, Donelan MB. Saunders May 1997.
4. Plastic Surgery. Volume 3 The Face, Part 2. McCarthy JG ed. Philadelphia: Saunders 1990.
5. Burn reconstruction. In: Achauer BM ed. New York: Thieme 1991.
6. Inventory of potential reconstructive needs in the patient with burns. In: Brou JA, Robson MC, McCauley RL. J Burn Care Rehabil 1989; 10:555-560.

11

Daily Work

Steven E. Wolf, Art Sanford

The following is included as a description of daily tasks that take place in our burn units. Topics such as the process of daily rounds and caring for wounds will be discussed. They are intended as guidelines for the care of burn patients.

PATIENT ADMISSION

HISTORY AND PHYSICAL

You have learned how to obtain a medical history and physical assessment skills in medical school. Be thorough. In burned patients, a couple of points should be emphasized. Patient evaluation includes an AMPLE history: allergies, medications, preexisting illness, last meal, and the events of the injury including time, location, and concomitant results. A history of loss of consciousness is sought. When, where, and how did the injury occur? With children, stories that do not match the injuries are suspicious for child abuse. What time did the burn occur? What was the initial treatment, including any narcotics or sedation that was administered and resuscitation at an outlying center? What is the immunization status, particularly for tetanus. For electrical injuries, the voltage that caused the injury is documented. For chemical injuries, the type of chemical and the duration from the injury are noted.

WOUND ASSESSMENT

An accurate initial description of the wounds, including depth assessment and extent of injury is accurately documented, preferably on a cartoon of the body (see figures in wound management chapter). If forms cannot be found, this may be drawn in the progress notes. Treatment that has been administered including the type of dressing and any escharotomies and fasciotomies are recorded. The wounds are gently debrided under sedation or anesthesia if necessary. Blisters are removed during this process. After complete evaluation, consultation is made with the responsible faculty, with a decision for the wound treatment. This is generally done with either topical antimicrobials, or a biologic/synthetic dressing. If topical antimicrobials are chosen, silvadine with mycostatin is generally the choice except

12

for the face, which should have neomycin/mycostatin. Ears are treated with sulfamyalon to prevent chondritis.

ADMISSION ORDERS

These are tailored for the burn size. In general, this will require a burn size calculation to guide resuscitation volume. For those with other trauma, x-rays and CT scans may be needed. All special procedures such as CT scans or arteriograms require a progress note describing their necessity. Tetanus prophylaxis is given as appropriate. Major injuries (> 30% TBSA) receive empiric antibiotics to cover staphylococcus and gram-negative organisms. Hypothermia should be avoided by limiting body exposure and warming the patient's room. Comfort measures including sedatives and analgesics are given after the initial assessment. Nutritional support is given immediately, either by mouth for minor burns (milk, Resource®) or via a nasoenteric tube for major burns. For those who are mechanically ventilated, attention must be made to the ventilator settings, particularly in the setting of inhalation injury. Serial exams of the vascular and neurologic status of extremities that are at risk are made. Elevation of injured limbs with topical collagenases can be used for marginally "tight" limbs that do not clearly require escharotomy. Labs including a blood count and electrolytes are drawn daily for the immediate phase of care. Consults for physical and occupational therapy, nutrition, respiratory therapy, psychiatry, photography, and social work are placed for all patients at admission. A list of medications and their recommended doses are included in Table 12.1.

DAILY ROUNDS

Rounds with the burn team are made daily at 7:00 AM. All burn wounds are inspected unless there was a recent operation. In general, the operative dressings are removed on postoperative day 3 down to the fine mesh gauze. Clinical circumstances may dictate that the wounds be inspected earlier at the discretion of the senior physician. All wounds are completely exposed on postoperative day 4. Donor sites are exposed on the day of the operation after arrival to the hospital room or on postoperative day 1, and are available for daily inspection thereafter. Wounds that are treated conservatively should be seen daily to inspect for signs of invasive infection. Ominous signs include a surface appearance of fungus or black spots. Increasing edema and erythema around wounds also increase suspicion. If there is any question, the wound should be biopsied and sent to pathology and microbiology. The pathologists do rapid sections to look for organisms invading into viable tissue. The microbiologists identify the organism, and the quantitative counts. The wounds are then dressed until the following day.

All personnel who participate in the dressing changes wear gowns and gloves which are available just outside the room. Other personnel who are only looking at the wound take care not to touch either the patient or the furniture in the room in an effort to avoid passing organisms between patients. After removing the gowns

12

Table 12.1. Medication dosage guidelines

Vitamins & Minerals	0-2 Years	2-12 Years	> 12 Years
Multi Vitamin	Poly Vi Sol 1 ml	Poly Vi Sol 1 ml Or Chewable Tab	Vi Deylin 5 ml or Theragran
Ascorbic Acid	250 mg QD	250 mg QD	500 mg QD
Folic Acid	1 mg QMWF	1 mg QMWF	1 mg QMWF
Vitamin A	2500U	5000U	10000U
Zinc Sulfate	55 mg	110 mg	220 mg
Elemental Iron	< 30 kg Dose = 2 mg/kg/dose PO TID		
	30 kg Dose = 65 mg PO TID or $FeSO_4$ 325 mg PO TID		
Antifungal Prophylaxis Mycostatin Oral Suspension	5ml QID	5ml QID	5ml QID

H-2 Blockers

Ranitidine Dose = 2 mg/kg/dose PO or IV q8h.
If gastric pH is less than 4, increase dose by 1 mg/kg up to a maximum of 8 mg/kg/dose PO or IV q8h

Treatment with Ranitidine is for the entire period of acute burn hospitalization.

If patient has had an endoscopically documented ulcer, Ranitidine should be prescribed for 6 weeks from the time the ulcer was documented.

Diuretics

Furosemide:	IV: 0.25 mg/kg/dose q6h up to 1 mg/kg/dose
	PO: 0.5 mg/kg/dose q6h up to 2 mg/kg/dose

Spironolactone:	0-2 yrs	6.25 mg PO q12h
	3 yr-12 yr	12.5 mg PO q12h
	> 12 yr	25 mg PO q12h

Human Growth Hormone   0.2 mg/kg/dose SQ qd

Beta-Adrenergic Blockers

Propranolol:	0.25 mg-0.5 mg/kg/dose IV q6H, titrate to decrease heart rate by 25%
Metroprolol:	0.75 mg/kg/dose IV q12h, titrate to decrease heart rate by 25%
Acyclovir:	Mucocutaneous ASV 750 mg/m²/day
	8 mg/kg/24h q8h IV x 7 days

Herpes Zoster in Immunocompromised Patients:
7.5 mg/kg/dose q8h IV
250-600/m²/dose 4-6 x day PO
Adult dose 800 mg 4-6 x day PO x 7-10 days

Varicella-Zester: 1500 mg/m²/day q6h or 30 mg/kg/day q8h IV
20 mg/kg/dose (max 800 mg/dose) PO 4-5 x day x 6 days
Begin treatment at earliest sign or symptom

12

Amikacin:	22.5 mg/kg/day q8h PO 1.5 gm max/day
Amoxicillin:	25-40 mg/kg/day q8hr PO > 20 kg Use adult dose Adult dose 250–500 mg PO q8hr
Amphotericin-B:	Test dose: 0.1 mg/kg x 1 up to 1 mg Initial dose: 0.25 mg/kg/day increasing by 0.125-0.25 mg/kg/day until 1 mg/kg/day as tolerated (given QD or QOD. Infuse over 6 h. Premedicate with Acetaminophen and Diphenhyramine at dosages based on weight.
Ampicillin:	50-100 mg/kg/day q4h IV Mild to moderate infection 150-200 mg/kg/day q4h IV Severe infection 50-100 mg/kg/day q6h PO Mild to moderate infection > 20 kg Use adult dose Adult dose 250-500 mg q6h PO
Augmentin:	< 40 kg 20-40 mg/kg/day q8h PO > 40 kg 250-500 mg/dose q8h PO
Aztreonam:	200 mg/kg/day q6h IV 8 gm max/day
Cefazolin:	25-100 mg/kg/day q8h IV 12 gm max/day
Cefoperazone:	25-100 mg/kg/day q12h IV 16 gm max/day
Cefotaxime:	< 50 kg 100-200 mg/kg/day q6-8h IV >50 kg 1-2 mg q6-8h IV 12 gm max/day
Cefotetan:	40-60 mg/kg/day q12h IV
Cefoxitin:	80-160 mg/kg/day q6h IV 12 gm max/day
Ceftazidime:	90-150 mg/kg/day q8h IV 6 gm max/day
Ceftriaxone:	50-75 mg/kg/day q12h IV 4 gm max/day
Cefuroxime:	50-100 mg/kg/day q6h IV Adult dose: 750 mg-1.5 mg/dose q8h IV
Chloramphenicol:	50-100 mg/kg/day q6h IV or PO
Clindamycin:	16-40 mg/kg/day q8h IV 2.7 gm max/day 8.58 mg/kg/day q8h PO 3 gm max/day

12

cont'd.

Dicloxacillin:	12.5-5.0 mg/kg/day q8h PO (up to 2 gm/day) > 40 kg should receive adult dose Adult dose 125-250 mg q8h PO
Erythromycin:	10-20 mg/kg/day q8h IV 30-50 mg/kg/day q8h PO
Fluconazole:	3-6 mg/kg/day IV or PO Immunocompromised: 12 mg/kg/day IV or PO Adult doses: 200-400 mg IV or PO on Day 1 Followed by 100-200 mg PO or IV
Gentamicin:	< 40 kg 7.5 mg/kg/day q8h IV > 40 kg 5 mg/kg/day q8h IV
Imipenem/Cilistatin:	> 12 yrs 50 mg/kg/day q6h IV ≤ 12 yrs 75 mg/kg/day q6h IV 4 gm max/day
Itraconazole:	Adult dose: Loading dose 200 mg PO TID for 3 days, then 200 mg POQD: If ineffective may increase by 100 mg increments to 400 mg PO QD
Mebendazole:	(round, hook or whipworm) 100 mg PO BID x 10 days
Metronidazole:	Giardiasis–5 mg/kg/day PO TID x 10 days Amebiasis–35-50 mg/kg/day PO TID x 10 days
Miconazole:	Children > 1 yr 20-40 mg/kg/day q8h IV
Nafcillin:	100-200 mg/kg/day q4h IV Adult dose: 500 mg-2000 mg q4-6h IV
Penicillin G:	25,000-100,000 units/kg/day q4h IV Adult dose: 2-24 million units/day q4-6 h IV
Penicillin VK:	25-50 mg/kg/day divided 96h PO Children ≥ 12 yrs or adult doses: 125-500 mg PO q6-8h
Piperacillin:	200-300 mg/kg/day q4h IV 24 gm max/day
Ticarcillin:	200-300 mg/kg/day q4h IV 24 gm max/day
Tobramycin:	< 40 kg 7.5 mg/kg/day q8h IV > 40 kg 5 mg/kg/day q8h IV
Vancomycin:	40 mg/kg/day q6h IV CHS infections 60 mg/kg/day Adults 500 mg q6 h or 1 pm q12h IV
Zosyn:	100 mg/kg/days IV q6h

and gloves in the patient room, each participant washes their hands prior to going to the next room.

During the wound inspection, the events of the previous day and night are reviewed with the team, including any pertinent changes in vital signs or physical exam. All laboratory and x-ray results are discussed (see included worksheet on Table 12.4). After this review, plans for the day are made which should be reflected in the physician's orders. After rounds are complete, the operations for the day or the outpatient schedule are attended to.

In the afternoon, brief rounds are made with the team where the events of the day are discussed. Potential problems should be identified for the personnel on call.

OPERATIONS

When patients are admitted, the operating room should be notified to prepare for the operation the subsequent day. The operating theater is warmed with adequate supplies garnered, such as multiple electrosurgical units. The burn size should be calculated in square centimeters to give an estimate of the blood loss. For example, a 50% TBSA burn in a 2.0 m² man will be 1.0 m² burn surface area. One m² is equal to 10,000 cm² (100 cm x 100 cm). Blood loss is generally 0.5-1.0 ml of blood per cm² excised. So this man should have 20 units of whole blood or reconstituted whole blood (one unit of packed red blood cells added to one unit of fresh frozen plasma) available for the operation. An estimation of the amount of cadaver skin required is made and ordered as well. For a massive burn (> 80% TBSA), enough skin to cover the whole wound is ordered, with a decreased amount for lesser wounds. Fresh cadaver skin is best if it is available, although frozen cadaver skin can be used.

A preoperative note is prepared for each patient the day before his or her operation. This note should contain the indication for the operation, the planned procedure, documentation that appropriate consent has been obtained, NPO orders if indicated, and that blood and skin have been requested.

On the day of the operation, the airway is secured by the anesthesia staff with subsequent bronchoscopy and bronchoalveolar lavage specimens obtained. The dressings are then removed in the operating theater under the supervision of the surgeons. The entire body surface area is prepared with betadine and sterile drapes placed under the patient. For most burns, the entire body is prepared in order to allow for intraoperative decisions about the donor sites that are procured and the amount of the wound to excise. A Foley catheter is then placed as dictated by the clinical situation. The operation is then begun and completed, followed by application of bolsters or bulky dressings to the grafted areas.

After the operation is complete, the postoperative orders are written with all the tenets described above in the admission orders kept in mind. An operative note is written describing the date, surgeons, operative findings, wound excised

12

and grafted in cm², donor sites, estimated blood loss, intraoperative fluids, and operative complications. Lastly, the details of the operation are dictated for later transcription.

All bedside procedures such as central vein cannulation, Swan-Ganz catheter placement, escharotomy, bedside sharp debridement, and bronchoscopy are documented with both a procedure note and a dictated note.

Please find included a list of medications commonly used with their recommended doses (Table 12.1). Also find the target serum levels for some antibiotics (Table 12.2). Lastly, we have included some recommended medications for anxiolytics, itching, nausea, and bowel cleansing (Table 12.3).

Table 12.2. Serum level norms

Amikacin		Acetaminophen	
Trough:	5-8 µg/ml		(1h post dose)
Peak:	25-30 µg/ml		= or < 10 µg/ml
			Toxic: > 50 µg/ml
Vancomycin		**Imipramine**	
Trough:	5-10 µg/ml		(8h post dose)
Peak:	30-40 µg/ml		150–300 µg/ml
			Toxic: > 500 µg/ml
			Do not advance if PR int. > 0.2
Gentamicin			
Trough:	< 2 µg/ml		
Peak:	5-10 µg/ml	**Phenytoin**	
			neonates: 6-14 µg/ml
			peds/adults: 10-20 µg/ml
Tobramycin		**Phenobarbital**	
Trough:	< 2 µg/ml		pediatric: 15-30 µg/ml
Peak:	4-10 µg/ml		adult: 20-40 µg/ml

12

Table 12.3. Anxiolytic (after pain control)

Criteria: First—Address pain management
             Second—Address posttraumatic stress disorder (PTSS) problems and then
             Third—Use anxiolytics

Lorazepam dose: 0.03 mg/kg/dose PO or IV q4h

Acute patients: Taper benzodiazepines: reduce dose by 50% every 2nd day
Reconstructive patients: > 15 days on benzodiazepines, taper slowly, reduce dose every 3rd day (may be tapered post discharge if necessary)

Itch
Step 1:   Use moisturizing body shampoo and lotions.

Step 2:   Diphenhydramine 1.25 mg/kg/dose PO q4h scheduled

Step 3:   Hydroxyzine 0.5 mg/kg.dose PO q6h and
           Diphenydramine 1.25 mg/kg/dose PO q6h
           Alternate medication so that patient is receiving one itch medicine every 3 hours
           while awake.

Step 4:   Hydroxyzine 0.5 mg/kg/dose PO q6h
           Cyproheptadine 0.1 mg/kg/dose PO q6h and
           Alternate medication so that patient is receiving one itch medicine every 2 hours
           while awake.

Management of Postoperative Nausea and Vomiting

Droperidol: 0.025-0.05 mg/kg/dose IV q4-6h PRN

Bowel Regimen

Start with 1 and 2 any time narcotics are given
   1) Prune juice   < 5 yrs-2 oz
                                                                     > 5 yrs-4 oz
                                                                     > 10 yrs-6 oz

   2) (Colace) Diacetyl sodium
      Less than 6 yrs of age   10-60 mg/day
      Children 6-12 yrs of age   40-120 mg/day
      Children more than 12 yrs   100-200 mg/day

Then add one of these if patient becomes constipated:
   3) Mineral oil   1-3 oz day
   4) Mini-enema (colace-glycerine) if no B.M. by noon
   5 SBI enema if no B.M. by 1500 hours.

12

Table 12.4. Daily rounds worksheet

Date:

Name: _____ **Age:** _____ Home: _____
Burn Date: _____ **Admit Date:** _____
Height: _____ Weight _____ TBSA: _____
% of Burn: _____ **% 3rd:** _____ SA Burn: _____

PBD#:   POD#:   for   Genitourinary
                                        <u>I/O summary</u>: (   )
Overnight concerns   <u>urine output:</u> <u>cc/kg/h</u>
                                        Fluid needs calculated* (% met last 24 hours)
                                        <u>lytes</u>: BUN   crt   Na K   Cl Mg P Ca
Vital Signs   *foley (yes/no) issues:*
<u>T</u>:   <u>Tmax</u>:   <u>at</u>   GU meds:

Respiratory   **Wounds**
RR   Grafts
<u>ABG</u>: pH   PCO2 pO2 02sat on   HCO3 BE   <u>Type</u> <u>Location</u> <u>Donor site(s)</u>
<u>Ventilator</u>: mode   RR   TV   02sat F102   PEEP PIP
<u>CT output:</u>
CXR:
Pulm PE
Pulm meds: Cultures
                                                          <u>DateAmt./OrganismLocation</u>

Cardiovascular
<u>P</u>   <u>BP</u>   <u>CVP</u>
Cor PE   State of wounds/
dressings:
Cor meds   State of donor sites:
                                                          <u>Antimicrobial meds:</u>
Hematology
<u>Blood given</u>: PRBC   whole   other   Neuro/Pain:
<u>Colloid:</u>
<u>Labs</u>: Hgb Hct WBCplt   glucose   ibili
       TP   alb   AST ALT AlkP GGT osm   *If OR*
Gastrointestinal   **blood ordered***:
<u>NCT residuals:</u> <u>NGT guaiac</u>   **skin ordered:**
<u>Stool</u>   <u>stool guaiac</u>   <u>emesis:</u>
Feeds
Caloric needs calculated:*   *(% met last 24 hours)* Assessment:
Abd PE:
GI meds: Plan:

                                                 *use formula card to calculate

Index